Christmas in Cincinnati

WENDY HART BECKMAN

THE History PRESS

Published by The History Press
Charleston, SC
www.historypress.com

Front cover, top left: *Cincinnati Enquirer* photo; *top center*: *Cincinnati Enquirer*/ Liz Dufour; *top right*: *Cincinnati Enquirer*/Cara Owsley; *bottom*: Christmas decorations at Fountain Square. Cincinnati & Hamilton County Public Library. Joseph S. Stern, Jr. Cincinnati Room.
Back cover, top: Library of Congress; *inset*: *Cincinnati Enquirer*/Shae Combs.

First published 2021

Manufactured in the United States

ISBN 9781467148313

Library of Congress Control Number: 2021943814

I dedicate this book to the people and the city of Cincinnati, my adopted home.

Catawba Wine
Henry Wadsworth Longfellow

This song of mine
Is a Song of the Vine,
To be sung by the glowing embers
Of wayside inns,
When the rain begins
To darken the drear Novembers.

It is not a song
Of the Scuppernong,
From warm Carolinian valleys,
Nor the Isabel
And the Muscadel
That bask in our garden alleys.

Nor the red Mustang,
Whose clusters hang
O'er the waves of the Colorado,
And the fiery flood
Of whose purple blood
Has a dash of Spanish bravado.

For richest and best
Is the wine of the West,
That grows by the Beautiful River;
Whose sweet perfume
Fills all the room
With a benison on the giver.

And as hollow trees
Are the haunts of bees,
Forever going and coming;
So this crystal hive
Is all alive
With a swarming and buzzing and humming.

Very good in its way
Is the Verzenay,
Or the Sillery soft and creamy;

But Catawba wine
Has a taste more divine,
More dulcet, delicious, and dreamy.

There grows no vine
By the haunted Rhine,
By Danube or Guadalquivir,
Nor on island or cape,
That bears such a grape
As grows by the Beautiful River.

Drugged is their juice
For foreign use,
When shipped o'er the reeling Atlantic,
To rack our brains
With the fever pains,
That have driven the Old World frantic.

To the sewers and sinks
With all such drinks,
And after them tumble the mixer;
For a poison malign
Is such Borgia wine,
Or at best but a Devil's Elixir.

While pure as a spring
Is the wine I sing,
And to praise it, one needs but name it;
For Catawba wine
Has need of no sign,
No tavern-bush to proclaim it.

And this Song of the Vine,
This greeting of mine,
The winds and the birds shall deliver
To the Queen of the West,
In her garlands dressed,
On the banks of the Beautiful River

(Emphasis is author's. Punctuation is Longfellow's.)[1]

Contents

A Word

About twenty years ago, I was working on a book about the National Parks. I was thrilled with the fantastic web pages of the Department of the Interior, especially those of the National Park Service. At that time, we writers were on the cusp of printing out all the resource materials we found when doing our research or just noting the URL of a web page, along with identifying information for footnotes. I usually did a combination of the two. (I'm a slow adapter.) Then two things happened that impeded my book progress.

First, the Internet account of the National Indian Trust was hacked. As a result, the Interior Department (which controlled the trust) immediately shut down its whole web system. I think of this event as the "Four I's": the Indian Trust, Interior Department and Internet Incident. Many native and indigenous people were deeply affected, but for me, it was a mild inconvenience. I was able to fall back on the information I had printed out and relied on mailed letters and telephone calls for new research.

The second incident had a small effect on my book but an enormous emotional impact on me and the rest of the world: the September 11, 2001, attacks. Not only were communication lines cut, but National Park Service sites themselves were also shut down. I lost access to Ellis Island and the Statue of Liberty for weeks, for example. Communication with freelance writers became a low priority—and rightly so.

In the midst of a pandemic, researching a book is a little challenging. People whom I would normally talk to were furloughed or, worse yet, laid off. Those left behind were trying to do the work of many absent coworkers. My work could still proceed at a slower pace but with constant reminders that at least I had work when many others weren't so lucky.

My heart goes out to our frontline workers and those who have lost loved ones to COVID-19. In the spirit of the season that I hope this book will bring you, I wish you well. I wish you peace. I wish you hope.

A candle lights the darkness.

Acknowledgments

When trying to capture the history of our city in a book, it's wonderful to have such venerable institutions as ours. Thanks to Jill Beitz and the folks in the Cincinnati History Library and Archives at the Cincinnati Museum Center and to Larry Richmond in the Genealogy and Local History Department of the Cincinnati and Hamilton County Public Library. (If I type "publ" into my computer, it automatically takes me to the Cincinnati Public Library's Online Research Databases. I think I'm addicted.)

Many, many thanks to Jeff Suess, Beryl Love and Lisa Gillespie at the *Cincinnati Enquirer*. I also greatly appreciate the Herculean efforts made by Cynthia Beischel, author of *Virginia Bakery Remembered*, to get me a photo from Virginia Bakery.

Before I jump into the first chapter, I would also like to acknowledge the passing of Jim Aglamesis, of Aglamesis Bros. shops in Oakley and Montgomery, while this book was in progress. He truly was a sweet and sincere man.

A big thanks to my editor, John Rodrigue, who lit the idea for this book and saw it through to completion.

I

Introduction

When my oldest son was eight or nine years old, I was a diversity consultant and also taught a course on cultural diversity at a local university. I tried to make sure that all three of my sons were aware that people have different perspectives, perceptions, paths and beliefs, among other things. One day, when we were talking about Santa Claus and his Christmas Eve ride around the world, this son asked how many people in the world were Christians. I said that about a third of people believed in Christianity, with the next largest group being Muslims, and that the greatest concentration of Christians was in the United States and Europe. He thought for a minute, then said, "So I guess Santa Claus doesn't work as hard as we thought he did."

Nevertheless, we know that Santa works *very* hard to deliver gifts to Christians (and even some non-Christians) around the world. In Cincinnati, that's not all, however. We also celebrate St. Nick's Day on December 6, which is the Feast of St. Nicholas (or on December 19 for people in Eastern Christian countries who use the old church calendar). On the evening of December 5, children leave their shoes outside their bedroom doors for St. Nick to fill—usually with cookies, candy, books or trinkets. Often chocolate oranges or gold coins are given to represent when St. Nicholas paid in gold the dowries of three young poor women.

Not having grown up in Cincinnati, I didn't know what a big deal St. Nick's Day was until my first son (yep, same one) came home from kindergarten on December 6. I noted his sad demeanor as I picked him up at the bus stop. He informed me about St. Nick's Day and said that St. Nick had forgotten him. So St. Nick made a hasty delivery to his bedroom doorway early on December 7 of chocolate, a Beanie Baby, a book and a note of apology.

Many people (especially we transplants from New England) wish for a "white Christmas," where the ground is covered with snow. Others, however, don't like the "s word," as it is frequently called here. In fact, one (somewhat grumpy-sounding) editor at the *Cincinnati Enquirer* opined on December 27, 1850, "In the morning the prospect was that we should have a most disagreeable day, as snow fell pretty plenteously; towards noon, however, the clouds cleared away and old Sol came forth in usual splendor." He said the streets were filled from dawn to dusk with people "looking for Christmas," which he assumed they had found. The Broadway House, Walnut Street House, Dennison House, Pearl Street House, Gibson House, Henrie House and United States Hotel invited him to feast at their facilities, but he declined, saying, "because we make it a point to dine with our better half on such occasions." Shows and entertainment were offered at the Olympic Theatre, National Theatre and Wood's Museum. The editor concluded "that the day came, and that it has passed away, as we hope to see many another come and go, with an equal share of enjoyment, an equal share of happiness, and an equal share of satisfaction to all."[2] These places no longer exist, but the spirit lives on in the city.

Some aspects of Christmas remain the same, and some have changed. When I was four or five, my father used to climb up on the roof with some of the sleigh bells that my mother collected. My brother and sister played along and announced that Santa and his reindeer had arrived! Neither my husband nor I have ever climbed up on our roof. Still, children eagerly wait for Santa on Christmas Eve, hoping to see or hear some sign of the "jolly old elf."

Nowadays, kids who have access to a television, a telephone or the Internet can track Santa's progress, thanks to the North American Aerospace Defense Command (NORAD) at www.noradsanta.org. For more than sixty-five years, NORAD—previously known as Continental Air Defense Command (CONAD)—has tracked the sleigh and reported Santa's progress. This happy arrangement began with a small phone number error. Air Force colonel Harry Shoup was alone on duty one night in 1955 when the unlisted phone rang. His senses were alerted as he answered, only to find that a fairly young child was on the other end of the line. (A local newspaper running a Santa promotion had listed a similar number.) Realizing that a mistake had been made, Colonel Shoup assured the caller that CONAD had Santa in its sights and would ensure his safety as he made his rounds.

That started a tradition that carried on to NORAD when it was formed in 1958. The Department of Defense considers tracking Santa to be one of its greatest public outreach programs. More than fifteen million unique visitors from more than two hundred countries and territories follow NORAD online through the website, Facebook, Twitter, YouTube and Instagram. More than 130,000 callers talk to the military and civilian volunteers who staff the lines on Christmas Eve.[3] Shoup's children said he was fondly known as "Colonel Santa" after that first call.

If seeing Santa's trajectory isn't enough for you, or if you can't wait until Christmas Eve, Cincinnati plays host to Santa each year (except for 2020). The city hosts thousands of Santas. We're talking "Santacon." The first Santacon started with only twenty-seven Santas in 2007. In 2019, more than ten thousand were expected. No special training is required—just a red Santa suit, a charged cell phone and good shoes. The Santacon website (www.cincinnatisantacon.com) does provide some of the music that might be sung, in case your Santa is out of practice. The website also has tips for where to stay, where to eat and how to get started. Santacon has been described as one of the country's largest pub crawls.

Today, Christmas has become secularized, so that the holiday is often celebrated by many people who don't consider themselves religious or by people who follow other faiths. In fact, many of my Jewish friends have told me that Hanukkah is not a big deal in the Jewish faith. (The most important holidays would be Yom Kippur and Rosh Hashana, the high holy days.) However, while being surrounded by Christian kids with their stockings and trees, some Jewish kids felt slighted. So Hanukkah became more of a focus and is celebrated far more here than it is in Israel. Cincinnati can be thanked (or cursed) for that!

In Cincinnati, home of Reform Judaism,[4] two rabbis wanted to reconnect the Jewish youth with the synagogues, so they introduced gift giving. With the influx of European immigrants toward the end of the nineteenth century, Jewish families increasingly wanted to celebrate faith, family and home in a way that they had not been able to do in Europe. They wanted to celebrate as Americans, but also as Jews.[5]

In an interview with National Public Radio's Steve Inskeep about her book *Hanukkah in America*, author Dianne Ashton said, "There was a lot of social change, urbanization, industrialization and migration," after the Civil War.

She said that people in the United States began to think that "sentimental home celebrations would help to stabilize all of the social changes."[6]

Christmas is celebrated not just in our churches, but also in our music, food, shopping and other activities. When I was growing up, our Christmas Eve family tradition was to gather around our Steinway grand piano while my mother played. (Sometimes she was still wearing the apron from cooking dinner or making cookies.) The rest of us held candles with doilies to protect our hands. One by one, each of us would get to choose a Christmas carol as our candle was lit by the last chooser. My mother would then search through her stacks of Christmas songs and carols to find the best version of our requested piece. My brother and father were both baritones, but Dad was low while my brother took the higher parts. My sister, mother and I were all altos, but my sister and I would take turns singing the soprano part. Dad would request "O Tannenbaum" ("O Christmas Tree"), which we would sing in German. We usually also sang "Silent Night" in German, with my brother and me emphasizing the "cht" in "nacht." Mom and I often sang "Il Est Né, le Divin Enfant" in French. Sometimes those of us who played other instruments would get them out and play a duet with the piano. My brother usually had a special piece he played on his trumpet against our mother's playing "Silent Night." We always sang "We Three Kings," with Mom designating who would be Melchior, Balthazar and Gaspar to sing that king's solo. We sang until it was Christmas, at the stroke of midnight, then we went to bed. I didn't realize until I got married that not every family does this. In fact, most of them don't.

Luckily, now I live in Cincinnati, the "City That Sings."[7] In 1977, Cincinnati was chosen by *Redbook* magazine for its 1978 annual Christmas feature. Food and nutrition editor Elizabeth Alston was in charge of the feature. "Cincinnati was recommended to us as the nicest city in Ohio," she said. "What we're looking for is what makes the holidays in Cincinnati. The little traditions." She listed some of her other favorite things about Cincinnati, which weren't any surprise to the city's residents:

- Cincinnati has both a sophisticated feeling and a small-town feeling. It has the best of both worlds.
- It's got a rich cultural tradition. We particularly liked the Krohn Conservatory and the zoo, as well as all the parks, fountains and churches.
- We liked all the different neighborhoods where people seem to know and talk to each other.[8]

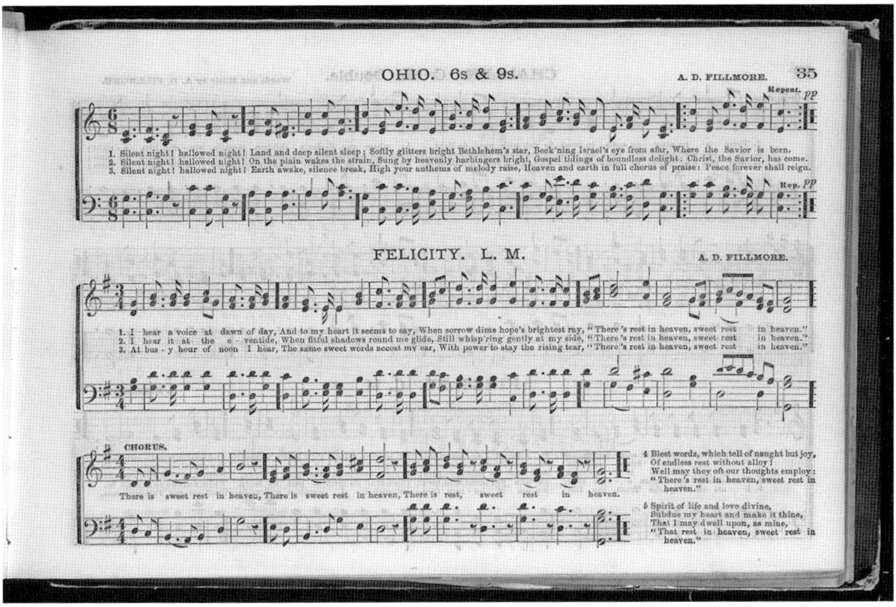

"Ohio," composed by Augustus D. Fillmore, Cincinnati, 1865. *Library of Congress.*

In 2018, Cincinnati was named by WalletHub as one of the top twenty-five cities for Christmas celebrations. The Queen City came in at thirteenth, with Orlando on top. (No other Midwest town made the top twenty, but Louisville came in twenty-fifth.) WalletHub ranked the cities based on traditions and fun, observance, generosity, shopping and costs. Specifically, they looked at "events and ice skating rinks…donations to charity, shopping centers, and Christmas markets per capita."[9] In an informal poll on Facebook conducted by the author, most responders noted their fondest Christmas memories were of going to church and spending time with family and friends. These shared memories ground us in love and tradition.

And that, as Linus said, "is what Christmas is all about."

2
History

Settling Cincinnati

The indigenous people now known as the Mound Builders were some of the earliest occupants of what we now call the Cincinnati area. However, by the end of the seventeenth century, the people of the Mound Builder culture had disappeared from southwest Ohio. About a hundred years went by with no other groups filling the void. Previously farmed fields lay fallow. Then the Iroquois entered Ohio after being driven out of New York. They spread quickly throughout the state, fighting other tribes and completely wiping out some, like the Erie. The Iroquois spread themselves too thin and were left vulnerable to attack from tribes coming in from the west, north and east.

The Miami tribes came in and established a stronghold on the west side of the state, eventually giving their name to many landmarks that still exist today, such as Miami University, the Great Miami River to the west of Cincinnati, the Little Miami River to the east and the Maumee River to the north. By now, the British and French had also discovered Ohio and battled for control of the region. All of this was taking place in a country that we now think of as the United States of America. Back then, this area was better described as an utter state of chaos.

George Rogers Clark led an expedition in 1780 of more than one thousand men with the goals of driving the Native Americans back and "teaching them a lesson" for their recent attacks on settlers in Kentucky and Ohio.

Documents published by the secretary of state in the late 1800s contain a description of the construction of two blockhouses directly across from the mouth of Kentucky's Licking River on August 1, 1780 (which describes where Cincinnati is). Clark's men were to guard these blockhouses for fourteen days until his return, and then the buildings were to be abandoned. Eventually, they were destroyed with no evidence of their exact location.

John Cleves Symmes was given a charter by the new Continental Congress to settle the area. For sixty-six cents an acre, Symmes purchased a large section of land for himself, bordered by the Ohio, Little Miami and Great Miami Rivers, hoping to establish a settlement there. Matthias Denman, Israel Ludlow and Robert Patterson bought eight hundred acres from Symmes. Surveyor John Filson—with Denman, Ludlow and Patterson—named the plot of land Losantiville. They declared that the name meant "city across from the mouth of the Licking River." "L" was for the Licking River; "os" is Latin for "mouth"; "anti" means "opposite"; and "ville" is French for "town" or "village."

So, Losantiville it was—for about a year. Then General Arthur St. Clair, newly named governor of the Northwest Territory, named it Cincinnati after the Society of the Cincinnati, of which he was a member. Around Cincinnati even today you can still find remnants of the name *Losantiville*, such as Losantiville Country Club in Pleasant Ridge and Losantiville Avenue in Golf Manor.

Cincinnati counts 1788 as its birth year. It could have been earlier, but fear got in the way. Captain William Lytle brought his family down the Ohio from Pennsylvania in April 1780. Lytle's river party consisted of a fleet of flatboats and immigrants from England, Ireland and Scotland. Flatboats were boxy and flat, with no keel, and were mostly used for transporting goods, not people. They could be up to one hundred feet long and were very difficult to steer. They carried goods downstream but could not go back upriver. At the end of their journey, the boats were usually dismantled, with the wood salvaged for other uses, such as new homes for the boatsmen or passengers.

As Lytle's flotilla of flatboats neared its objective, the group noticed a band of Native Americans encamped at the mouth of the Licking River. Lytle's party attempted to run them off but was unsuccessful, so the group continued floating down to Louisville. However, the Lytles didn't all stay in Kentucky. Lytle's son, another William Lytle (who became General William Lytle II), and his wife, Eliza, eventually returned to Cincinnati. This William Lytle purchased eight acres of land in what later became known as Lytle Square in downtown Cincinnati's neighborhood of Fourth, Lawrence and Third Streets. The Lytles became neighbors of the Taft and Longworth families.

Christmas was first celebrated in Cincinnati in 1788, as described in a WLW radio show on December 23, 1959, by Herbert Koch, the vice president of the Ohio Historical and Philosophical Society. Excerpts from the *Adventures in America* broadcast are provided here. Koch's account came mostly from Judge Isaac Dunn, who had attended the Christmas feast as a boy of about six years old[10] in 1788 and had written a letter to a friend in 1857 describing the day.

> *Koch: This week, we are celebrating Christmas. On Fountain Square this week in Cincinnati, two great trees stand as symbols of the Yuletide spirit, and in innumerable homes Christmas trees, holly wreaths, mistletoe, and good cheer hail the happy season....*
>
> *Columbia, which was to become a part of Cincinnati...consisted of four blockhouses and fifty settlers....Although on that Christmas day, the river carried a heavy floe of ice, the day was comparatively mild and a feast was laid out on rough tables at the river's edge. A few Indians dropped by and watched curiously. The principle dish was stew, which was cooked in two ten-gallon kettles, and potpie....*
>
> *In Marietta, the capital of the great Northwest Territory, the governor, General Arthur St. Clair, issued a Christmas proclamation, for even in this new wilderness, Christmas was to be recognized. The proclamation was given in 1788 in the thirteenth year of the independence of the United States. The hard-bitten governor wrote: "For as much as it is incumbent on all men to acknowledge with gratitude their infinite obligations to Almighty God for benefits received, and to implore His superintending care and providence for future blessings, I have thought proper to set apart a day for that purpose, and do hereby ordain that Thursday, the 25th of December, be observed as a day of solemn thanksgiving and praise that the people may, with one voice in sincere thanks, express their grateful sensations...and I do hereby prohibit all servile labor on that day."*[11]

Although Ohio's governor St. Clair declared Christmas 1788 a holiday, the day was not routinely considered a holiday until much later. In fact, back in 1659, the Massachusetts General Court had made it clear that the day should be like all the rest and decreed that "anybody who is found observing, by abstinence from labor, feasting or any other way, any such days as Christmas day, shall pay for every such offense five shillings." Just a dozen years before St. Clair's declaration, General George Washington had "observed" the non-holiday by crossing the Delaware River the night of December 25, 1776. Of course, the birth of Christ had been "assigned" the date of December 25 by fourth-century religious leaders.[12]

Episcopalian bishop Philander Chase, who came to Ohio in 1817, bemoaned the lack of attention paid to the religious aspects of the chosen date in a letter to his wife: "The devil has stolen from us…Christmas, the day of our spiritual redemption, and converted it into a day of worldly festivity, shooting and swearing."[13]

In 1869, historian Edward Deering Mansfield shared his 1826 Christmas experience as a young man. He recalled that the day had dawned crisp and cold. The Ohio River had even frozen over during the night, so instead of ferries or other types of boats, tradesmen just drove their wagons across the ice to do business in the other state. A friend of Mansfield's, Charles Schultz, had ordered oysters from Baltimore; they arrived just in time for the Christmas feast. Oysters on Christmas was a tradition that easterners had brought to Ohio. One man from the East even said that he would find living in Cincinnati impossible, as the city had no oysters. Mansfield further noted in his piece of reminiscence that the only church open was Episcopalian.[14]

The *Daily Gazette* announced on December 24 that Mrs. Trollope's famous bazaar would hold a dance in its ballroom on Christmas Eve 1930. Men's tickets were $1.50, and refreshments were to be served to the ladies. There was no exchanging of gifts or cards.[15] Novelist Frances "Fanny" Trollope had been enticed to come to America from Europe and had chosen Cincinnati as the "honored" recipient of her vision. Her bazaar sold goods and held lectures and dances in its many rooms. (It bombed badly and became known as "Trollope's Folly." She made her offense and bitterness clear in her scathing book *Domestic Manners of the Americans*.)

Ohio declared Christmas to be a legal holiday in 1857, followed by Kentucky seven years later.[16] Christmas was finally declared a federal holiday in 1870, when President Ulysses Grant (an Ohioan) made it official, along with Independence Day and Thanksgiving (although he did not set a specific date for Thanksgiving). At this point, Grant was looking for ways to reunite the nation after the Civil War. Christmas tended to be celebrated in the South, but not in the North. Resistance came from Puritans, Pilgrims, Quakers and Anabaptists, who were moving inland from the Northeast. These groups associated Christmas with pagan worship and celebrations and also with the Roman Catholic and Anglican churches.[17] The Dutch Reformed and Lutheran churches also observed the holiday.

By the late 1880s, Christmas was firmly established as both a religious and a shopping holiday. Advertisements in the *Cincinnati Enquirer*, *Cincinnati Post-Times Star* and *Daily Gazette* made the latter point clear. George Wartenberg, in his 1959 *Cincinnati Enquirer* article, described it as a foretaste of "the Great Swap": "the most enormous merchandising event of the year for stores; the ever-widening circle of those who must receive gifts or Christmas cards, the bigger, better, shinier tree, the illuminated plywood reindeer prancing over the split-level house, the spate of popular holiday songs in bad or indifferent taste, and the appearance of a Santa Claus on every street corner."[18]

Bah, humbug!

CHRISTIANITY IN CINCINNATI

The settlers who had established homes for themselves in late eighteenth-century Cincinnati were overwhelmingly Christian. Not only is Cincinnati still very Christian (of those who practice any faith), but it is also very Catholic. Cincinnati's first two waves of immigrants came from Germany and Ireland and were mostly Catholic. Thus, combined with the more recent immigrants from countries in Central and South America, Roman Catholics represent the largest group of Christians in the city. (In fact, a Cincinnati McDonald's franchise owner invented the Filet-O-Fish sandwich in Cincinnati for meat-free Fridays, especially during Lent.) Not only did these immigrants bring their religious beliefs, but they also brought their cultural traditions—hence the popularity of St. Nick. However, Cincinnati (like other areas in the country) is seeing a decrease in people who identify with a specific religion or denomination.

Julie Irwin Zimmerman described our religious makeup in *Cincinnati Magazine*: "The Public Religion Research Institute finds that the Cincinnati region ranks just 18th for percentage of Catholic residents, putting us behind not only Boston, New York and Pittsburgh—the three cities with the highest concentration in the country, where more than 32 percent of residents identify as Catholic—but also Miami, Houston, Las Vegas and Detroit. What's more, the institute reports that our rate of unaffiliated folks is 2 percent higher than the national average, and higher than just about any other Midwestern metro region, including Chicago, Indianapolis, Pittsburgh, Cleveland and Milwaukee."[19]

According to the 2010 Religion Census Study (2020 results are not available yet), the largest Christian denomination is Roman Catholic, with 402,000 members in the Cincinnati metro area. The next-largest denomination is evangelical Protestants, which is the only religious denomination that is growing, both here and nationally. The people who consider themselves not religious or not affiliated with a specific denomination are also growing in number and are by far the largest population.[20]

CHURCHES IN CINCINNATI

The Cincinnati area is home to numerous churches and temples. On the west side of Cincinnati, especially, it is said that one cannot spit without hitting at least two churches and a Catholic school.

Roman Catholic Mass was celebrated in Cincinnati for the first time in 1811 by Dominican priest Father Edward Fenwick. This Mass was celebrated in a home on Walnut Street. The first Catholic church was not erected until 1818 and was considered to be outside of the Cincinnati city limits: it was at Liberty and Vine Streets. The church celebrated its first Mass on Easter Sunday, April 11, 1819. Cincinnati was then designated by Pope Pius VII as an Episcopal diocese, with Edward Fenwick, OP, as the first bishop.

Bishop Fenwick purchased land on Sycamore Street and moved the church to its present site. He dedicated the church to St. Peter in 1826. John Baptist Purcell succeeded Fenwick in 1832 and established the Athenaeum next to the church as a men's college and school, the first such Catholic institution in the Northwest Territory. In 1840, the name of the college was changed to St. Xavier College when Bishop Purcell asked the Society of Jesus (the Jesuits) to take over the school. The Sycamore site continued to host a college and a high school until 1912, when the college moved to its current location. In 1919, the college and high school split. The college's name was changed in 1930 to Xavier University, and four years later, the high school and university became financially independent.[21] The high school moved to its current location in Finneytown in 1960.[22]

St. Francis Xavier Church was and is one of the most magnificent churches in downtown Cincinnati. A November 23, 1882, article in the *Cincinnati Post* detailed the major restoration of the church, reporting that the workers were exerting "strenuous efforts to have the edifice ready for divine service on christmas [*sic*] day." The seventy-foot ceiling had stars in it that functioned as ventilation ducts. Tradesmen named in the article are Banman, the plasterer; the Robinson Bros. for the floor; the (renowned) Robert Mitchell furniture company for the pews; and "Mr. Nottingham," who was in charge of the "steam-heating apparatus." The article concluded, "Christmas day will be a day of joy to the scattered congregation of St. Xavier."[23]

While St. Xavier Church was under the watch of Bishop (later Archbishop) Purcell, he also turned his attention to building another church: St. Peter in Chains Cathedral. Located at Eighth and Plum Streets, its construction began in 1841. It was formally dedicated on November 2, 1845. The Cathedral Basilica of St. Peter in Chains was designated the Cathedral of the Archdiocese in 1851 (with a brief break during which St. Monica in University Heights assumed the title). St. Peter in Chains, just south of Cincinnati City Hall, is easy to spot with its 220-foot white marble spire. Greek-themed mosaics make the interior awe-inspiring.

Cincinnati today *still* has no lack of churches. In the downtown area alone, comprising roughly 170 blocks, you can find more than thirty churches. The traditions run from a church that still offers a German Mass to nondenominational evangelical churches with professional audio and video equipment. At Christmastime, many churches sparkle with candles and lights, garlands strung on ornate walls and evergreen trees decorated with Chrismons.[24]

With the city's strong Catholic traditions, it is not surprising that a favorite activity on Christmas Eve and Christmas Day is attending Mass. Many of the Protestant churches also offer Christmas Eve services, sometimes holding a separate children's service in the afternoon or early evening. Truth be told, some of those "children's services" are also attended by those who can't make it to midnight and who no longer care if mommy is kissing Santa Claus.

The downtown churches tend to offer old-fashioned surroundings with lots of wood and stained glass. Christ Church Cathedral (Episcopalian) was founded in 1817 and was consecrated as a cathedral in 1993.

Begun in 1841, St. Mary of the Annunciation (Roman Catholic) in Over-the-Rhine (OTR) is the oldest church still standing and also has the oldest clock tower. The tower was built in 1843 around a tree, and then the tree was demolished. It has three bells: St. Joseph, St. Mary and Little Anne. The abolitionist Levi Coffin cast the first bell. (Coffin, the Cincinnati leader of

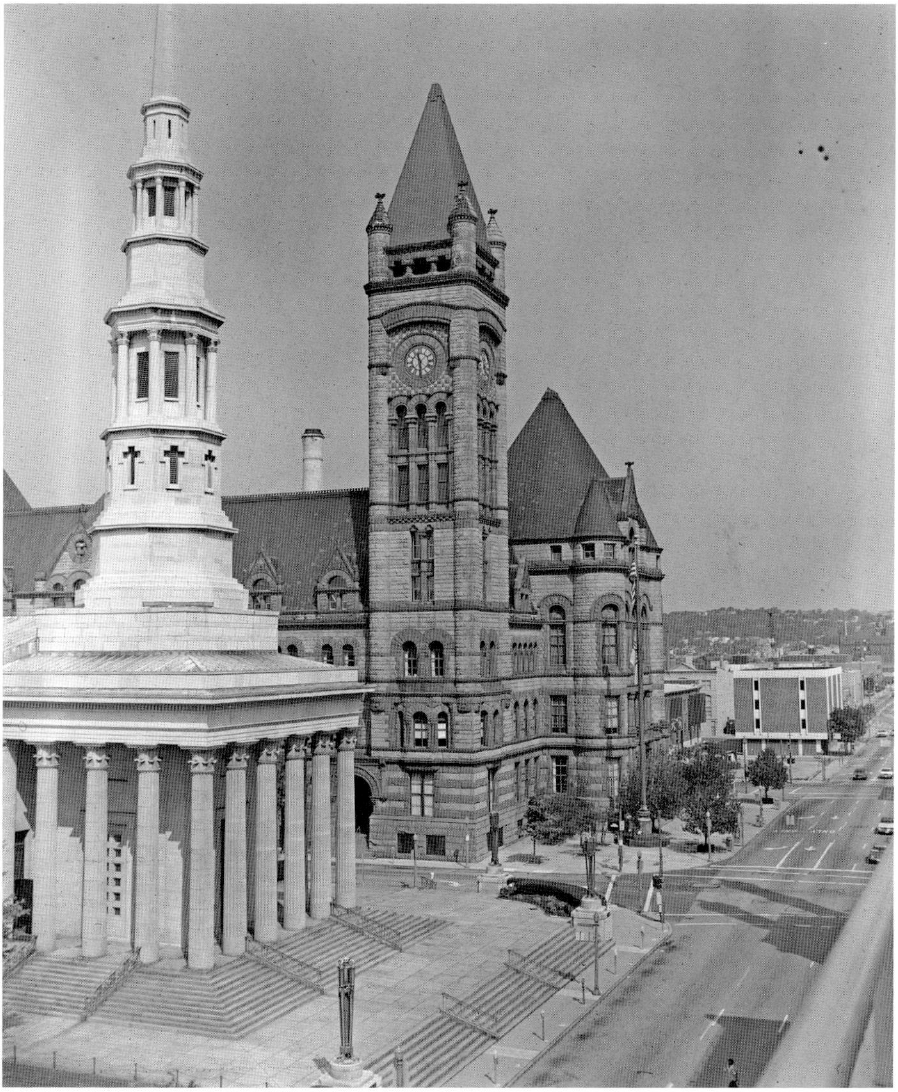

St. Peter in Chains Cathedral (*left*) and Cincinnati City Hall. *Library of Congress.*

the Underground Railroad in Cincinnati, was credited with saving the lives of thousands of slaves as they escaped to the North.)

St. Mary's tower was the tallest point in Cincinnati, so it was used as a fire tower, and Little Anne was rung in warning. After another St. Mary's Church was established in 1907 in Hyde Park, it became known as "Old St. Mary's Church."[25] Services are still offered in Latin and German.

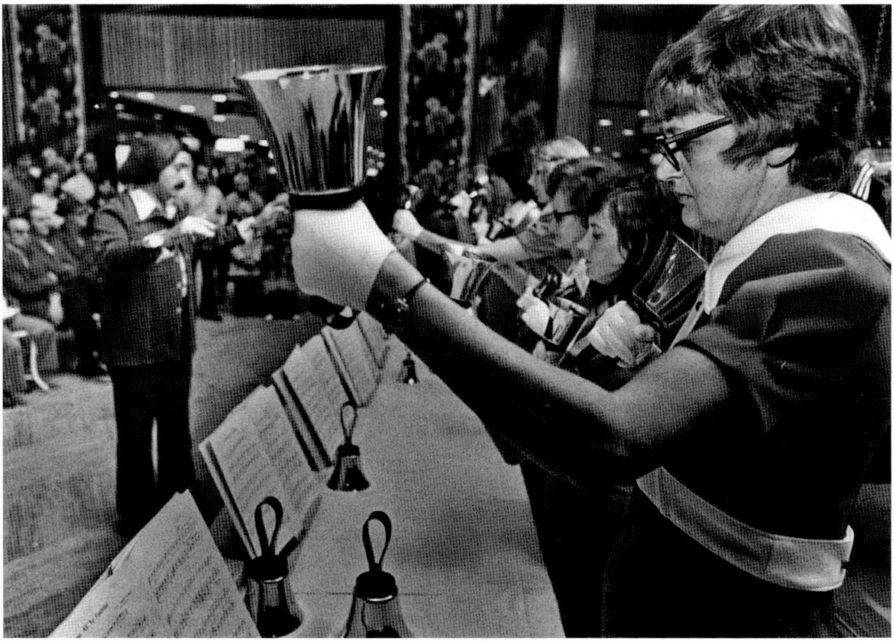

Jane Hughes (*right front*) rings bass bells as minister of music of the Latonia Baptist Church, while Charles Wells directs the annual bell ringing offering to emphasize the Christmas season, December 20, 1975. Cincinnati Enquirer *photo*.

Other churches near downtown include St. Louis Church (Catholic), St. Mary Church (Baptist), Covenant First Presbyterian, St. Xavier (Catholic) and Pilgrim Presbyterian. Across the Ohio River in Covington, Kentucky, is the Cathedral Basilica of the Assumption. Its façade was inspired by Notre Dame Cathedral, and its interior was styled after the Abbey Church of St. Denis, also in Paris, France.

Crossroads Community Church, an evangelical nondenominational church, is renowned for its Christmas presentation. Founded in 1996 in a former Home Quarters Warehouse (HQ) box store in the neighborhood of Oakley, Crossroads has expanded to numerous locations, including Mason, Corryville, Eastgate and Over-the-Rhine, as well as other cities and states. It is famous for its lively, participative services.

For eleven years, Crossroads presented *Awaited*. The church describes it as "a story full of risk, rejection and unexpected rescue by a long-awaited King. It is the story of how God relentlessly pursues each of us with his love and freedom, no matter who we are, what we've lived through or where we've come from. It is a story that has the power to change us all."[26]

In 2017, Crossroads announced that it would no longer be presenting *Awaited* because of its cost (more than $1.5 million each year), logistics and staff fatigue.

However, after a one-year hiatus, *Awaited* returned to Cincinnati in 2019 at a new location: the Aronoff Center for the Arts. With a change in venue came a change in price. Previously offered at no cost, tickets at the Aronoff range from $25 to $100.[27] *Awaited* was recorded in 2017, so it can also be found on the church's website. This was a blessing when the pandemic hit in 2020, allowing people to still enjoy its message.

3
Things to Do

White Christmas

What do Hollywood, Bing Crosby and Danny Kaye have to do with Christmas in Cincinnati? Not much, but their *White Christmas* costars have a lot to do with our great city and its surroundings. Rosemary Clooney and Vera-Ellen play sisters in Irving Berlin's 1954 feel-good movie. Both Clooney and Vera-Ellen hailed from the Cincinnati area, where Clooney was in a sister act in real life with her younger sister Betty. In *White Christmas*, Clooney plays the older sister, but she was actually seven years younger than Vera-Ellen. (Another interesting juxtaposition of ages is Clooney's and Crosby's: they were paramours in the movie, but in real life, he was almost twice her age of twenty-six.)

Betty and Rosemary Clooney were natives of Maysville, Kentucky, along with their brother Nick. (Maysville is east of Cincinnati, across the Ohio River.) In the twenty-first century, the best-known Clooney is George, Nick's son, and he's known pretty well. Back in the day, however, his aunt Rosemary was just as big a star. (Her son Miguel Ferrar was also a well-known actor in his own right.)

Vera-Ellen Westmeier Rohe grew up in Norwood, which is just north of Cincinnati proper. Vera-Ellen carpooled to dance class with none other than Doris Day, another Cincinnati star in the making. (Of course, at that time, Day's name would have been Doris Mary Anne Kappelhof.) Vera-Ellen's

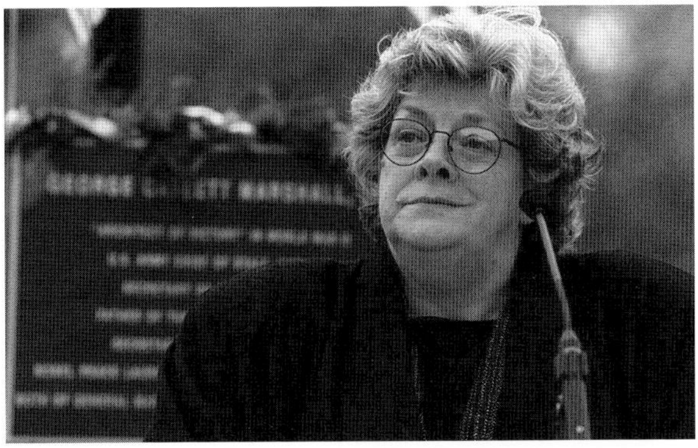

Right: Rosemary Clooney and her family dedicated the new memorial park, Marshall Park, in Augusta, Kentucky, her hometown, November 8, 1997. (While in town, Clooney also got married.) Cincinnati Enquirer/*Yoni Pozner*.

Below: Vera-Ellen (*center*), February 1952. Cincinnati Enquirer *photo*.

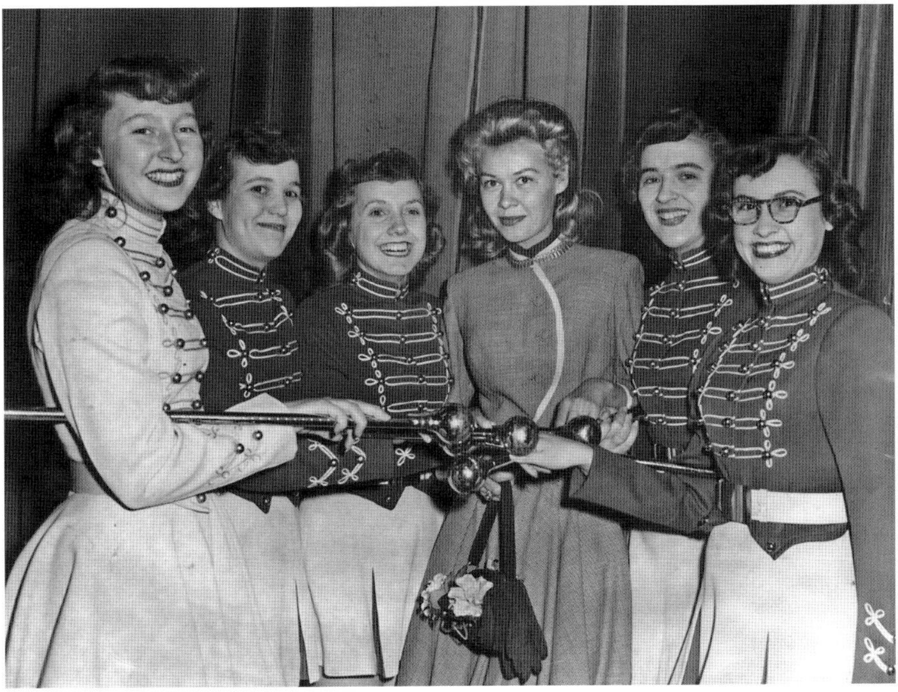

dancing talents far exceeded those of her male costars, so in her big dance numbers, she was paired up with uncredited professional dancers.

One uncredited dancer in *White Christmas*, who partners with Clooney in her nightclub scene, has a Cincinnati connection: George Chakiris. The Chakiris family had come to the United States from Greece in 1916. Against patriarch Aristotle's wishes, son Stylianos ("Steve") wanted to be an actor. However, Aristotle won, so Steve stayed in the family's confectionery business. He went to work for the Aglamesis brothers, Tom and Nicholas, who had a candy and ice-cream parlor in Norwood. In 1933, Steve's son

George was born. Seven years later, the family moved to California. There, George was able to achieve his father's dream: he became an actor. He won the 1961 Academy Award for his supporting role as Bernardo in *West Side Story*.[28] I can't help but wonder if Rosemary, Vera-Ellen or George ever sat together at Aglamesis's marble counter for a dish of peppermint ice cream! Probably not.

White Christmas has a simple plot, mostly to carry Berlin's songs, like "Count Your Blessings," and to showcase the cast's enormous talents. Clooney and Crosby, of course, were known as singers. Kaye was known as a singer and a dancer, but he could not keep up with Vera-Ellen's dancing, so he usually provided the comic relief while a professional dancer partnered with Vera-Ellen. Those dance lessons must have done their job!

Enjoying the Snow

Unlike the rest of the wonderful Irving Berlin music in the movie *White Christmas*, one of the more forgettable songs is "Snow."[29] Whereas Danny Kaye couldn't keep up with Vera-Ellen's dancing, she could not keep up with the other three actors' singing. Therefore, she didn't sing most of the songs. In fact, Rosemary Clooney's voice was dubbed in for some of them. However, Vera-Ellen actually sang on "Snow."

Cincinnatians can be forgiven for not caring for the song "Snow," as "the white stuff" (as it's commonly called now) is not always welcome here. But some people know how to enjoy it!

Cincinnati is unreliable as far as having a white Christmas. In the past 105 years, Cincinnati has had only sixteen white Christmases. A "white Christmas" is defined by the National Oceanic and Atmospheric Administration (NOAA) as having one inch of snow on the ground on Christmas morning. Because this happens so seldom in Cincinnati, I have my own definition: I call it a white Christmas if it's snowing on Christmas Eve as I drive to church or head home after the evening service, or if the ground and trees have been dusted with even a quarter of an inch of snow, or if the trees are coated with ice. I'm not choosy. I'll even accept it as a white Christmas if it's just really, really cold. That modification helped me when my parents visited from New England in 1983. On Christmas morning, the temperature in Cincinnati was twelve degrees below zero. Factoring in for windchill dropped it into the negative twenties!

Cincinnati has had its ups and downs when it comes to Christmas weather, according to the National Weather Service in Wilmington, Ohio.

Christmas Day Climate Extremes (1871–2019):

Coldest High Temperature: 3 degrees (1983)
Coldest Low Temperature: -12 degrees (1983)
Warmest High Temperature: 66 degrees (1893)
Warmest Low Temperature: 58 degrees (1889)
Most Precipitation: 1.12 inches (1957)
Most Snowfall: 3.7 inches (1909)
Greatest Snow Depth: 9 inches (2004)*

* "Christmas Day Climatology and White Christmas Probability," National Weather Service, accessed March 12, 2021, https://www.weather.gov.

Although snow has factored into some Christmas celebrations, it has not been enough for some of us. Being in a temperate zone, Cincinnati's snowfall is unpredictable even considering the winter as a whole. The highest one-day snowfall, on December 8, 1917, was a respectable 11.0 inches. Two years later, however, the one-day record for the most snowfall on one day was a mere 1.7 inches on December 19, 1919.[30]

Still, Cincinnatians enjoy getting out their flying saucers, snowboards, toboggans, Flexible Flyers and even (sometimes) cardboard or cafeteria trays no matter the depth of snow. Known as the "City of Seven Hills"—actually boasting far more than seven—Cincinnati offers lots of accessible slopes for amateur and professional snow fans.

Just west of Cincinnati is a fabulous recreation area called Perfect North Slopes (PNS). PNS achieved some international fame when Lawrenceburg native Nick Goepper won the Silver Medal in the men's slopestyle at the 2018 Olympics in South Korea and gave the resort several shout-outs.[31]

The slopes are great, but they're not perfect. The name comes from the owners, the Perfect family. Perfect North Slopes, near Lawrenceburg, was established in 1980 by Clyde Allen Perfect (who passed away while this book was being researched). In 1965, Perfect left his successful brick contracting business (called Perfect Brickwork—what else?) in Colerain

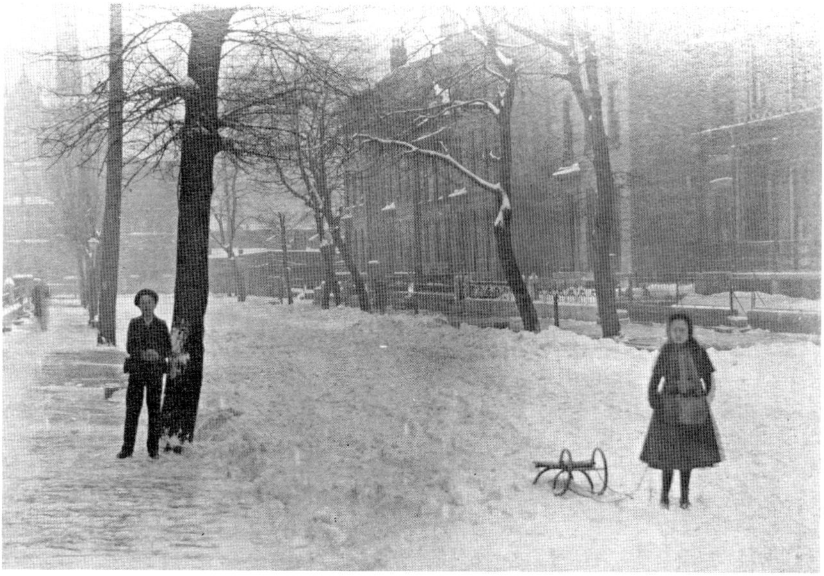

Children play in the snow, downtown Cincinnati, 1892. *Cincinnati & Hamilton County Public Library. Joseph S. Stern, Jr., Cincinnati Room.*

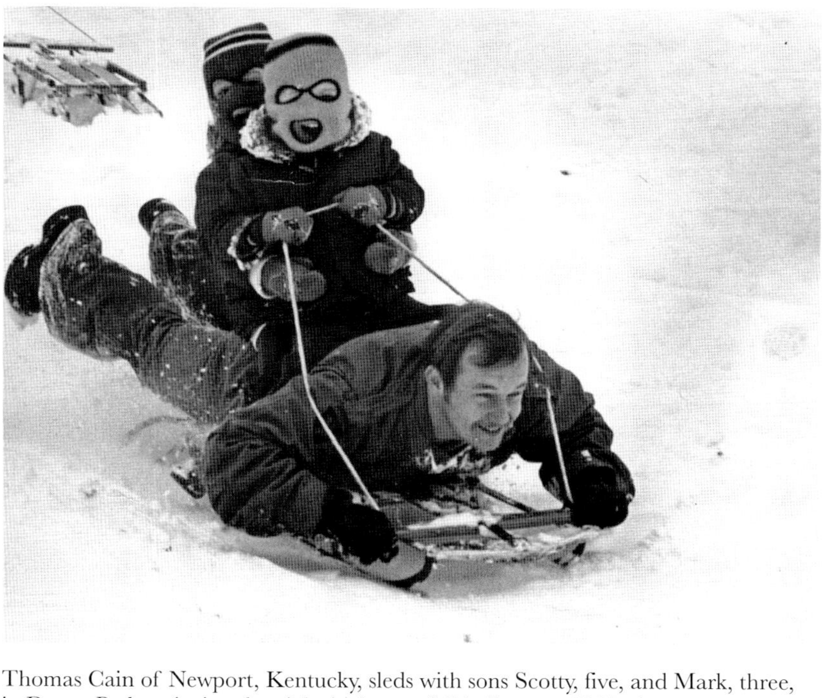

Thomas Cain of Newport, Kentucky, sleds with sons Scotty, five, and Mark, three, in Devou Park, enjoying the eight-inch snowfall in January 1977, the area's heaviest in eight years. Cincinnati Enquirer/*Bob Free.*

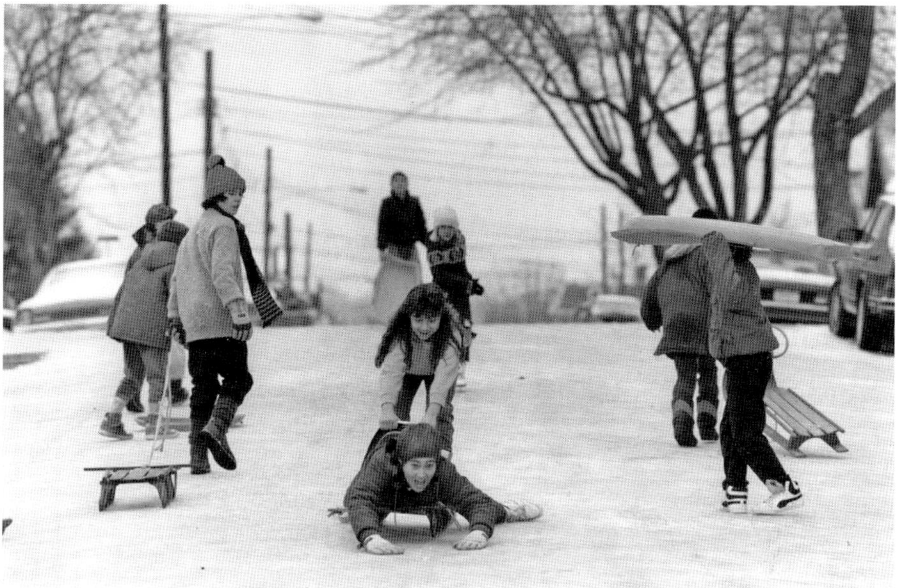

Michael McKinney, thirteen (*center*), gets a push from his friend Tanya Vetter, eleven. The pair took advantage of the day off from school to go sledding, March 6, 1989. Cincinnati Enquirer/*Jim Callaway*.

and, with his wife and five children, moved to a farm in Indiana. The family created Perfect Stock Farm. In 1980, Clyde Perfect sold the cattle and opened a ski area in its place. It originally had two ski slopes and a "bunny" slope for beginners. Altogether they had two handle tows and three rope tows. (With a rope tow, the skier is actually holding the rope itself. With a handle tow, the rope has a handle attached to it for the skier to grasp.) Back in 1980, weekday tickets were seven dollars, increasing to ten dollars on the weekend.[32]

Over the past four decades, PNS has expanded to welcoming snowboarding and tubing. (They weren't welcomed at first at many ski resorts.) Now the resort offers thousands of skis, poles, snowboards, tubes and helmets for rental. Five magic carpets, two rope tows and five chairlifts help skiers access the twenty-three runs: one expert, three most difficult, two advanced intermediate, twelve intermediate and five beginner slopes. Snow is guaranteed through a combination of snow guns and natural snowfall.

Some people like to enjoy the winter weather by strapping something smaller to their feet and spinning around a flat surface with no hills. Each year, part of Fountain Square is turned into an ice-skating rink. In 2020, reservations were controlled to allow for social distancing. Another change

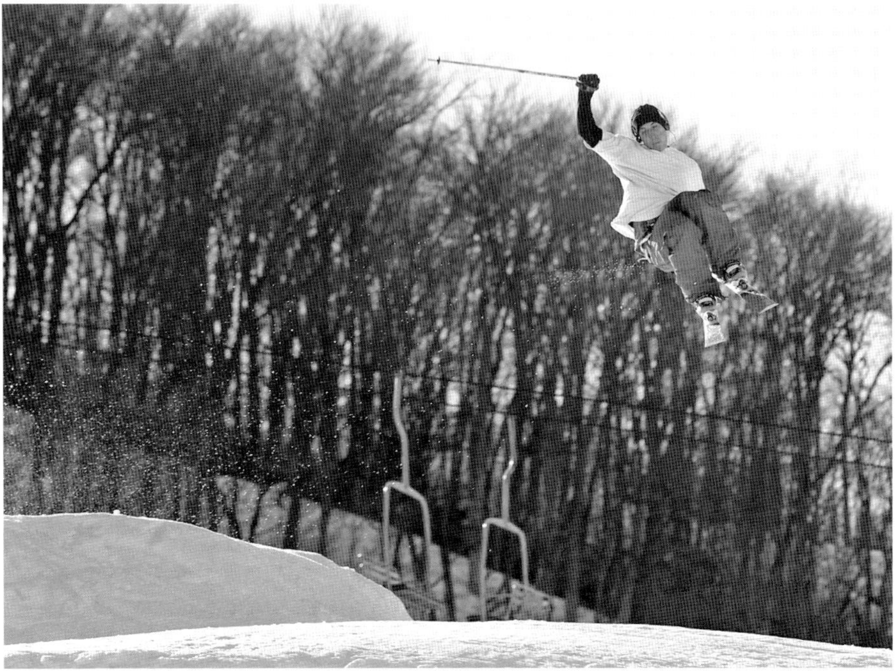

Jacob Schwab, twenty-two, of Crescent Springs, flies off a jump at Perfect North Slopes on January 10, 2012. Cincinnati Enquirer/*Patrick Reddy*.

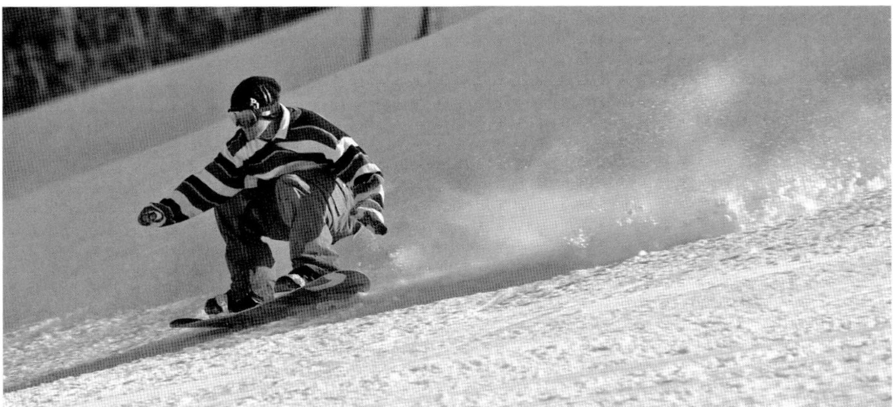

Snow flies as Stephen Hall, twenty-three, of downtown Cincinnati lands his snowboard off a jump at Perfect North Slopes, January 10, 2012. Cincinnati Enquirer/*Patrick Reddy*.

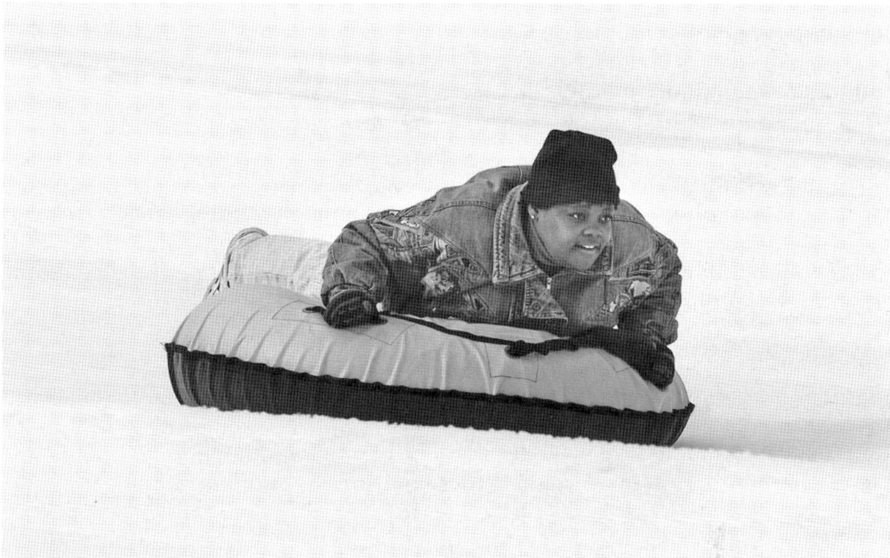

Cincinnati Enquirer reporter Shauna Rhone slips down the tubing hill at Perfect North Slopes, January 18, 2004. Cincinnati Enquirer/*Craig Ruttle*.

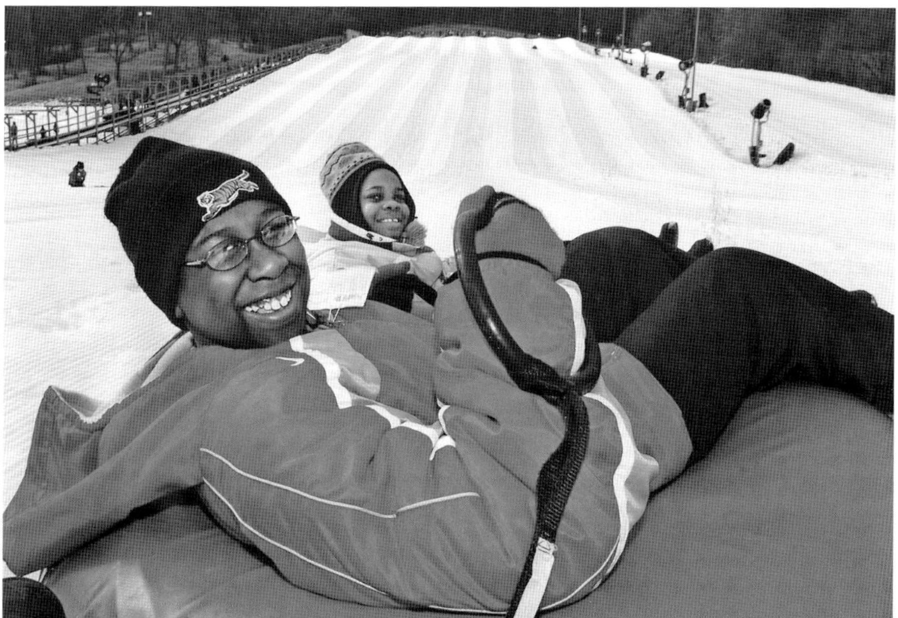

Lance Jackson, twelve (*left*), and Tosha Oliver, nine, of Forest Park, smile as they fly down the tubing hill at Perfect North Slopes, January 18, 2004. Cincinnati Enquirer/*Craig Ruttle*.

for 2020 was the addition of bumper cars. Never fear: the cars were separated from the skaters.

A fee is charged per person; ice skates are also available for rental. The rink is usually open once the weather turns cold in November, including Christmas Eve and Christmas Day.

The area around Fountain Square has been adapted for things besides skating rinks. One season that Cincinnatians still talk about is the winter of 1976–77, not just for the snow, but also for the dramatic temperatures. It was so cold that the Ohio River between Cincinnati and Covington, Kentucky, actually froze over. This cold weather was especially badly timed, as there was also a natural-gas shortage. Public buildings were directed to drop their thermostats to below sixty degrees Fahrenheit. Some schools closed. It was a time for some creative thinking.

One Catholic boys' school, St. Xavier High School (now in Finneytown, having moved from downtown in 1960), moved its classes. Someone at St. X had a connection to the Mabley & Carew Department Store in downtown Cincinnati on Fountain Square. So the young men found themselves attending classes in offices and storage rooms on the top floors of Mabley's. In a plan foreshadowing the "Nontraditional Instruction" during the pandemic of

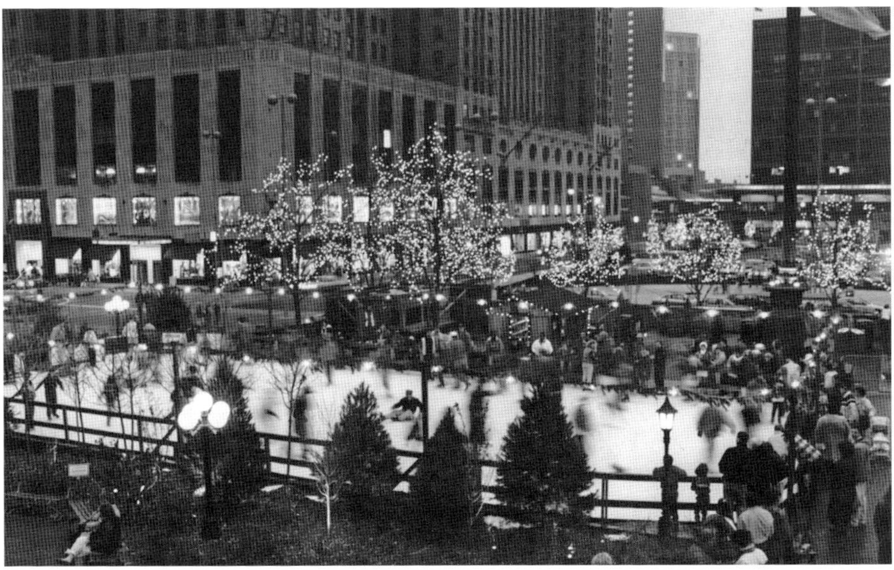

The ice rink at Fountain Square is the centerpiece of the annual Christmas display. Hundreds flock to the square throughout the day on December 22, 1991, as milder temperatures and the final weekend before Christmas teamed up to drive up activity. Cincinnati Enquirer/*Michael E. Keating*.

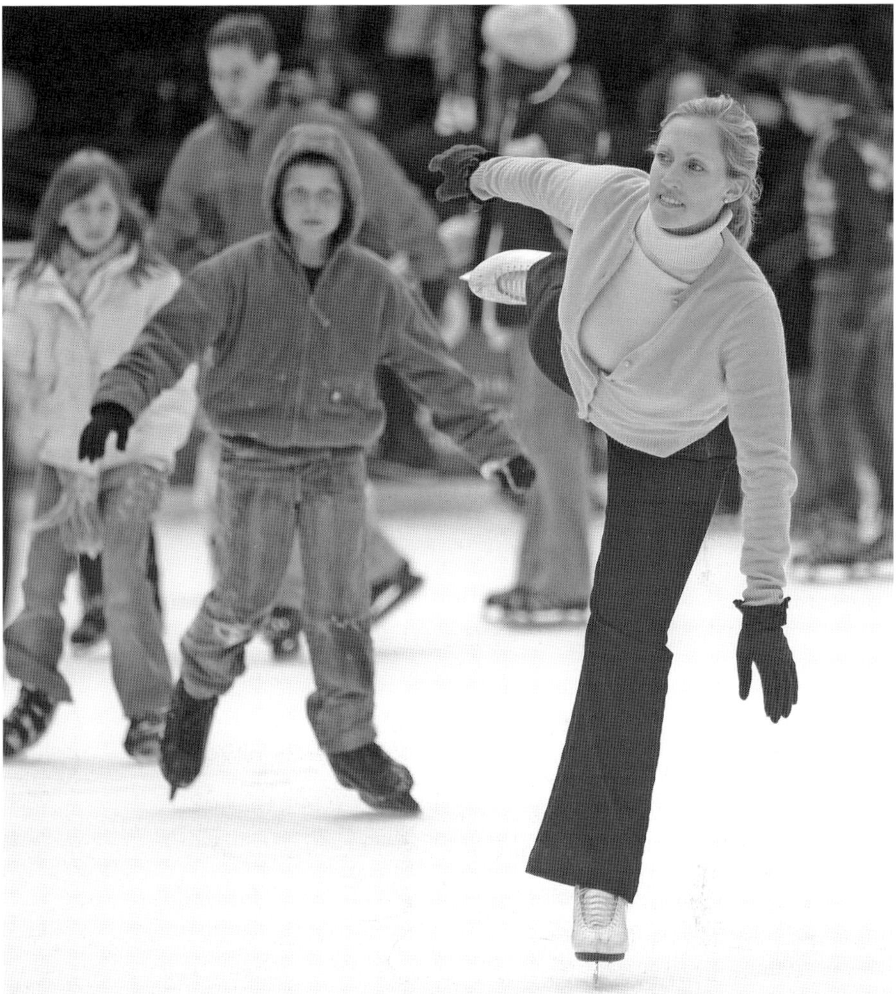

Jennifer Norlof of Madison, Wisconsin, makes her way around the rink while ice skating on Fountain Square, November 27, 2009. Cincinnati Enquirer/*Jeff Swinger*.

2020–21, the St. X students alternated what days they attended class: first-year, sophomore, junior, senior. My husband, who was a senior that year, thought that attending school in a department store was "pretty neat. We even had access to the employees' lounge," he says. "To get to the rooms, we had to walk through the store and take the elevators up."

A classmate of his, Nick Vehr, agrees. "We thought we were pretty special," says Vehr, CEO and executive counselor at Vehr Communications, former VP of economic development and marketing at Cincinnati

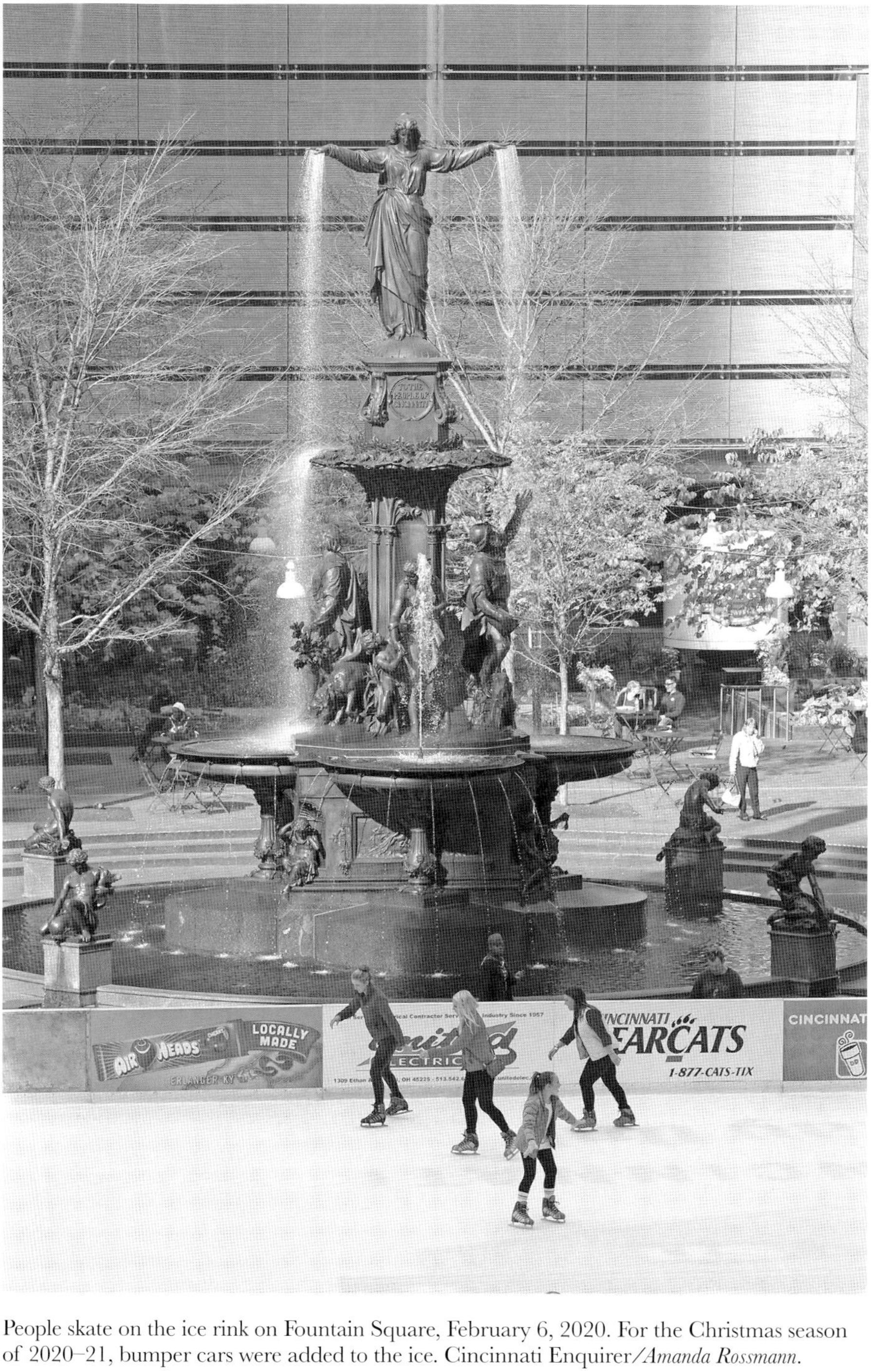

People skate on the ice rink on Fountain Square, February 6, 2020. For the Christmas season of 2020–21, bumper cars were added to the ice. Cincinnati Enquirer/*Amanda Rossmann.*

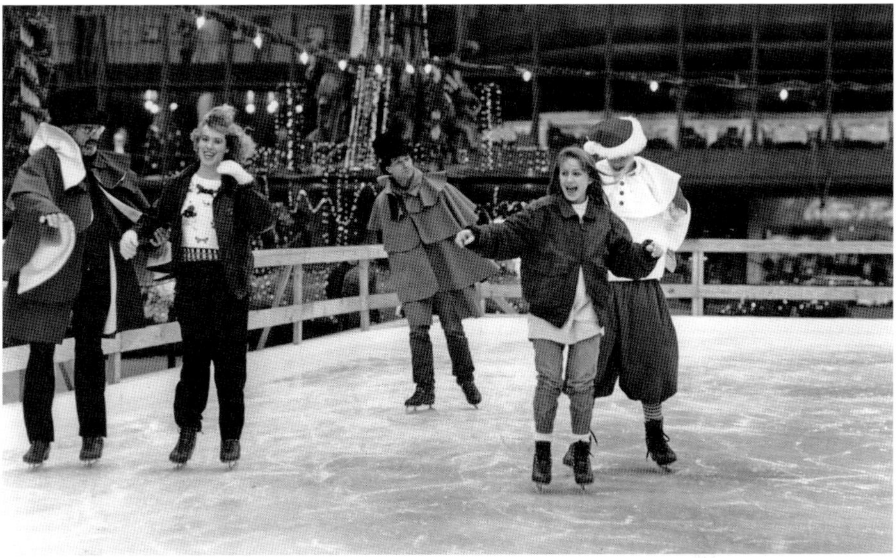

From left: Urban Knue of Sayler Park, Jennifer Bowers of Terrace Park, Jeff Weech of Clifton, Kelly Kock of College Hill and Scott Soward of Pleasant Ridge are among the first skaters to take a turn on the ice, November 30, 1990, at Fountain Square. The skaters in costume are volunteers from 'Tis the Season and Santa's Cottage, sent to the square to spread some holiday cheer. Cincinnati Enquirer *photo*.

USA Regional Chamber and former Cincinnati City Council member. "Heading downtown during the blizzard for classes at the Mabley & Carew store, walking through town in our St. X jackets (we actually thought people were impressed). It is a vivid memory yet today."

Vehr's younger brother Greg, senior VP of development at the Dragonfly Foundation and former VP at the University of Cincinnati, said he was interviewed by one of the TV stations. He describes it as the winter of all winters. "I was a freshman at St. X," he recalls. "We had makeshift classrooms at the old Mabley & Carew building near Fountain Square. I can't say that we learned much in the classrooms (I remember it being really loud), but it was truly an adventure to explore downtown and made great memories for us forty years later."

SHOPPING

Mabley & Carew played an important role in Cincinnati, and not just for providing academic facilities to teenagers. Mabley's was one of a handful of major department stores in downtown Cincinnati. Most of the stores began here in the nineteenth century; a few of them went on to become part of national chains. Some of them stayed local, one came here from New York City and another came from Minnesota. What ties many of them together are the precious Christmas memories their names evoke.

During this time, people approached shopping, especially during the holidays, as a daylong affair—something to look forward to and even dress up for. "The era of looking at a shopping trip downtown as a destination continued into the early 1970s. There was a special spirit to those times. People made an effort to get all dressed up for these expeditions—doing so was part of the adventure."[33]

Ladies wore dresses, stockings and heels for these shopping adventures. Therefore, many of the downtown department stores, and later on their counterparts in the suburbs, had tea rooms and cafés where holiday shoppers could rest their feet and fill their tanks. The McAlpin's Tea Room and the Kopper Kettle, Pogue's Camargo Room, Shillito's Tea Room and Mabley's Fountain Room were some of the favorites.

Not just a lunch counter or a lounge with vending machines, these tea rooms had genuine meal service, with delicious fare created by professional chefs and served by professional wait staff. In fact, the Shillito's Tea Room provided food for Ruth Lyons's show.[34] Shillito's Tea Room, located on the sixth floor, later became the Dining Room, then the 6th Floor Café in Lazarus.

Occasionally, entertainers were brought in. In the 1960s, patrons enjoyed a live radio show broadcast on WLW. McAlpin's *Good Morning Show* was hosted by Bob Braun until Nick Clooney was hired in 1966, as Braun was moving on to replace Ruth Lyons on her *50-50 Club*.[35] During the Christmas season, Santa Claus came to the tearoom for what was routinely a sold-out Santa Claus Breakfast. Besides its tea room, McAlpin's also had the Kopper Kettle, which served a broader audience. (I think I remember enjoying vanilla milkshakes at the Kopper Kettle.)

Pogue's had a few different venues for eating. In July 1964, it opened the Ice Cream Bridge, which served Graeter's ice cream. It provided the Soup Bar on the sixth floor, which was expanded from a capacity of 148 to 196 in 1977. Wine was served to the grown-ups; children enjoyed their Shirley Temples. Uncle Al and Captain Windy made regular appearances. During the weeks leading up to Christmas, it hosted breakfasts with Santa every Saturday morning.[36]

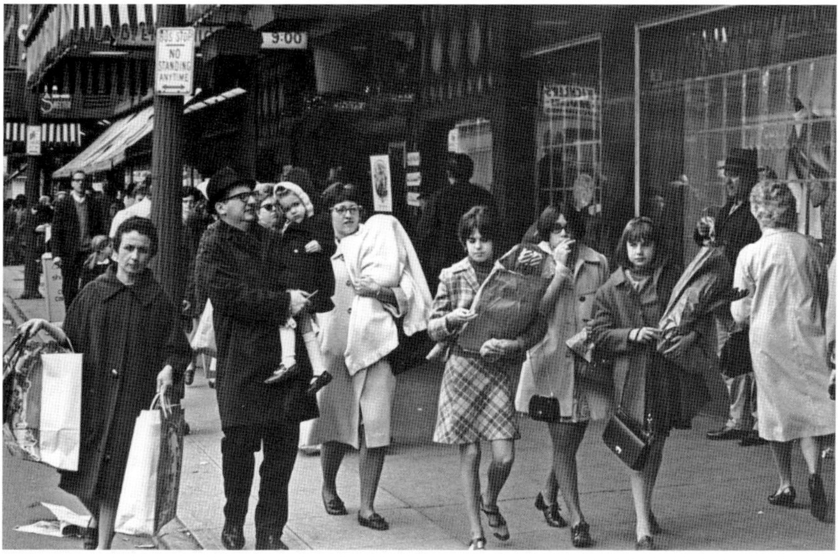

Cincinnati downtown shopping after the end of the transit strike, December 9, 1967. Cincinnati Enquirer *photo*.

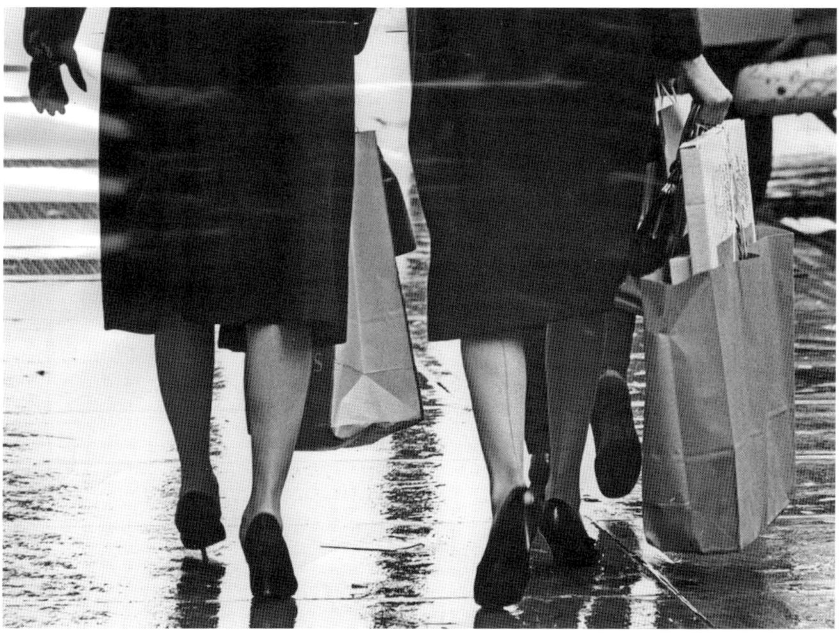

December 1964: The merchants anticipated another big day as last-minute shoppers converged on downtown, returning home at day's end with their arms full and their feet in agony. Cincinnati Enquirer *photo*.

Some tearooms provided a home in which the ladies could while away the hours playing bridge. Author Cynthia Beischel found that the women she interviewed enjoyed reminiscing about the tearooms. "The topic revived great memories not only of the era but also of their mothers, grandmothers, aunts and sisters. The tea rooms provided an environment that united generations."[37]

Just as their tearooms were slightly different, so were the stores themselves. For example, McAlpin's was known for its reasonable prices. Gidding-Jenny was more expensive and focused on personal service. C.R. Mabley declared that it was "thronged with customers of every class in society."[38]

On October 4, 1882, Mabley ran a rather long ad touching on this very topic with the headline of "THERE ARE A Great Many SHARP PEOPLE IN CINCINNATI" (original capitalization). The ad reads more like a letter from a parent giving advice:

> *There are many beautiful hat stores here, and their hats are good—just as good as ours, many of them. Prices are a little higher, well a good deal higher sometimes, and these sharp people come right up and buy their hats from us; they save a quarter, a half-dollar, and sometimes a dollar. It makes no difference to them if our hat store isn't as elegant as some others; they get the latest style of hats, and save money.…It would be hardly worth speaking of so obvious a fact, but for the moral, which is: buy when you find what you want, for to-morrow the style of pattern you want may be sold.*[39]

Other Mabley ads abandoned a helpful tone and went right for the jugular. Imagine being a parent whose children heard that C.R. Mabley & Co. was giving away a Shetland pony! And a saddle! The 1883 ad described the pony as a "perfect daisy, very gentle and kind and of a sweet disposition. It cost $200 and will be our Christmas Gift to some patron of our BOYS' HAT OR SHOE DEPARTMENT. It is beautifully marked, and as small as the smallest. Pony and Saddle now in our Show-Window."[40] Nowhere in the ad does it say the pony is actually a live animal. One can only wonder.

One store that has some of the strongest Christmas memories associated with it is Shillito's. John Shillito, one of the founding fathers of Cincinnati, established his store in 1830 to sell dry goods (fabrics, tobacco, sugar—literally, *dry* goods). Three generations of Shillitos served Cincinnati's citizens until the family moved to New England.

From 1830 to 1982, the Shillito stores bore John Shillito's name. However, in 1928—long before the store names started changing—the F&R (named for brothers Fred and Ralph) Lazarus Company bought the John Shillito

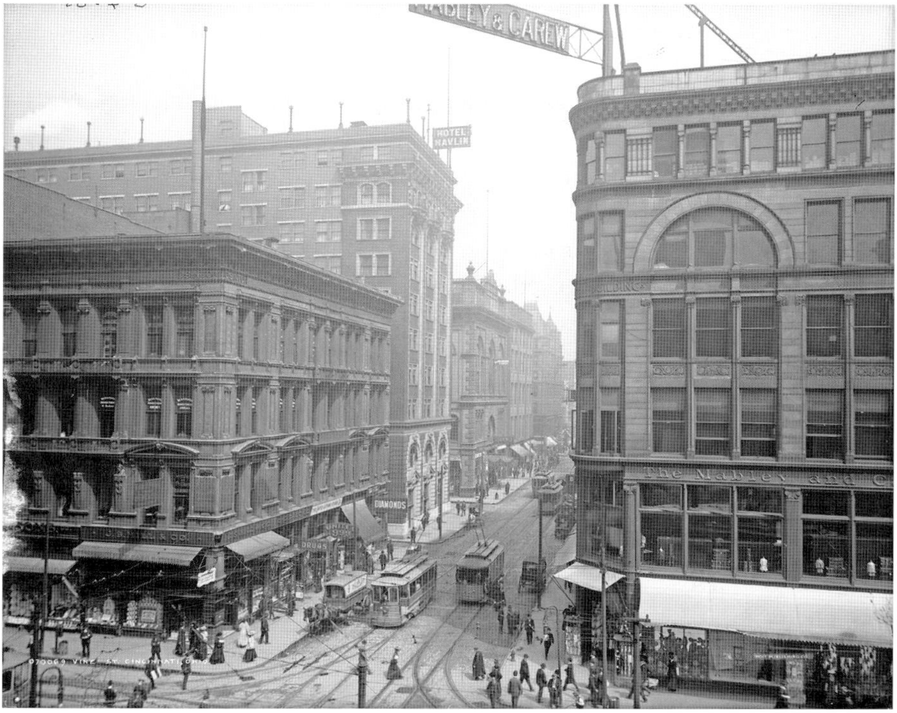

Mabley & Carew Department Store overlooks Fountain Square in 1907. *Library of Congress.*

Company. Why? Part of the reason was business: Shillito's had fallen from its proud past as king of the Queen City and ranked fourth in sales in the Cincinnati retail market. Another reason was sentimentality: Fred and Ralph's mother, Amelia, had grown up in Cincinnati and had bought her trousseau at Shillito's.

Shillito's was followed by the George W. McAlpin Company in 1852 (first as a wholesaler, then as a retailer), H.&S. Pogue in 1863, Alms & Doepke in 1865 (by 1900 the second-largest dry-goods store west of New York), Rollman & Sons Company (the "most progressive store") in 1867 and Mabley & Carew in 1877. Late to the party were the mall at Union Terminal in 1980 and Saks on Fifth Street. Saks Fifth Avenue originally came to Cincinnati with its high-end department store model but by the twenty-first century had switched to Saks Off Fifth, a deep-discount store under the same ownership.[41]

In 1929, Columbus-based F&R Lazarus joined forces with New York's Abraham & Straus and Bloomingdale's and Filene's of Boston to create

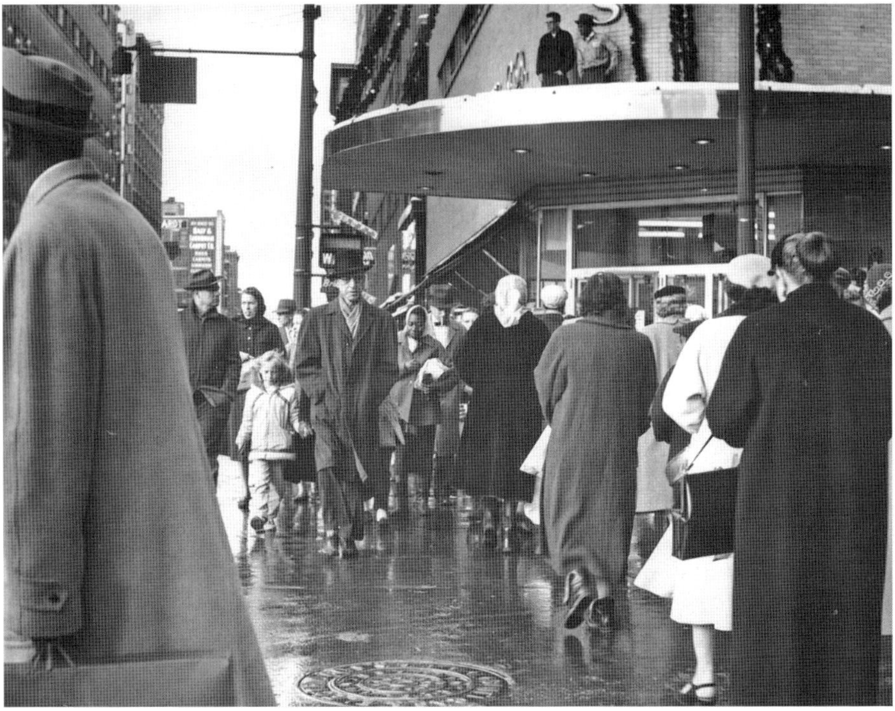

Downtown Cincinnati shoppers crowd the streets, December 1958. Cincinnati Enquirer *photo.*

Federated Department Stores, right before the stock market crash of 1929. When Fred Lazarus Jr., grandson of patriarch Simon Lazarus, became chairman of Federated in 1945, he moved the company headquarters to Cincinnati. Shillito's went through several name changes until finally becoming Macy's in 2005, matching the Federated Department Stores in New York. As such, we can claim a connection to the Macy's Thanksgiving Day parade!

One of the things that shoppers can also thank Fred Lazarus Jr. for is having Thanksgiving forever fixed as the third Thursday of November. To give retailers a longer shopping season before Christmas, Lazarus convinced President Franklin Roosevelt to buck the presidential trend and in 1939 made the change. Calendar makers, schools and football players weren't too happy about the confusion. It took an act of Congress in 1941 to settle on the third Thursday for good.[42] But after that, shoppers knew that the day after the *third* Thursday would kick off the Christmas shopping season. And people who worked in retail would know they would get little sleep on "Black Friday."

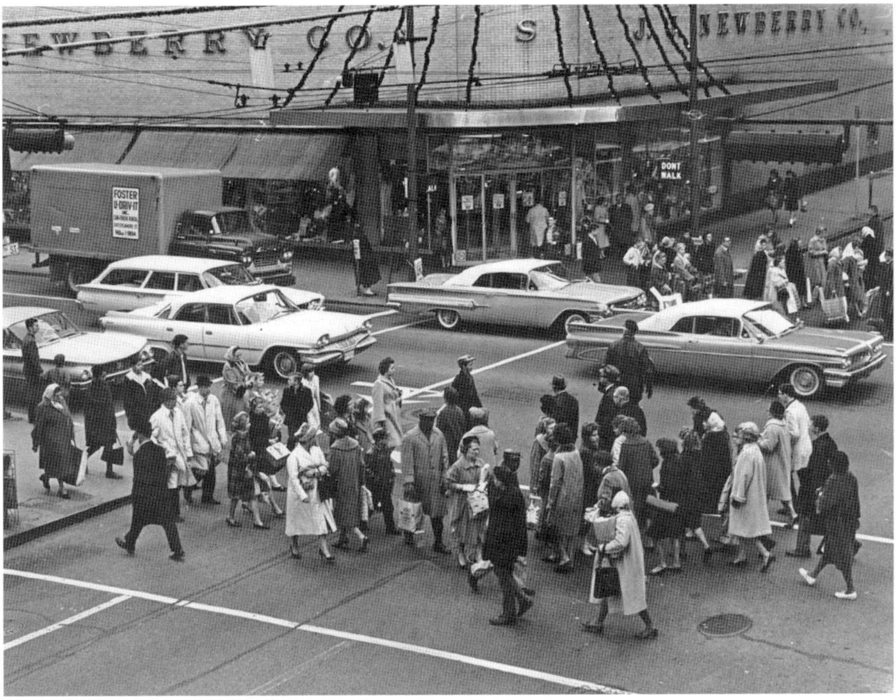

Downtown Cincinnati holiday shoppers, December 1962. Cincinnati Enquirer *photo*.

Cincinnatians of many ages remember Shillito's at Christmastime, with its display windows filled with Santa's elves, busy making toys for good little girls and boys. The elves began with Shillito's Christmas window displays in the mid-1950s. People stood spellbound in front of the elves as they painted and hammered, sawed and sewed, packed boxes and entertained cats, among other jobs. In the late 1970s, Shillito's decided to ramp up the elf action and had a team of fifteen workers create Santaland and refurbish the elves. In addition to the elves, Shillito's had "The Secret Gift Shop—for Little Shoppers Only."

The elves entertained young and old alike until 1996, when Lazarus moved its headquarters to Columbus. The elves left the building, making stops in various places before going up for auction in 2005. Bill Spinnenweber bought as many of the elves as he could and set about getting them in shape. He was surprised to find that they were already in good shape, a reflection of the care that went into creating them.[43] Before the 2020 pandemic hit, a rumor spread that the elves might make another appearance. We'll have to hope they've been vaccinated and can come out in future years.

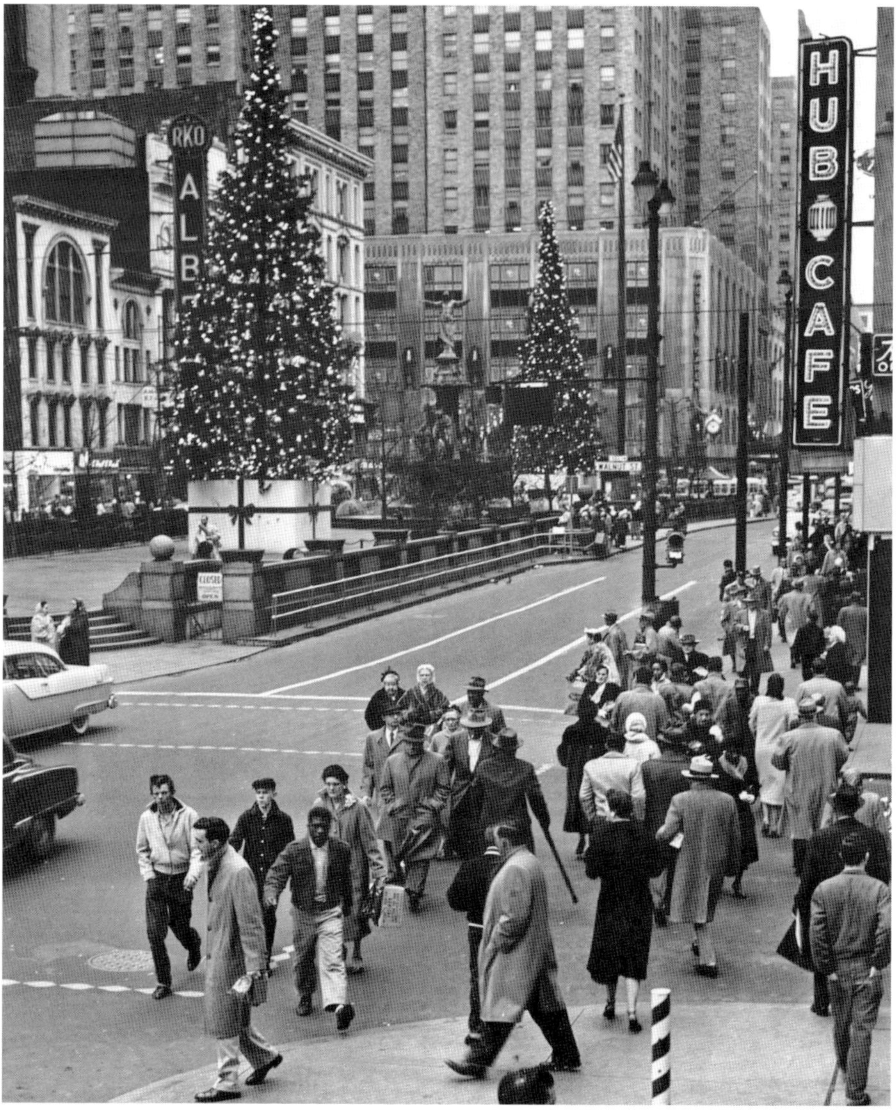

Above: Fountain Square in downtown Cincinnati during the 1956 Christmas season. Cincinnati Enquirer *photo*.

Opposite, top: On November 23, 1977, Becky Metz, two, strains for a wide-eyed look at Willy Wonka's chocolate factory helpers in the window at downtown Shillito's at Seventh and Elm Streets. Her mother, Polly Metz of Westwood, is just as pleased. Cincinnati Enquirer *photo*.

Opposite, bottom: Santaland at Shillito's goes back to the basics in December 1979 with its cute, animated elves living in a fantasy world. Cincinnati Enquirer *photo*.

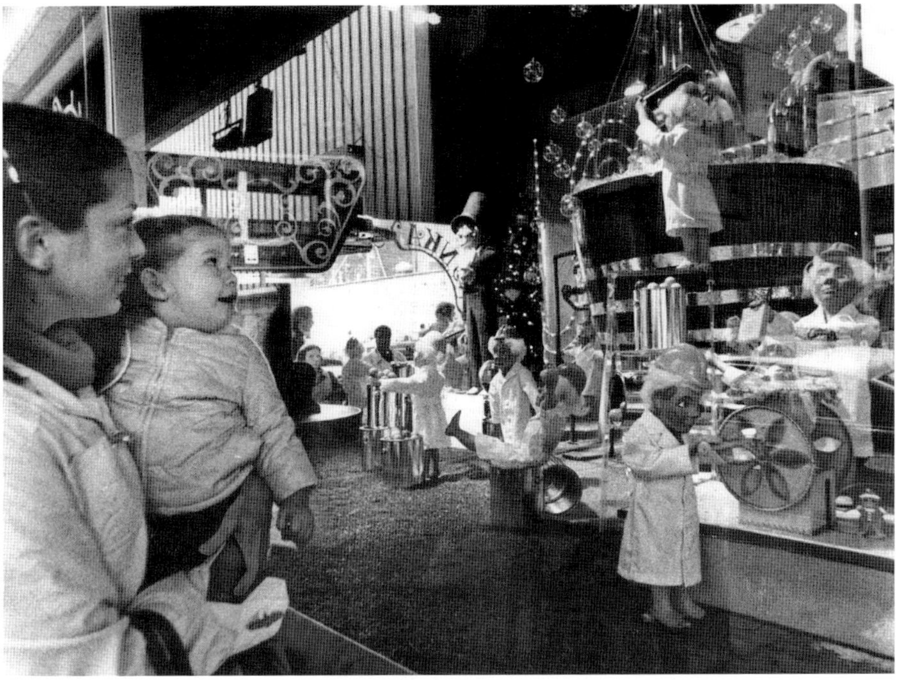

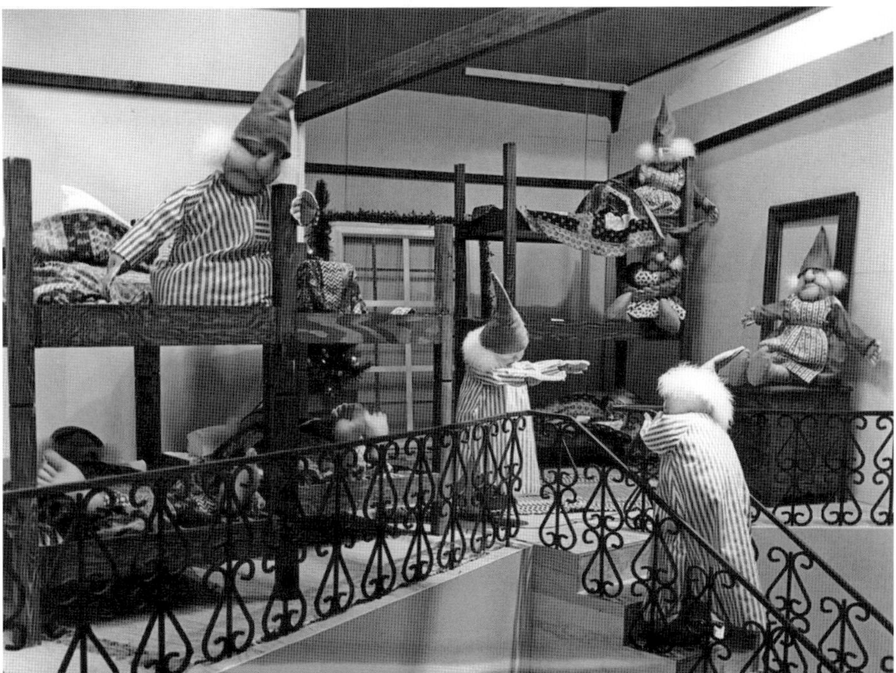

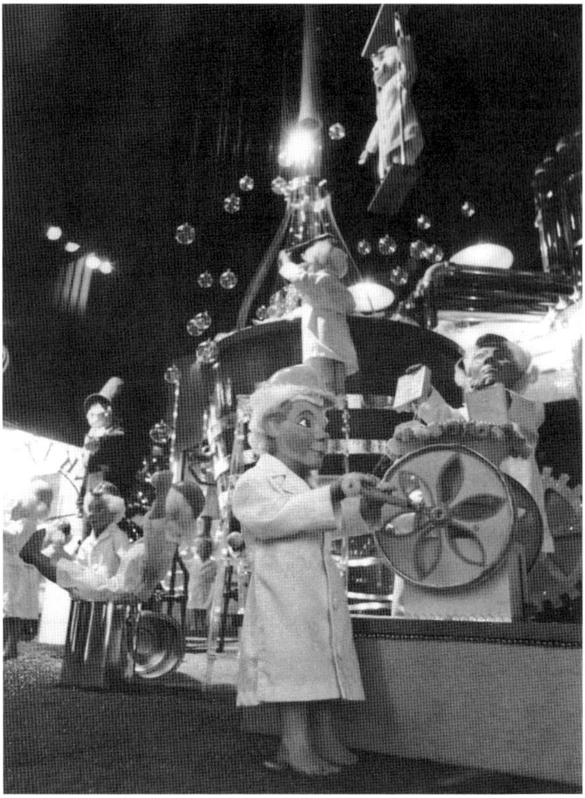

Shillito's Christmas display in the corner window at Seventh and Elm Streets, November 1977. Cincinnati Enquirer *photo.*

In 1977, Shillito's also featured scenes from Roald Dahl's novel *Charlie and the Chocolate Factory*, which in 1971 had been made into a movie, *Willy Wonka and the Chocolate Factory*. No merchandise could be seen in the store windows. The theme was carried inside, where shoppers could walk through Santaland.[44]

Rollman's had an animated display in its six windows along Fifth Street. The display, which had four thousand moving parts, was made to order in Germany and shipped in sixteen wooden crates. Five of the windows had one motor to control the action; the second window needed two motors. Each of the windows depicted a different section of Charles Dickens's *A Christmas Carol*. The first window showed Ebenezer Scrooge shaking his head and waving away men asking for donations. The second window depicted Scrooge rubbing his hands in front of his fireplace as the ghost of his former partner, Jacob Marley, appeared. Marley's chains ("that I forged in life!") could be heard distinctly inside the store. In the third window, Scrooge recalled his childhood. The fourth window showed the Cratchit family preparing Christmas dinner. In the fifth window, Scrooge sees that his bed covers have been stripped and are being sold at a pawn shop. The last window shows that Scrooge has seen the error of his ways and has given Bob Cratchit a raise. The words from *A Christmas Carol* corresponding to the action in each window were printed on an antique-looking scroll stuck to the window.[45]

Pogue's provided great holiday delight to its younger shoppers with two talking reindeer: Pogie and Patter. The two animals (just their heads, actually) were voiced by Pogue employees. One worker had to laugh when she walked by them and was greeted by name! In *Tea Rooms of Cincinnati*, Cynthia Beischel noted, "Those who spoke with Santa at Pogue's received a special helium balloon souvenir, consisting of an interior snowman balloon with an exterior clear balloon painted with snowflakes." Pogue's also had Dickensian-costumed carolers and a train set near the toy department.[46] In 1977, Pogue's created a walk-through "Enchanted Forest" in the Carew Tower Arcade. Moving, talking animals frolicked among the snowy trees.[47]

Seasonal concerts regaled shoppers at Mabley & Carew. The Carew Tower Arcade had an enchanted forest and Santa Claus in a gilded throne. Alms & Doepke, which occupied a full city block on Central Parkway, provided a full-sized carousel. Beischel writes, "For a nickel, a child got a ride and a big, fat candy cane."[48]

For the older shoppers, though, Gidding-Jenny was a special place for them. Then called J.M. Gidding & Company, it opened in 1907 as a high-grade women's department store specializing in clothing, makeup and jewelry. At the opening, the *Cincinnati Enquirer* described the building as a "work of art" with its mahogany, rich crimson carpets, marble cases and Rookwood ceramics. In 1939, another women's store, the Jenny Company, moved from its home in the Union Central Building across the street and right next to Gidding. They were merged in the 1960s under Genesco and became Gidding-Jenny.[49]

Writer Katie Laur remarked in an article in *Cincinnati Magazine* that Gidding-Jenny was "the jewel of the crown of Cincinnati's retailing community. You'd walk in the front door, smell the fragrance of Odalisque, the store's 'signature' scent, step onto the thick cream carpeting, and you were in holiday heaven." After the customer made her purchases, the purchase slip and money were placed in a pneumatic tube through which they were sucked up and scooted off to some unknown place. After the payment was approved, the bill of sale returned through the mysterious tube.

Laur described Gidding's at Christmastime as being extra special. "[At] Christmas, everything was gold at Gidding's: the wrapping paper, the bags,

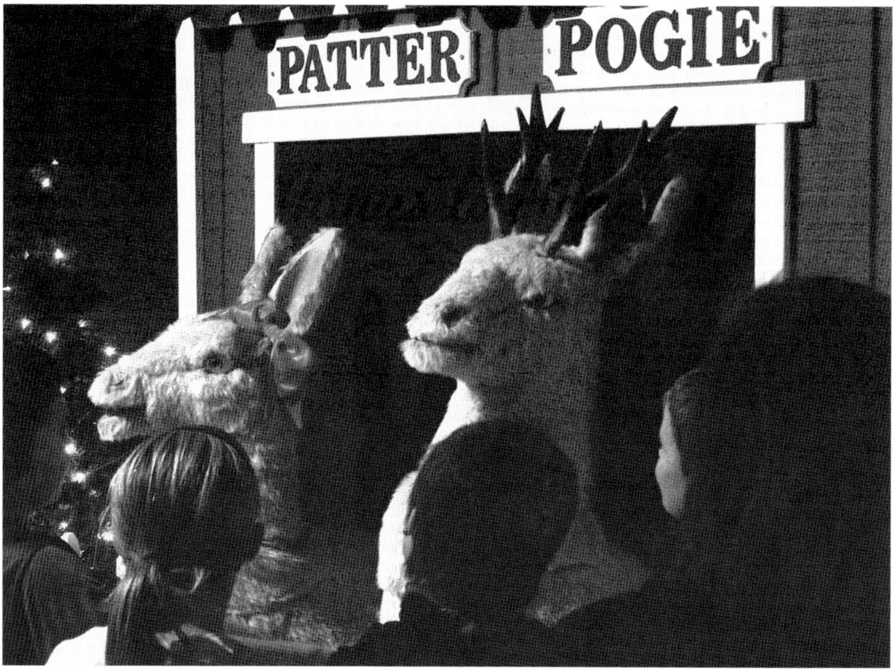

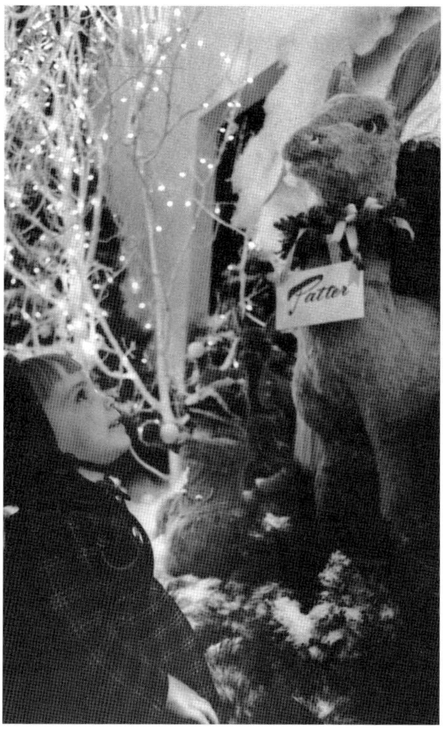

Above: Pogie and Patter entertained many H.&S. Pogue shoppers by engaging them in conversation as they walked by. One Pogue's employee was tickled when the reindeer called her by name as she passed them. Cincinnati Enquirer *photo*.

Left: The Enchanted Forest at Pogue's arcade featured two interactive talking reindeer, Pogie and Patter. Cincinnati Enquirer/*Ed Reinke*.

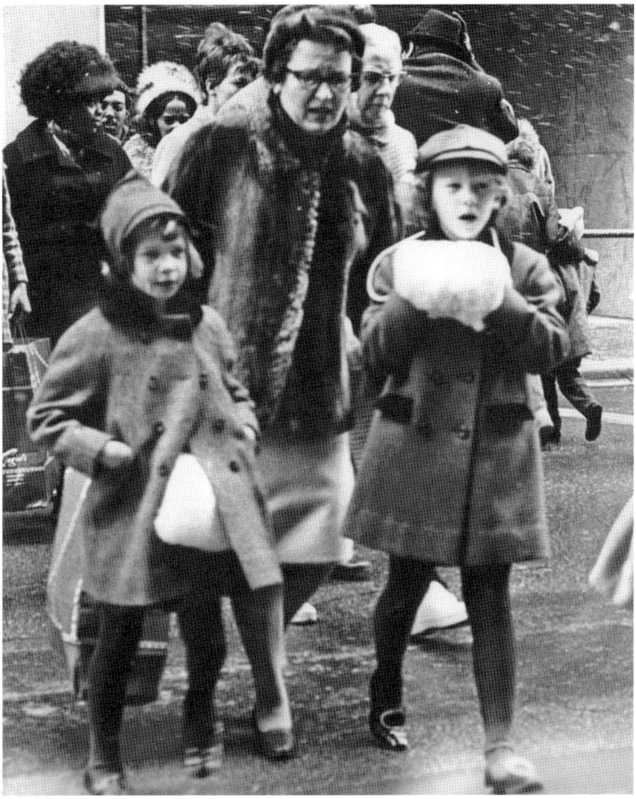

Downtown Cincinnati holiday shoppers cross the street, December 1968. Cincinnati Enquirer *photo*.

the bows were an orgy of gilt." Perhaps in the best stroke of all, the store served eggnog from a silver bowl. A man dressed in white scooped the eggnog and poured it into diminutive glass cups and sprinkled it with nutmeg. Laur really liked the eggnog: "It was spiked, too; it lowered your inhibitions and gave you a feeling of euphoria, as if you were floating on a cloud. To add to the luxurious holiday spirit, the store hired models to stroll around in fur coats and evening gowns."[50]

Gidding-Jenny had the same feel in its advertisements. Lithe models were hand drawn in pen and ink by some of the artists from the Art Academy of Cincinnati. One of those artists, Romilda Dilley, proudly displayed some of her Gidding-Jenny drawings even into her nineties. The descriptions in the ads transported potential shoppers with a promise of what they would find in the store. One ad from December 2, 1963, in the *Cincinnati Enquirer* offers the ladies "our refreshing two-piece dress in a textured weave of soft and acrylic fiber…bubbling over with holiday spirits…sparked with a detachable Christmas green chiffon scarf."

Gidding-Jenny's clientele decreased as shoppers turned to the suburbs instead of going downtown to shop, a fate faced by many downtown retailers. It closed its doors in 1995. In March 2021, the building was put up for sale.

Mabley's was sold to Elder-Beerman in 1978. The building was razed to make way for the redesign of Fountain Square (one of many).[51]

Union Terminal, located northwest of downtown, is a cat with nine lives. It was originally built to consolidate the tracks for the seven railroads found in Cincinnati. Construction started in 1928; the art deco half-dome construction began in 1931 and was completed in 1933. At that time, it was one of the largest train terminals in the nation. Eventually, though, ridership fell and the trains decreased. The Union Terminal Company sold Union Terminal to the city of Cincinnati in 1975.

The city hoped to pave the way for the long-term preservation of the Cincinnati icon. The city tried to rent the building for as little as one dollar a year but got no response. Finally, in 1979, a Columbus developer, Skilken & Company, proposed to turn the building into the "Land of Oz," an entertainment facility that would feature an ice rink, a theater and other entertainment venues. The proposal morphed into a mall, which opened in 1980 with a variety of vendors lined up on the concourse. The mall experienced success early on, but by 1984, it had lost most of its tenants. The last to go was discount retailer Loehmann's Department Store in 1985. The city looked for another tenant, and thus the Cincinnati Museum Center was born.[52] At that point, the Cincinnati Museum of Natural History and the Cincinnati Historical Society were looking for a new location, so they formed a museum in 1991. When the Children's Museum was flooded in the spring floods of 1997 and needed to relocate, it was a natural addition to the mix.

Although the mall is history, the Cincinnati Museum Center has a wonderful gift shop (as does the main branch of the Public Library of Cincinnati and Hamilton County) for holiday purchases.

Craft Affairs, Markets and Shows

Another great way to pick up unique gifts and decorations is by visiting any of the many craft shows, markets and fairs. One of these is the Germania Christkindlmarkt. ("Christkindlmarkt" is German for "Christ child market.") This coming year should be the 23rd Annual Germania Christkindlmarkt,

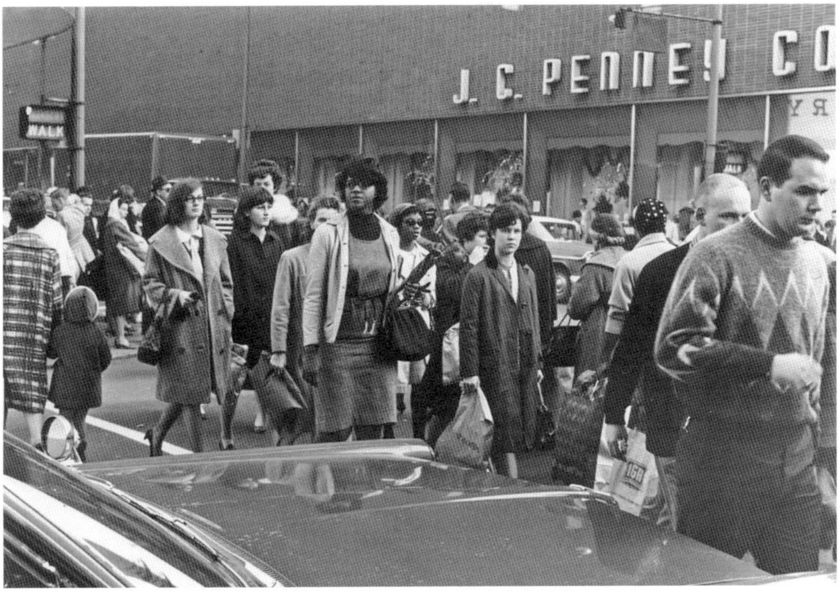

Downtown Cincinnati shopping on the day after Thanksgiving, 1964. Cincinnati Enquirer *photo.*

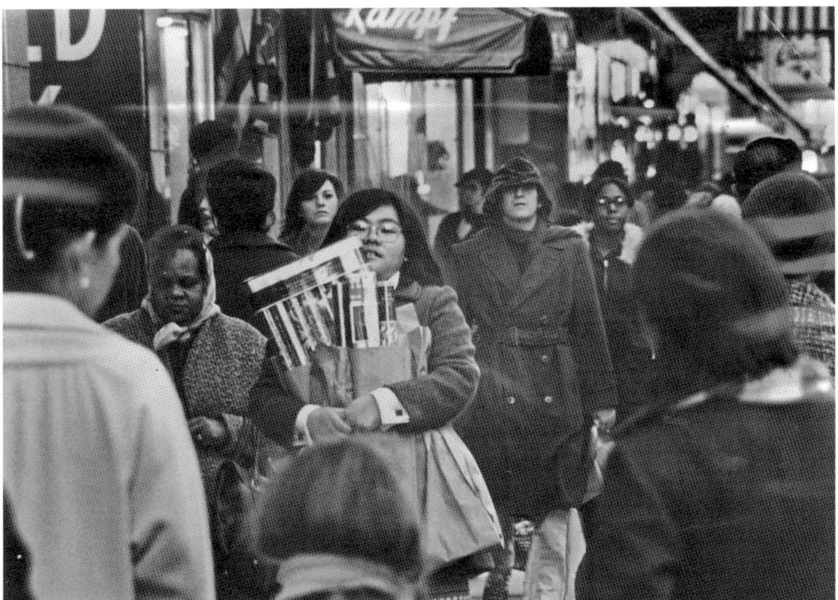

"And the Multitudes Turned Out Upon the Streets…"; "fear not, for thou canst still reach the market place before it is closed," December 24, 1970. Cincinnati Enquirer *photo.*

which is put on each year by the Germania Society. During the pandemic year of 2020, Christkindlmarkt went virtual, as did many others. It is traditionally held the weekend before Thanksgiving; in 2021, it is scheduled to take place on November 20 and 21.

According to the Germania Society's 1964 constitution, the society's purposes are to "maintain and perpetuate the German heritage (in cultural, educational, and social life of the German people), and to serve all German people in the Cincinnati area whether resident or visitor by doing all things necessary, convenient and incident thereto."

The Germania Christkindlmarkt is the oldest and most authentic German Christmas market in the Cincinnati region. It takes place at Germania Park in the Pleasant Run community north of Cincinnati. Shoppers can browse in comfort in heated, enclosed tents. Besides shopping for German steins, crafts, foods and other gifts, families can enjoy a children's lantern parade, a petting zoo, carriage rides and Christmas caroling. Of course, German music is everywhere. If you get hungry while you're shopping, try the *Dillgurkensuppe* (traditional dill pickle soup), *Bier*, *Kuchen*, *Glühwein* (hot mulled wine) and *die Süßigkeiten* (sweets).[53]

Other holiday fairs and craft shows can be found all around town. Here are some of the big favorites:

- 10/23/21, 10:00 a.m.–6:00 p.m., Home for the Holidays Craft and Vendor Show, Sharonville Convention Center, 11355 Chester Road, 45246
- 11/13/21, Winter Craft Show, EnterTRAINment Junction, 7379 Squire Court, West Chester, 45069 (It also has an online gift shop for train aficionados of every age: https://toys.entertrainmentjunction.com.)
- 11/12–14/21, Greater Cincinnati Holiday Market, Duke Energy Convention Center, 525 Elm Street, 45202
- 11/15/20, All Things Local/Art on Vine, Washington Park, 1230 Elm Street, 45202
- 11/20–21/21, Christkindlmarkt, Germania Park, 3529 West Kemper Road, 45251
- 11/27/21, Westside Market—Holiday Edition, 3719 Harrison Avenue, Cheviot, 45211
- 11/26–29/21, Greater Cincinnati Winterfair, Northern Kentucky Convention Center, 220 Madison Avenue, Covington, Kentucky, 41011

- 11/26–11/27 (?), Crafty Supermarket, Cincinnati Music Hall, 1241 Elm Street (Check for 2021 date at https://craftysupermarket.com.)
- 12/4–5/21, 8:00 a.m.–4:00 p.m., Findlay Market Holiday Market, 1801 Race Street, 45202
- 12/11/21, Delhi Township Holiday Market, Delhi Township Senior Citizens Center, 647 Neeb Road, 45233
- 12/14/21, 4:00–9:00 p.m., City Flea Holiday Market, Washington Park, 1230 Elm Street, 45202

Some of Cincinnati's area high schools also host craft shows that offer great Christmas gifts. Check out these schools for their 2021 dates:

- Colerain High School, 8801 Cheviot Road
- Lakota East High School, 6480 Lakota Lane
- LaSalle High School, 3091 North Bend Road
- Loveland High School, 1 Tiger Trail
- Milford High School, 1 Eagles Way
- McNicholas High School, 6536 Beechmont Avenue
- Oak Hills High School, 3200 Ebenezer Road
- Ross High School, 3601 Hamilton-Cleves Road
- Seton High School, 3901 Glenway Avenue
- Sycamore High School, 7400 Cornell Road[54]

Holiday Trains

While Union Terminal no longer houses a shopping mall, it still attracts young and old from near and far to its Holiday Junction. One of the key components of the event is the Duke Energy Holiday Trains. These trains have a long history and are very dear to Cincinnatians of all ages.

The trains were built by the Baltimore & Ohio (B&O) Railroad Company to train the U.S. military on how to operate a rail yard. After World War II, B&O Railroad gave the trains and display to the Cincinnati Gas & Electric Company, whose headquarters was on Fourth Street.[55] (CG&E became CINergy in November 1993, which was bought by Duke Energy in 2006.)

For sixty-five years, each season, a dedicated corps of volunteers assembled and dismantled the display, one of the largest portable model trains in the

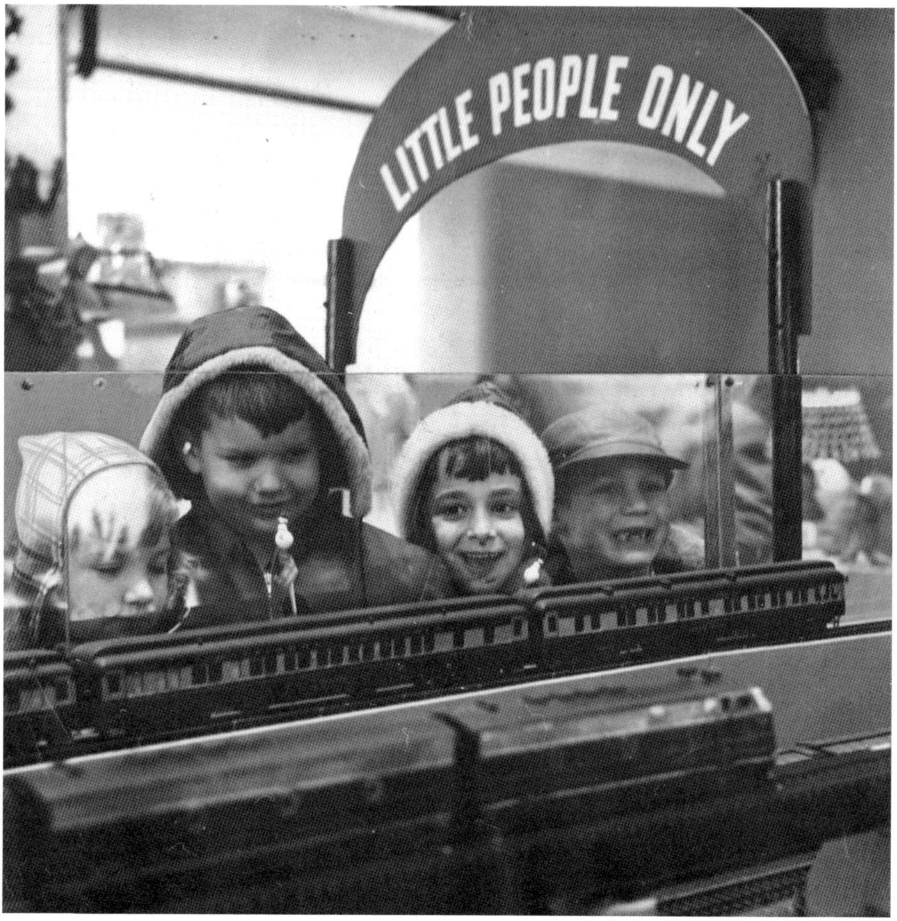

Whittier School youngsters (*left to right*) Plans Haydon, Jimmy Bridgeford, Emily Fowler and Jay Minser eye with pleasure the Baltimore & Ohio O gauge model train exhibit in the Cincinnati Gas & Electric Company lobby, November 30, 1960. Cincinnati Enquirer *photo*.

world, consisting of three hundred miniature cars, sixty engines, more than one thousand feet of track and an incredibly detailed diorama. It is considered an O gauge model railroad, which means that a quarter of an inch on the model represents one foot in real life.

After the display was taken down each year, it was shipped to the B&O Railroad Museum in Baltimore. Finally, in 2011, it was moved to the Cincinnati Museum Center to be conserved as a permanent exhibit. This meant the train would not need to be dismantled and shipped each year, alleviating many people's worries about potential damage to the aging train.

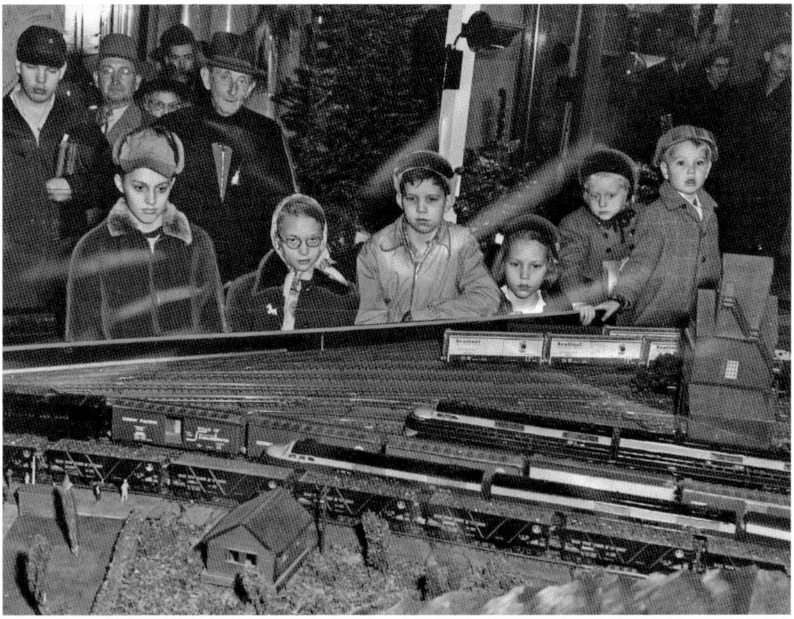

Young and old fans view the $50,000 model Baltimore & Ohio Railroad display for the fourth consecutive year in the lobby of the Cincinnati Gas & Electric Company on Fourth Street, December 6, 1950. Cincinnati Enquirer *photo.*

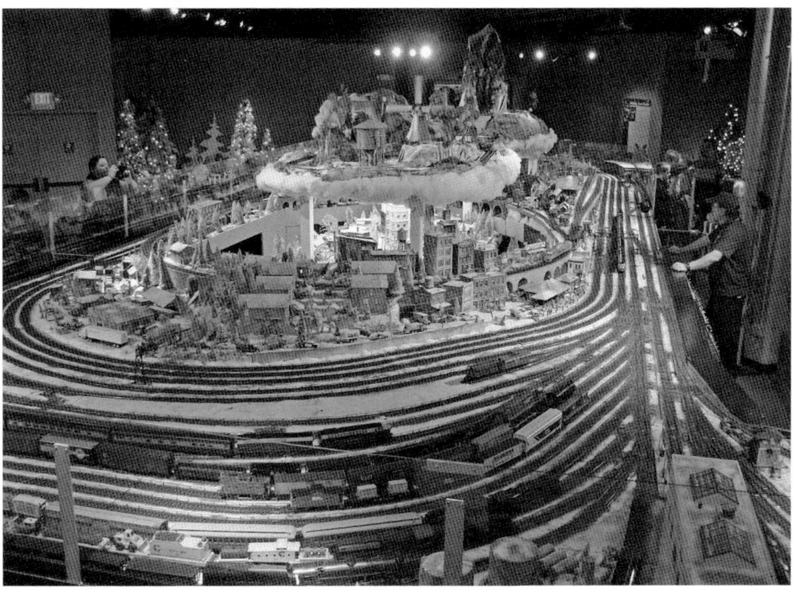

Though many "old-timers" still call these the CG&E trains, they have moved to the Cincinnati Museum Center and are now named the Duke Energy trains. *Courtesy of Denny Gibson.*

Starting in 2016, the Cincinnati Museum Center underwent a major $212.7 million renovation. It was decided that the seventy-year-old train display might not survive being moved, so it "sheltered in place" until CMC was ready to bring it out again.[56] That day arrived in November 2018, as the Holiday Junction featuring the Duke Energy Holiday Trains at Union Terminal enthralled local train enthusiasts once again.

Train enthusiasts in Cincinnati are lucky to have many trains available for watching. Just north of Cincinnati, in West Chester, is EnterTRAINment Junction, the largest indoor train display, as well as a railroad museum. In addition, EnterTRAINment Junction has a children's play area and the A-Maze-N Funhouse. Between Memorial Day and Labor Day, instead of just watching the model trains, visitors can ride the narrow-gauge train or ride around the track in an old hand-cranked railroad car. For the holidays, a special "Christmas at the Junction" is offered from the Saturday before Thanksgiving to New Year's. Visitors can see the North Pole and meet Mr. and Mrs. Santa Claus until Christmas Eve (after which Santa takes a much-deserved break). It is usually open on Christmas Eve but not on Christmas Day. Even better, for those who can't wait a full year for their Santa fix, from the last week of June to the last week of July, "Christmas in July" at EnterTRAINment Junction offers visitors a chance to check in with Santa.[57]

VISITING SANTA

Despite what my son concluded (see the Introduction), Santa is a very busy man. He is also a talented man, sometimes arriving by helicopter (as is often the case at the Cincinnati Museum Center). Across the Ohio River at the Newport Aquarium, "Scuba Santa" can be found "swimmin' with the fishes." Literally. At the Newport Aquarium, Santa swims with his elven helpers, carrying his big "Magic Book." Children gather at the window, pressing their hands and noses against the glass. (The Newport Aquarium is usually open on Christmas Eve but not on Christmas Day.)

Santa has rappelled down one of the skyscrapers on Fountain Square, after which the crowd enjoyed holiday fireworks. He has also been caught skating on the ice rink on Fountain Square.

In days gone by, shoppers could find Santa in most of the downtown department stores, sometimes accompanied by his reindeer or riding a train.

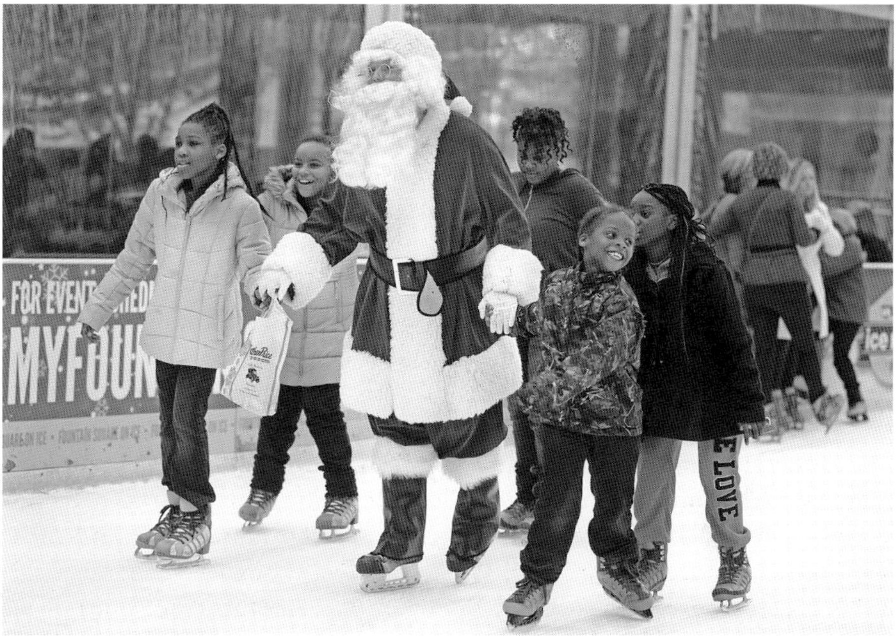

Santa skates with a group of children at the U.S. Bank Ice Rink on Fountain Square, December 13, 2015. Cincinnati Enquirer/*Liz Dufour*.

He often set up shop in the Carew Tower Arcade, ready for children to whisper their innermost Christmas wishes into his ear. Santa also makes stops at the Society for the Prevention of Cruelty to Animals (SPCA), because he loves animals. Sometimes joined by Mrs. Claus, he has been seen all over the city at Christmastime.

Sometimes, Santa has to work harder than usual to deliver the best gift to each good little girl and boy. Occasionally, brave parents might push their luck and plunk more than one child at a time on Santa's lap. In 1963, Ralph Gollahon, who was in charge of Shillito's display, estimated that more than fifty thousand children sat on the laps of the store's three Santas.[58]

In 2020, many places that usually hosted Santa had to "reimagine" (as Bass Pro Shops put it) how Santa could interact with the children but still maintain the proper social distance. So Santa learned how to Zoom.

The pandemic was a scary time for adults and children alike. Kids wondered if Santa was going to be able to carry out his duties and if Santa was at risk for COVID-19 because he was ignoring the travel restrictions. One little six-year-old spoke for many at a CNN town hall with Dr. Anthony Fauci, the director of the National Institute of Allergy and Infectious

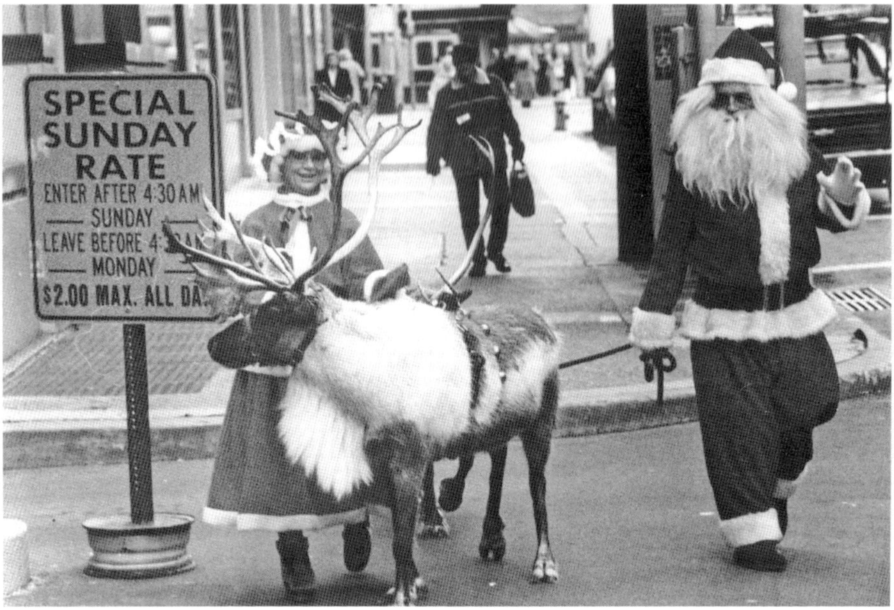

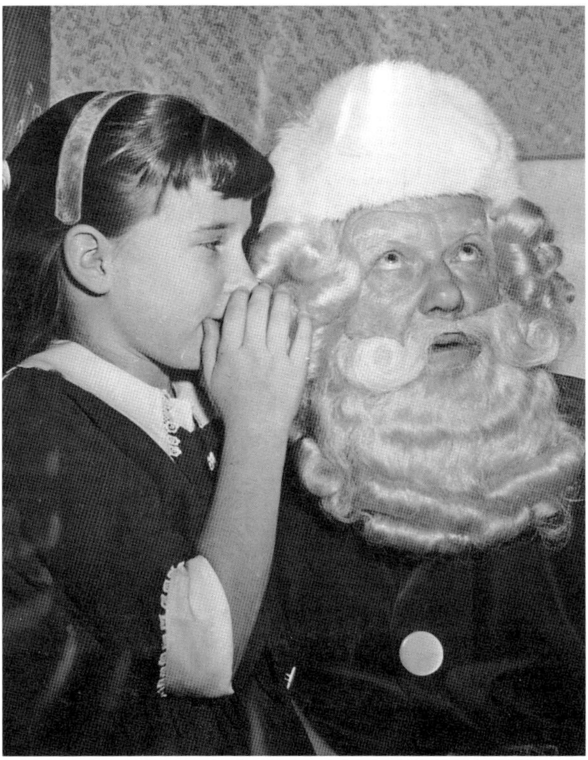

Above: Santa and Mrs. Claus (Bill Rehrig and Alice Henning) stroll along downtown Cincinnati streets on December 3, 1991, accompanied by one of Santa's reindeer. The reindeer is part of the Fountain Square holiday display. Cincinnati Enquirer *photo*.

Left: "'Twas three weeks before Christmas, but Santa was here. / And wherever you looked, kids were bending his ear. / He listened and nodded and patted their curls / and asked if they'd been model-type boys and girls, / and thought, as the lines seemed to stretch without end, / 'I'll be back Christmas Eve—if my knees will unbend!'" Cincinnati Enquirer/*Fred Straub*.

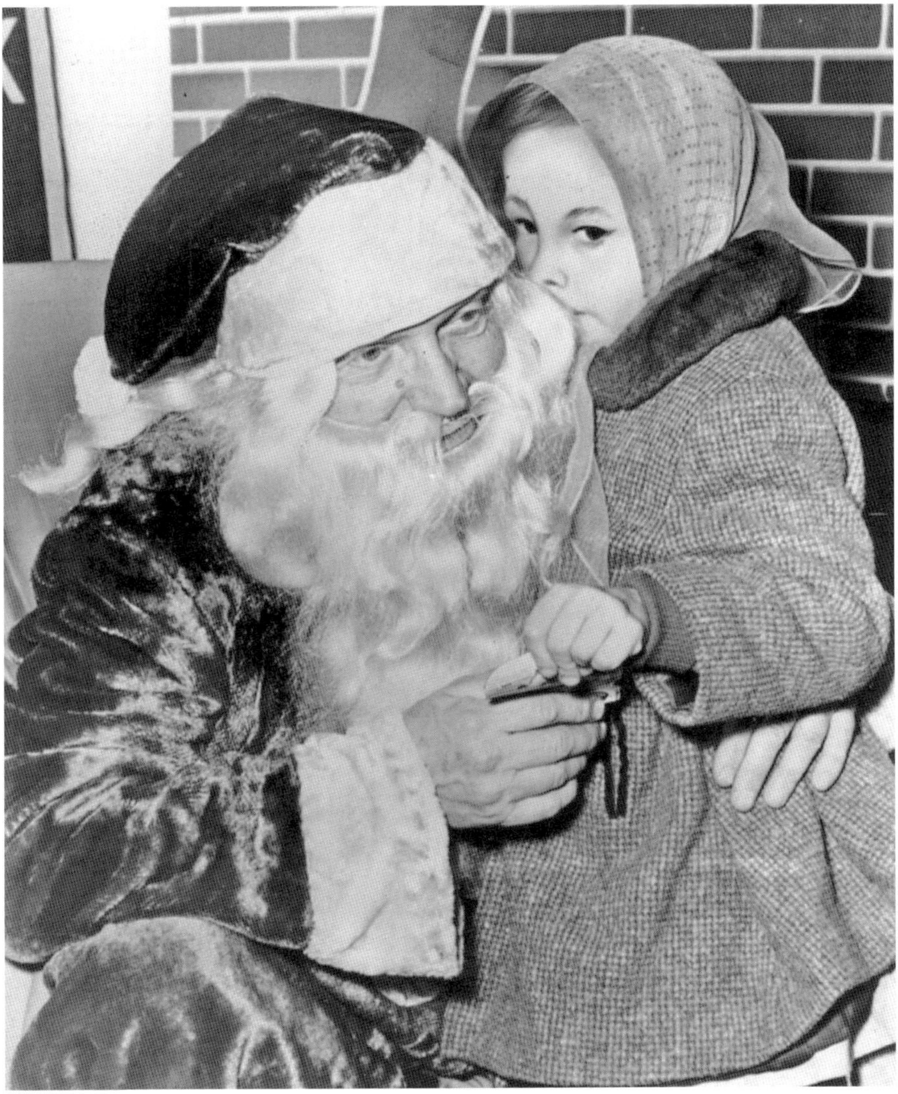

An unidentified little girl visits with Santa Claus, December 11, 1967. Cincinnati Enquirer *photo*.

Diseases. Paxton from Geneva, Illinois, asked, "Will Santa still be able to visit me in coronavirus's season? What if he can't go to anyone's house, or near his reindeer?" Dr. Fauci reassured the youngster, telling him that he had thought that children might be worried, so he personally went up to the North Pole and vaccinated Santa himself. The good doctor then checked Santa's immunity and found he was "good to go."[59]

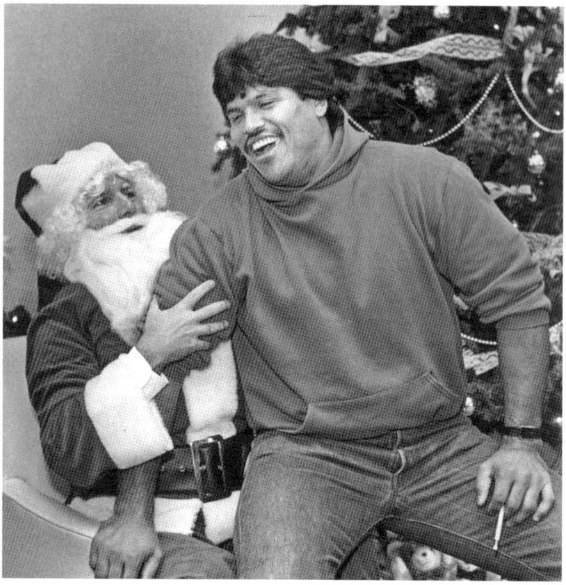

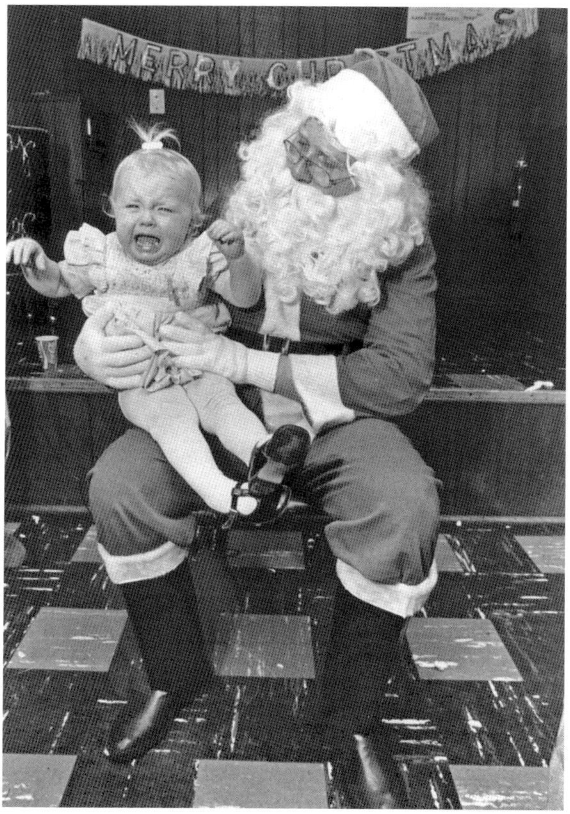

Top: Cincinnati Bengals all-pro offensive tackle Anthony Munoz breaks into a laugh as he puts his 280-pound frame on Santa Claus's lap while visiting economically disadvantaged children at a holiday celebration at Avon Products Inc., December 6, 1985. Cincinnati Enquirer/*Rick Norton*.

Left: Melissa Brunner, fifteen months, the daughter of Mr. and Mrs. Daniel Brunner of Price Hill, figures there's got to be a better way to spend a Friday night than sitting on some chubby guy's lap. "C'mon, Mom, get me out of here!" Santa Claus visited the Price Hill Christmas party at the Chambers-Hautman American Legion Hall and told about three hundred young people that they'd best not pout. December 5, 1980. Cincinnati Enquirer *photo*.

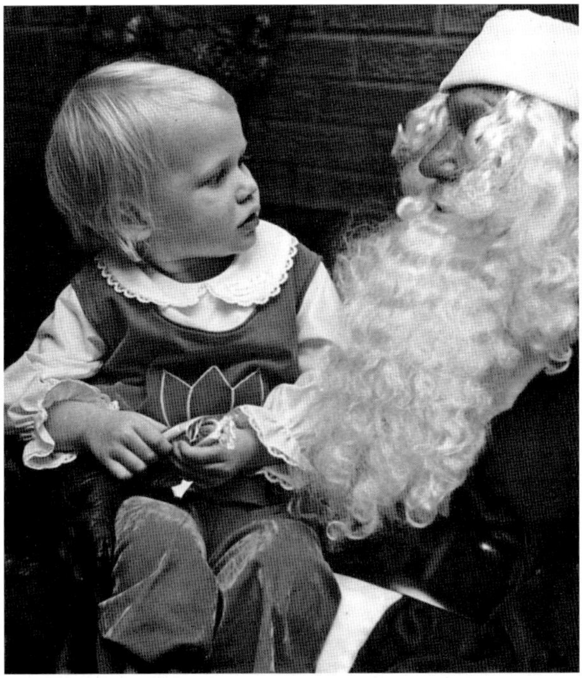

Little Charlie Mescher uses telepathy to communicate with Santa Claus Flesch. The Beechwood School PTA, Fort Mitchell, brought Santa and Mrs. Claus to the school so that the children would have an opportunity to talk with Santa himself. More than eight hundred children and parents came to the school for a day of games and songs with storybook characters, December 24, 1975. Cincinnati Enquirer/*Bob Free.*

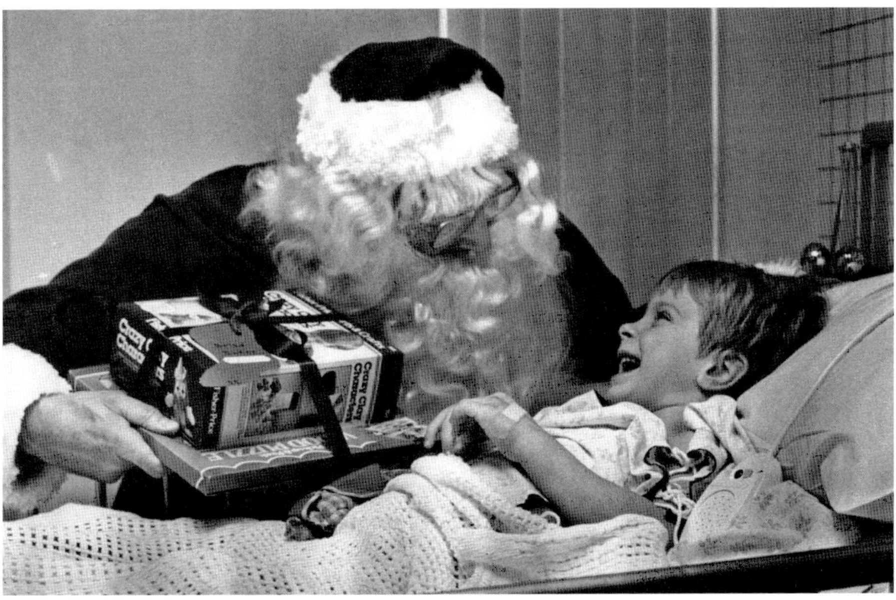

Santa Claus, who in this case also goes by the name of Dr. Roger Giesel, hands gifts to a delighted Brian Baker, a patient at Cincinnati Children's Hospital. It was Giesel's twenty-fifth year as the hospital's Santa. December 21, 1983. Cincinnati Enquirer/*Fred Straub.*

Santa needs to take care of his health, especially because one of his most important tasks is visiting ill and injured children in the hospital. For years, the patients in Cincinnati Children's Hospital and Medical Center have greatly enjoyed the attention of the jolly old elf.

One such Santa was pediatrician Dr. Roger Giesel, who visited patients as Santa for twenty-five years. As a young doctor, Giesel did his internship at a time when doctors were being drafted. In December 1955, he was sent to Stuttgart, Germany, where he treated Americans at the one-thousand-bed U.S. Army Hospital. He found himself "volunteered" to be Santa Claus, and he came in by helicopter. Now ninety-three, he says, "I was impressed with myself," with a chuckle (but not a "ho, ho, ho"). In 1957, when he returned to the States, he went to work at Cincinnati Children's Hospital. "They were looking for a Santa Claus for the Ruth Lyons Christmas party, so I volunteered."[60]

DONATING

When Santa makes the rounds in the hospitals, he is lucky to be helped by elves—not those in Shillito's windows or those at the North Pole, but an auxiliary set of elves far south of the North Pole. They're called "Cincinnatians." One of the activities that Cincinnatians excel at is giving. Some of the best drives for toys and other items are held by the local TV stations.

The Neediest Kids of All (NKOA) started in 1952. WKRC (then under Taft Broadcasting) was a huge supporter from the start. The *Cincinnati Enquirer* jumped on board in 1964, and iHeartMedia Cincinnati joined in 1999. According to the *1955–'56 Campaign Report for "Neediest Kids Of All,"* the board members, NKOA officers and anyone else affiliated with the organization would not derive any financial benefit. Furthermore:

> *It is agreed by the Board, officers and members, that help to children shall be forthcoming on aid-projects adopted without regard to race, creed or color.*
>
> *All projects undertaken by "Neediest Kids Of All" shall have the full support of all members of this organization who are members for the sole reason of their belief that kindness, help and guidance for children create fine citizens for the future.*[61]

NKOA collects money, toys, clothing, eyeglasses and shoes and seeks educational opportunities for children. In the 1954–55 campaign, $9,676.43

was collected.[62] That's almost $99,000 today. In the 1955–56 campaign report, Hulbert Taft Jr., president of Radio Cincinnati Inc., reported that at that year's Christmas party, 750 school-age children and 250 preschoolers were served. An additional one thousand families received gift bags, which were delivered to their homes. More than $7,500 was received in cash donations. Cincinnati's children received a total of two thousand shopping bags, brimming with gifts, holiday sweets, fruits and nuts. Many local organizations have played a role: Albers Super Markets, E. Kahn's and Sons Company, Geo. Wiedemann Brewing Company, Hamilton Specialty Insurance, L. Schreiber & Sons Company and employees of the Cincinnati Public School system. The campaign and publicity efforts were supported by South-Western Publishing Company, Cincinnati Parent Teacher Association, Cincinnati Board of Education, the College of Music, the *Cincinnati Enquirer*, the *Cincinnati Post*, the *Cincinnati Times-Star*, Cincinnati Teachers Association, Cincinnati Chamber of Commerce, Jr. Chamber of Commerce, Cincinnati Police Department and even the U.S. Army and Air Force. Cincinnati was blessed with a lot of toy, book and other manufacturers that also stepped up to the plate: Artcraft Paper Company, Baxter Toy Company, Cardinal Craftsmen, Kenner Products, Kruse Hardware, MacGregor Company, Merry Manufacturing, Sears Roebuck & Company, Cincinnati Cordage and Paper Company, J.J. Schmidt Inc., Toy Manufacturers Association and Stuart Manufacturing Company.[63]

In the major flooding experienced by Cincinnati in 1997, NKOA collected and disbursed $175,000 for flood relief. Through their efforts, NKOA has benefited children in the seventeen-county tri-state area in more than seven hundred schools and Head Start sites, as well as foster children in the juvenile court system.[64]

Toy Team 9 has been a joint effort by WCPO Channel 9, Kroger, Cumulus Radio and local nonprofits since 2011. In 2019, it collected 10,613 toys in a five-hour period on December 7.[65] As so many other outfits did, its efforts went online for a virtual drive, but the organization was still able to collect $18,701 to purchase toys for children.

The gem of the holiday drives is the Ruth Lyons Children's Fund. In the 1930s, Ruth Lyons worked for Cincinnati radio station WKRC. During the horrendous flood of 1937, she broadcast nonstop—both to provide comfort and to seek donations. A less traumatic and less known achievement reflected her musical talent. Every week she composed a new song to perform while accompanying herself on the piano. In 1958, two of her songs, "Christmas Song" (also known as "Have a Merry, Merry Christmas") and "Let's Light

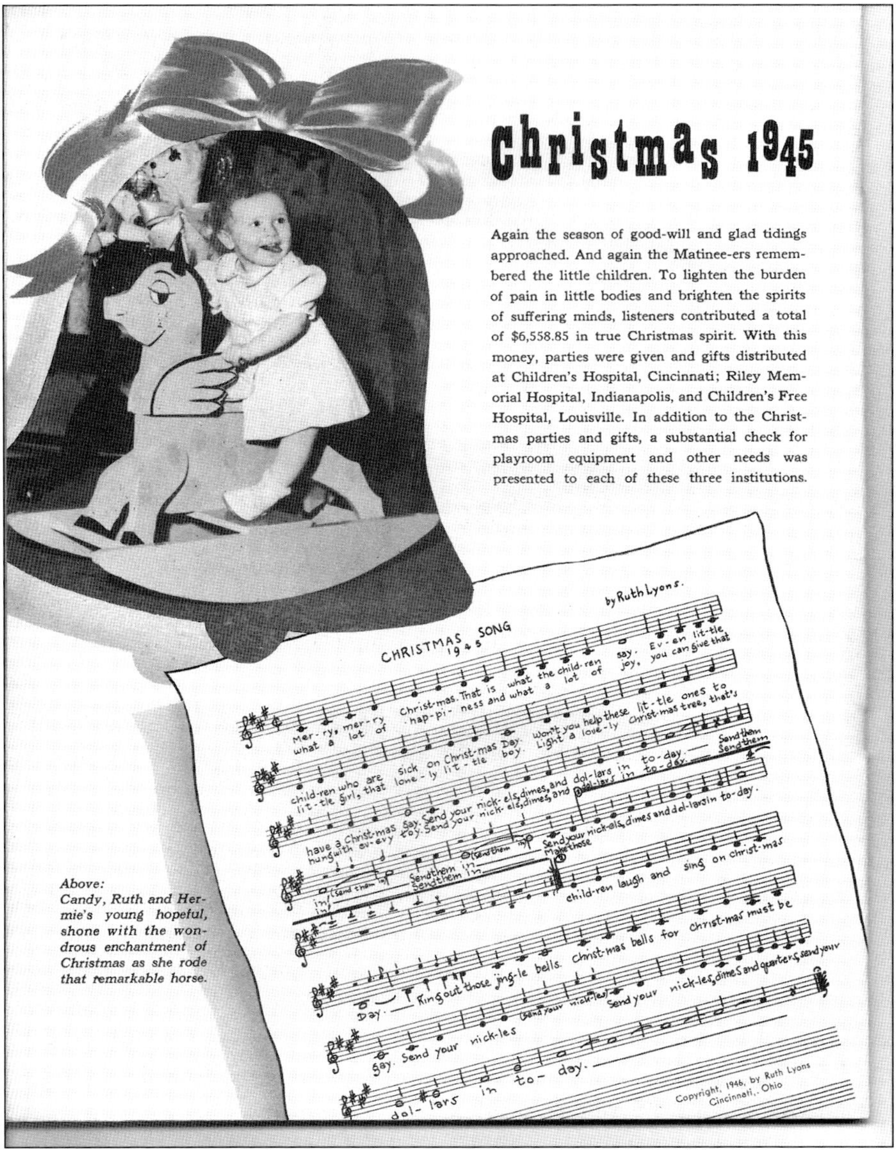

Candy Lyons rides her rocking horse in this booklet from *WLW*. *WLW photo*.

the Christmas Tree," were played on the Union Central Life Insurance chimes. Union Central vice president Marshall Hunt selected the songs for the tower chimes to play.[66]

In 1942, Lyons left for WLW (the "World's Largest Wireless") and WSAI. *The WLW Consumer's Foundation* featured Lyons, Frazier Thomas and organist

Arthur Chandler. The show was later renamed *Your Morning Matinee*, then *Morning Matinee*. Her trademark was to always use a handheld microphone wrapped in flowers.

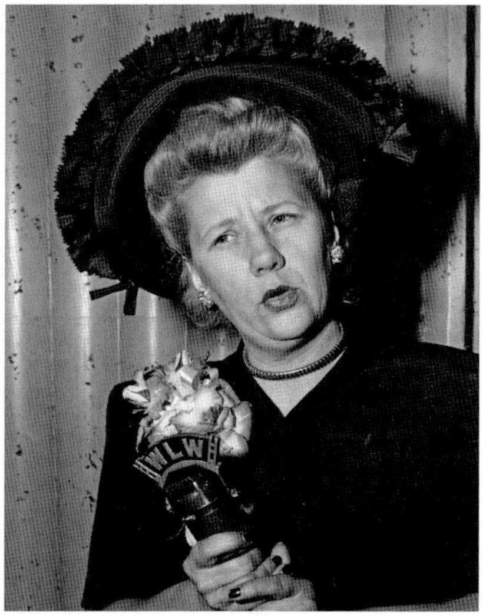

Radio and television pioneer Ruth Lyons started a Christmas fund in 1939 to buy toys for children at area hospitals. Cincinnati Enquirer *photo*.

Lyons's magnum opus, *The 50 Club*, created in 1949, was so named for the fifty lucky women attending the daily luncheon and broadcast. In the 1950s, because of incredible response to the show, the luncheon was expanded to fill two studios, and the show was renamed *The 50-50 Club*. By then, the show was being simultaneously broadcast on WLW radio and WLWT-TV, NBC's first affiliate outside of the East Coast. The show was carried by NBC nationally for eleven months in 1951 and was broadcast in color in 1957 by WLWT. It remained on the air with Ruth Lyons as the host until her retirement in January 1967, at which time her "sidekick," Bob Braun, took over.[67]

Lyons's word was gold: one mention by her of an advertiser's product and the merchandise would fly off the shelves. Sponsors waited more than a year to get advertising time. One request from Lyons generated instant response. People waited up to five years to get tickets to be in the audience. When the city of Cincinnati held a "Ruth Lyons Day" in 1957, more than one hundred thousand people had to be turned away.

However, Ruth Lyons's personal life was not all white gloves and roses. In 1944, she and her husband, Herman Newman (an English professor at the University of Cincinnati), adopted a little girl named Candace. "Candy" became a fixture on her mother's show. The three enjoyed life, going on many cruises as a family. Two things marred this idyllic existence: in December 1964, Lyons suffered a stroke. One month later, Candy was diagnosed with breast cancer. Surgery followed immediately at Holmes Hospital. By February 1966, however, Candy's cancer was clearly winning, so the family decided to go on one more cruise. They boarded the SS *Michelangelo* on June 3, 1966, for a trip to Europe. Candy got gravely ill during the cruise and had to be hospitalized in Italy. After her treatment, they boarded the ship for

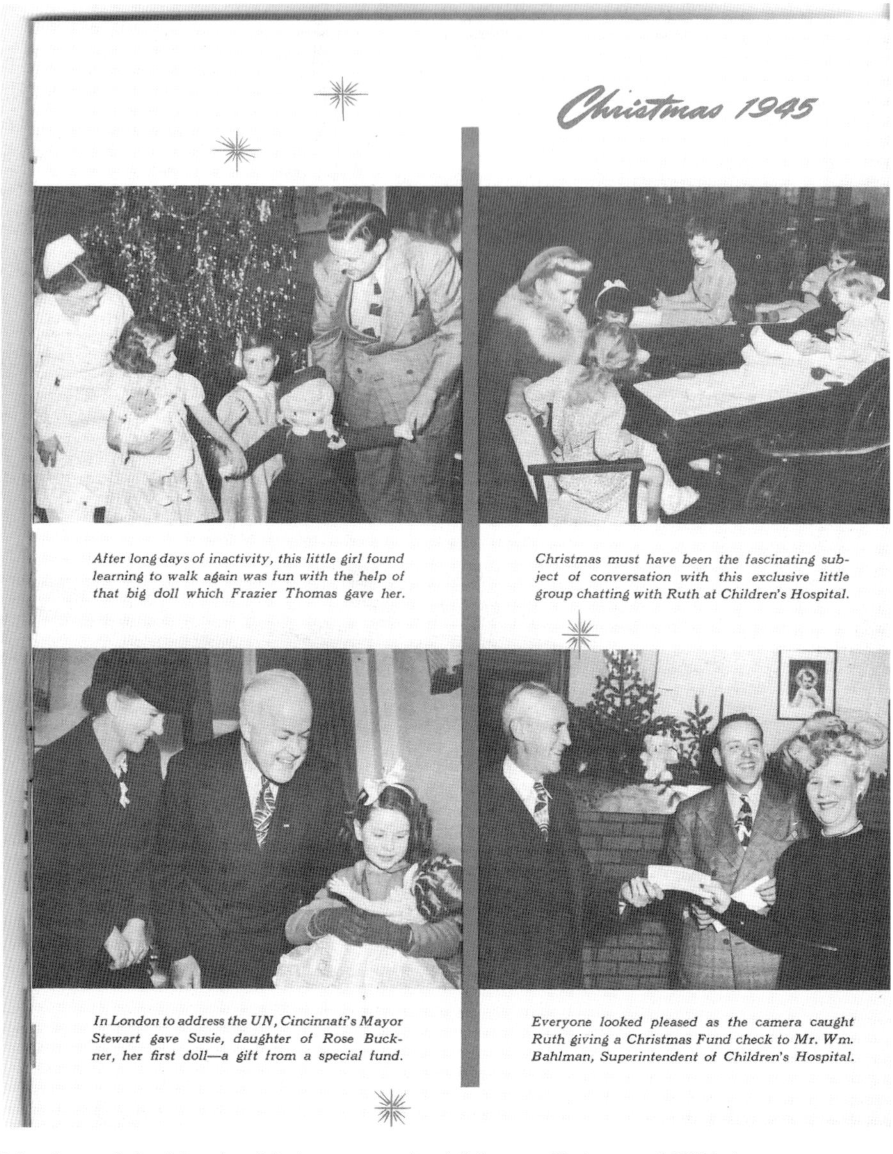

Members of the Morning Matinee entertain children at Christmas. *WLW photo.*

home but didn't make it. On the evening of Father's Day, June 19, 1966, she died peacefully around 10:00 p.m.

Even years before this tragedy, Ruth Lyons was devoted to children. In a visit to Cincinnati's Children's Hospital, she noticed that the children didn't have enough toys to play with. At Christmastime, she began a drive to collect

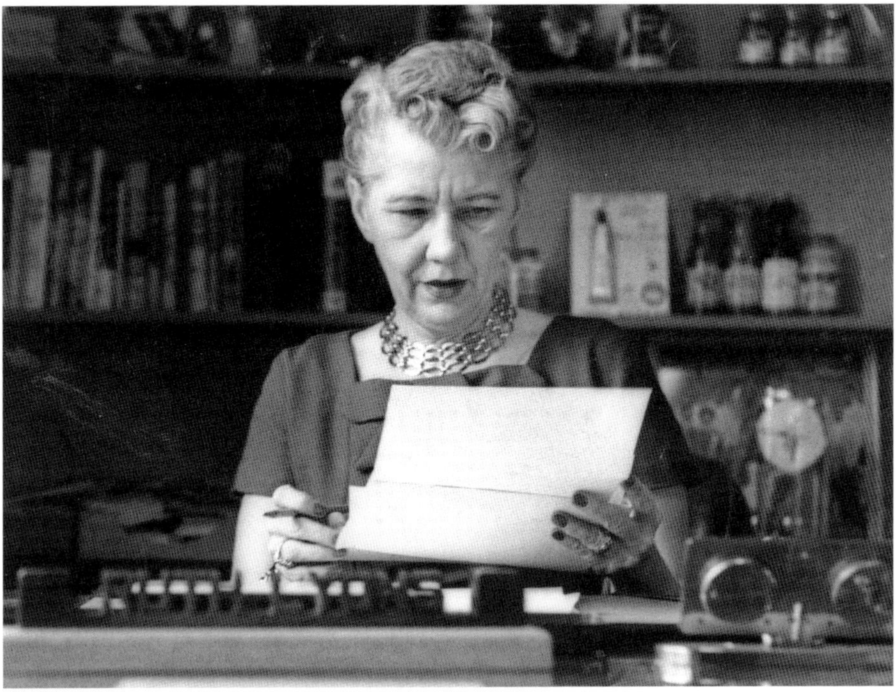

Ruth Lyons ruled the noontime airwaves with her *50-50 Club*. She doubled as a tireless, behind-the-scenes executive for Crosley Broadcasting Corporation. March 15, 1959. Cincinnati Enquirer/*Allan Kain*.

toys for children who were hospitalized for the holidays. Thus the Ruth Lyons Children's Christmas Fund was born in 1939. Ruth worked herself and her staff tirelessly on the fund.

The fund eventually grew too large and was turned over to the bank for control. But that didn't prevent Lyons from participating personally. She visited the Cincinnati Children's Hospital carrying stuffed bears, dolls and other toys. When my husband was four years old and had his tonsils removed at Children's Hospital, he received a stuffed animal from the fund.

In 1996, the fund was renamed the Ruth Lyons Children's Fund to reflect two different things: the fund (and its volunteers) worked all year, not just at Christmas; and the recipients weren't restricted to Christian kids. After more than eighty years, the fund is still going strong, assisting the Division of Child Life at Cincinnati Children's Hospital Medical Center, one of the leading pediatric hospitals in the nation. Many of today's Cincinnati families have been touched by the kindness of Ruth Lyons, not just at Christmas but throughout the year.[68]

In 2020, the fund partnered with Graeter's and CinFed Credit Union to sell decorative plates with delicious Graeter's holiday cookies. All told, the fund has given more than $21 million to area hospitals.

SENDING CARDS

Like people in other cities, historically, Cincinnatians have loved to send Christmas cards. Most depict general Christmas scenes with Santa, presents and lots of evergreens. Some also depict Cincinnati scenes, especially Fountain Square with its lights, the Tyler Davidson Fountain and (of course) the Christmas tree.

A *Penny Paper* ad from November 1, 1882, describes "Herold, pen artist and card writer," who was inviting the public to peruse his "fine line of visiting cards, the neatest and latest styles. Christmas and New-Year Cards [*sic*] of the most elegant patterns in stock. Card writing of every description done in the most artistic manner."[69]

On October 27, 1882, a Mr. Coville gave a Christmas card to each lady attending the performance of *Taken from Life* at Robinson's. These must have been no everyday Christmas cards, for they were described as

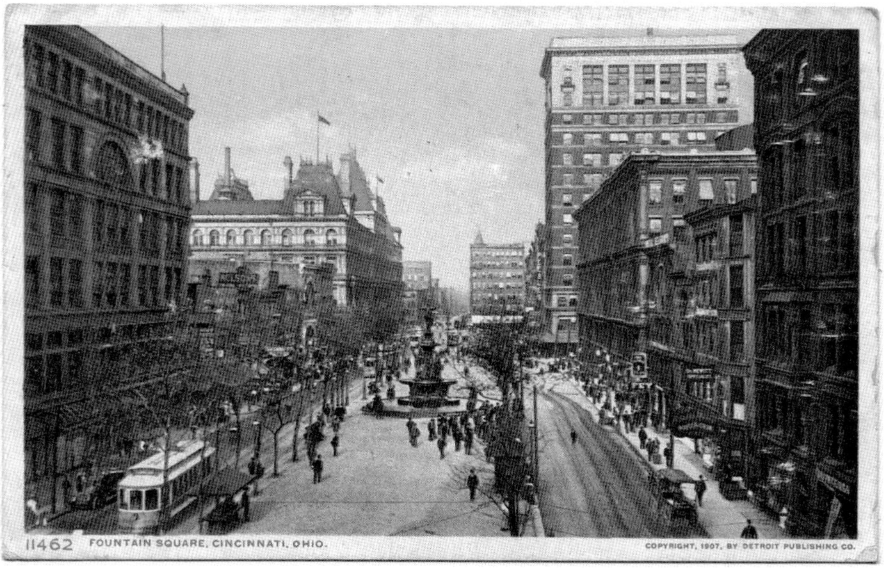

A postcard of Fountain Square. *Public Library of New York.*

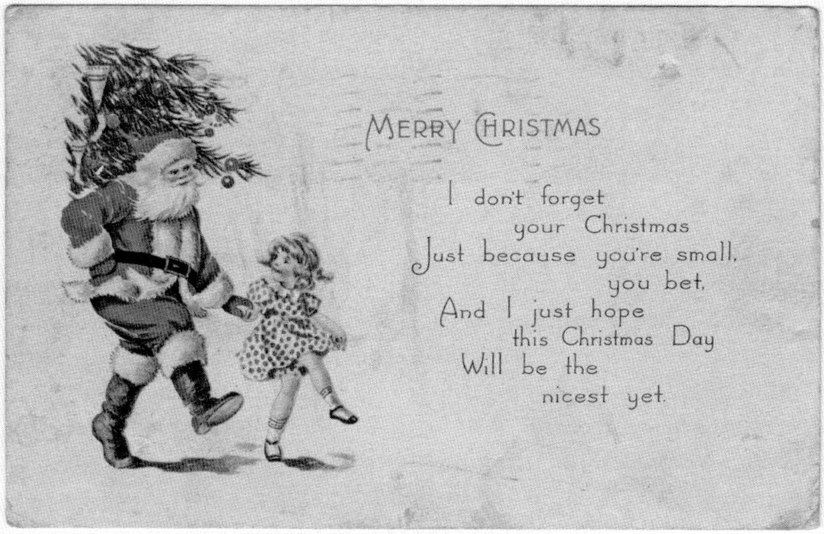

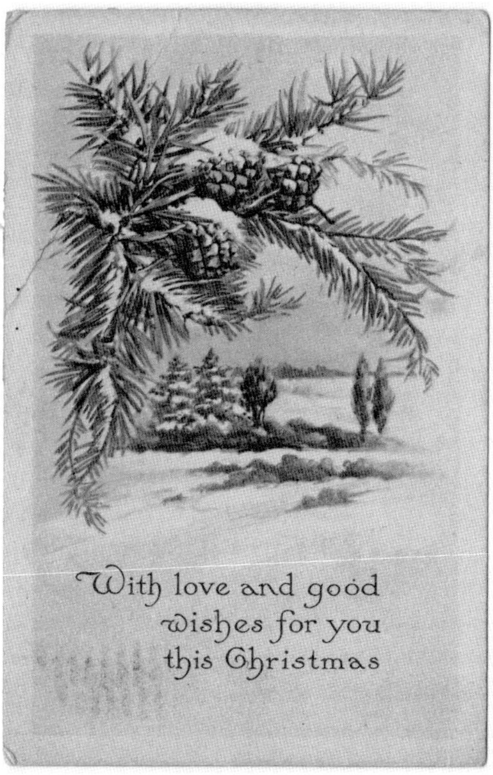

Above: Merry Christmas! postcard. *Public Library of New York.*

Left: A Cincinnati postcard with delicate pine boughs. *Public Library of New York.*

"a beautiful souvenir, one of the costliest ever given away in this city." The cards contained the picture of an ideal figure in colors and were bordered with satin fringe. On the back of each one was the program of the evening's performance.[70]

Tucker, Ziegler & Company, "Booksellers and Stationers," opened its store on December 1, 1883, announcing it with an ad in the *Cincinnati Post* listing its variety of printed goods, inkstands, paperweights and "a full line of Prang's Christmas cards."[71]

L. Prang & Company cards were popular in Cincinnati, as they were in many cities across the country. Louis Prang had learned from his printer father how to print in multiple colors (chromolithography). With government upheaval and ensuing political problems, young Prang left Prussia for the United States. (A 1939 article in the *Cincinnati Post* opened with, "It took a European revolution to give Americans the habit of sending Christmas cards."[72]) In Boston, he formed a partnership, Prang & Mayer, with a fellow chromolithographic printer, Julius Mayer, but it didn't last long.[73] Prang created his own printshop, L. Prang & Company, and became one of the leading chromolithographers in the country. Besides Tucker, Ziegler & Company, Prang's Christmas cards were also carried by a variety of merchants. An ad in the November 27, 1880, *Cincinnati Enquirer* announced that Robert Clarke & Company had spent $2,000 on "four exquisite designs" for "Prang's Prize Christmas Cards."[74] Unfortunately, Prang was muscled out of the greeting card business by foreign competitors.

Cincinnatians had an advantage in finding perfect cards: one of the nation's leading producers of greeting cards and wrapping paper was right here in Cincinnati. Gibson Greetings, located in Roselawn, produced cards of all kinds and wrapping paper for every occasion. Established in 1850 by Scottish lithographer George Gibson's sons, it printed bonds, stock certificates and business cards. The family had been importing German Christmas cards but began to create its own line of cards in the 1870s.[75] It became the third-largest producer of cards, behind Hallmark and American Greetings.

An article in the business section of the *Cincinnati Post* in 1984 glowed about Gibson's success. Written as a letter to England's Sir Henry Cole, the mastermind behind the first Christmas cards, the article said that Gibson Greeting Cards had sold thirty-seven million Christmas cards that season and that Christmas cards and wrapping paper accounted for one-fifth of the company's annual revenue. Gibson was one of the first companies to offer fringe-edged Christmas cards, which had been imported from Germany.

Christmas cards changed some with the times, but a common theme has been love and fellowship, along with the Christ child and the Nativity, as well as Santa and snow. George Elliston, a groundbreaking female journalist, remarked in 1940, "Santa Claus is on the way out in Christmas-card land." She said old Santa was "conspicuous by his absence." She bemoaned (or scoffed at) the absence of "Scotties" (Scottish terriers), who had been so popular the year before: Scotties with gift boxes handing red ribbons from their mouths; Scotties perched on, under and around Christmas trees; Scotties to the right of the fireplace and to the left of it; Scotties everywhere. Nobody knew just why or how they had "cornered" Christmas. Evidently, candles had taken the place of the Scotties. Bells and holly remained popular. She concluded with the "crux of the matter," which was this: "It is religious. [Angels] fly on many cards, the Nativity is featured on dozens of them, the star of Bethlehem is ever present and the camels of the wise men, the shepherds and their sheep are to be found everywhere. The most famed madonnas of the artworld are at the command of any lover of fine art, reproductions on cards as easy as a penny apiece."[76]

Some cards that might have been "cute" when they were sold don't stand the test of time. A Gibson card from the 1930s read, "If you'd let St. Nick try your pie so tempting and delicious, he'd stay for Christmas dinner and help you with the dishes!" During the Second World War, Christmas cards embraced a military theme. One Gibson card showed a soldier holding a bayonet on Santa Claus while shouting, "Halt! Who goes there?" One article concluded with the judgment that "while Christmas cards change, the ritual of sending them seems firmly implanted."[77] Not quite.

Greeting cards in general took a big hit with the advent of personal computers, the Internet, email and social media. Cell phone calls and text messaging replaced carefully thought-out written greetings. Facing this shared crisis, the U.S. Postal Service continued to raise the price of stamps almost yearly. First-class postage for the first ounce was eight cents in 1971, eighteen cents in 1981, twenty-nine cents in 1991, thirty-four cents in 2001, forty-four cents in 2011 and fifty-five cents in 2021. Forever stamps and "shape-based postage pricing" were introduced in 2007. Forever stamps could be bought in bulk at one time with the knowledge that they would cover first-class postage, regardless of the current price. "Shape-based postage pricing" added another dimension beyond weight. It added three dimensions: height, width and length. That meant that a card that was an odd shape could cost more, even if it was only an ounce.[78]

Environmental concerns caused the company to change several aspects of its products, such as going to water-soluble inks and using recycled paper products. Another quiet threat came from the cottage industry of scrapbooking and stamping. With a variety of materials available, including templates online, many people took to making their own cards.

American Greetings went through a series of owners in the late twentieth and early twenty-first centuries; it closed its last U.S. plant in 2020.[79] Although Cincinnati no longer has a nationally ranked greeting card company, the oldest and youngest Cincinnatians still appreciate finding printed greetings in their mailboxes, whether they're icons on a screen or boxes at the curb.

MOUNT ADAMS REINDOG PARADE

In case your dog is feeling left out of the festivities, Cincinnati has a Christmas activity for Toto, too: the Mount Adams Reindog Parade. Each year on one afternoon in December, the Mount Adams Business Guild sponsors the parade. Admission to the parade is a voluntary donation to SPCA Cincinnati.

First, get your dog all gussied up as befits the season. Then make your way to Mount Adams. Registration is held the same day as the parade, which follows the streets in Mount Adams. Santa leads the parade with the grand marshal. Awards are given to the dogs (or perhaps their owners) in categories such as small dog (less than twenty-five pounds), large dog (more than twenty-five pounds), dog/owner look-alike and multiple dogs. Many of the businesses in Mount Adams have dog-friendly patios for a little libation after all the hard work.

The parade was virtual in 2020, but it should return in its original furry form in 2021.

WINTERFEST

Winterfest (with a lowercase *f*) began in 1982 in an effort to expand the Kings Island season beyond the summer. The folks at Kings Island conducted consumer research the previous winter: they polled housewives. They asked the women how they would feel about a winter opportunity besides going

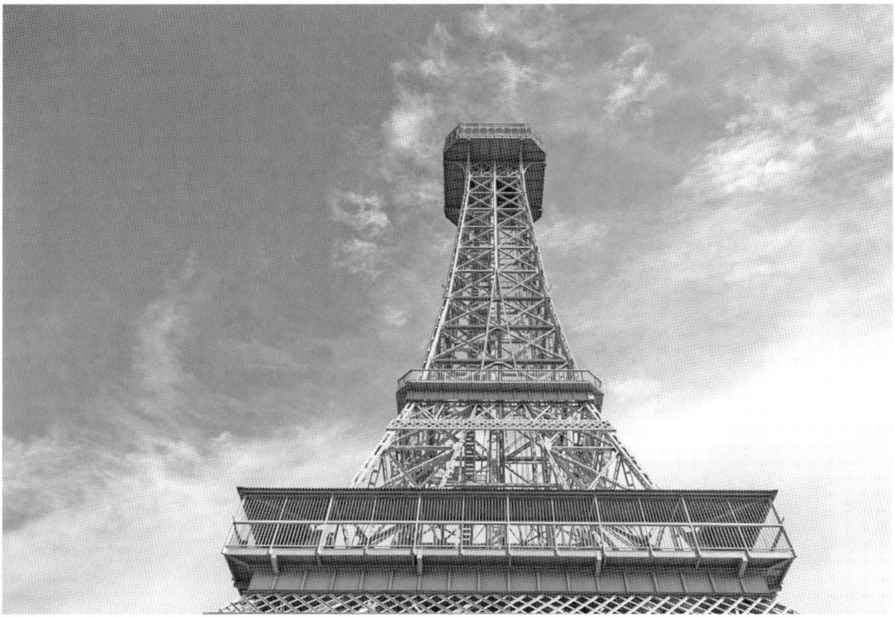

Kings Island's Eiffel Tower. *Library of Congress.*

downtown, something that might become a new Christmas tradition. The women said that they would enjoy such a place and thought their husbands and children might, also.[80] They were right.

Kings Island predicted that its new Winterfest experience would be a "celebration of Christmas, winter, snow, freezing breezes, and frost-bitten noses."[81] A full-page ad in the *Cincinnati Enquirer* described Winterfest as being "Where Winter Comes Alive": "We took one of the most magical places on Earth, wrapped it with shiny holiday trimmings and filled it with the delicious aroma of homecooked treats, happy songs and the most enchanting gifts." The ad promised one of the world's tallest Christmas trees (a 30-foot tree was placed on top of the 314-foot Eiffel Tower), which could be seen from I-71.[82]

When Kings Island's Winterfest opened, it was believed to be the first major amusement park to open in the winter. (Some Kings Island associates like to point out that they preceded the Cincinnati Zoo & Botanical Garden's "Festival of Lights" by a year.) At first, the celebration would be small, focusing on International Street, the Eiffel Tower and the ice-skating rink created from the Royal Fountain. Admission was $2.50, with a $1.00 add-on fee for skating and an additional $1.00 to rent skates.

A Herculean effort went into converting the Royal Fountain into a skating rink. The six-hundred-thousand-gallon fountain was replaced with a combination of sand, gravel and ice for enjoyment by five hundred skaters. The fountain's pool was first lined with a 180-by-80-foot plastic liner, which was then covered with two inches of sand, nine inches of gravel and one and a half inches of ice. Even with eight hundred tons of gravel and one hundred tons of sand, the contents weighed less than a fountain full of water. One reason for this is that the ice level would be below that of the water. (In addition, there are no air holes between molecules of water.) At the end of Winterfest, park workers stored the sand and gravel and used it for various repair work around the park.[83]

Unfortunately, the week that Winterfest was supposed to open for the first time, the temperatures hovered in the fifties and sixties. Every snow-cone maker and ice machine in the park was put into use, and twenty thousand tons of crushed ice were dumped into the fountain. The next day, Tuesday, another twenty thousand tons were dumped in the rink.[84] The workers crossed their frozen fingers. With future improvements to the massive refrigeration units, ice skating could continue even with temperatures in the sixties. This was important with Cincinnati's history of fluctuating temperatures in the wintertime.[85]

Pre-opening publicity highlighted the 2,400 six-inch white lights that would be on the Eiffel Tower, the 25,000 lights that would light up International Street and the half-mile each of 3.5-foot-wide red ribbon and garland that would be used. In addition to the tree on top of the Eiffel Tower, three hundred more trees would be placed around the open areas of the park, which were few. A new 28,000-square-foot facility[86] was dubbed the "Festhaus" with 1,500-capacity seating and foods from Germany, Italy and Mexico, as well as special holiday entertainment.[87] Speaking from personal experience, that Festhaus was a great place for warming up, inside and out!

Response was immediate, positive and strong. The first night, November 26, KI managers budgeted for an attendance of five thousand people, but with the warm weather, only two thousand found themselves in a Christmas mood. The next night, they again anticipated five thousand guests—and got twenty thousand![88] Fans looked forward to the next Winterfest—and they weren't disappointed. From 1982 through 1991, fans flocked to the amusement park to get in the spirit of the season.

In 1983, Taft Broadcasting (which also owned Coney Island) sold Kings Island to Kings Entertainment Company (KECO). The sale became final in 1984, with Taft maintaining 30 percent ownership of Kings Entertainment.

Then Cincinnati millionaire businessman Carl Lindner bought Taft in 1987. There was a perceived conflict between the mission of Lindner's American Financial Corporation and KECO. Finally, a solution was attained by a ten-year management agreement so that American Financial owned Kings Island, but KECO managed it.[89]

In 1992, Paramount approached Lindner, its largest stockholder, and presented him with a deal to buy Kings Island. Lindner was reluctant at first but eventually agreed. The deal was finalized, reuniting KI with Carowinds and Kings Dominion under a new division called Paramount Parks. Kings Island now became Paramount's Kings Island.[90]

Paramount itself went through major changes during this period. In 1994, Viacom acquired Paramount Communications, which had been part of CBS. In 1995, Westinghouse bought CBS, which was then merged with King World and acquired by Viacom. Many other mergers and acquisitions ensued; finally, Viacom split into the second version of CBS Corporation and Viacom.[91] The new owners were overwhelmed with taking over the park, rebranding it and handling what was going on at the corporate level—all while handling the load of a busy summer season. Winterfest was not to happen again in the 1990s.

In 2005, Paramount's Kings Island announced that Winterfest would be held once again. By now, the park had expanded, so "WinterFest: Home for the Holidays" expanded, too (and gained an upper-case *F*). This time, there would be more rides operating during the winter festivities. The Kings Island and Miami Valley Railroad was given a new theme as the White Christmas Express and was built around the theme of homecoming after World War II—just like the movie starring Bing Crosby, Danny Kaye, Rosemary Clooney and Vera-Ellen. Swan Lake, which was near the Beast roller coaster, would have nightly light shows with fireworks synchronized to Christmas music. The spirit expanded, as well. This time, "miles and miles" of garland decorated International Street. More than three million lights dazzled the eyes and directed the feet to the many available attractions. As grand marshal, Santa Claus led a nightly parade from the Nickelodeon area to International Street, then to the Coney Island Mall. The Nickelodeon area itself was transformed into "Santa's Christmas Town," with sights that reminded parents of the great downtown department stores' Christmas displays. Festhaus had also been given a makeover. As WinterFesthaus, it offered full meals (including turkey dinners), as well as a new Graeter's and LaRosa's. The Paramount Theater now hosted *Santa's Toy Factory*, a live production, including snow

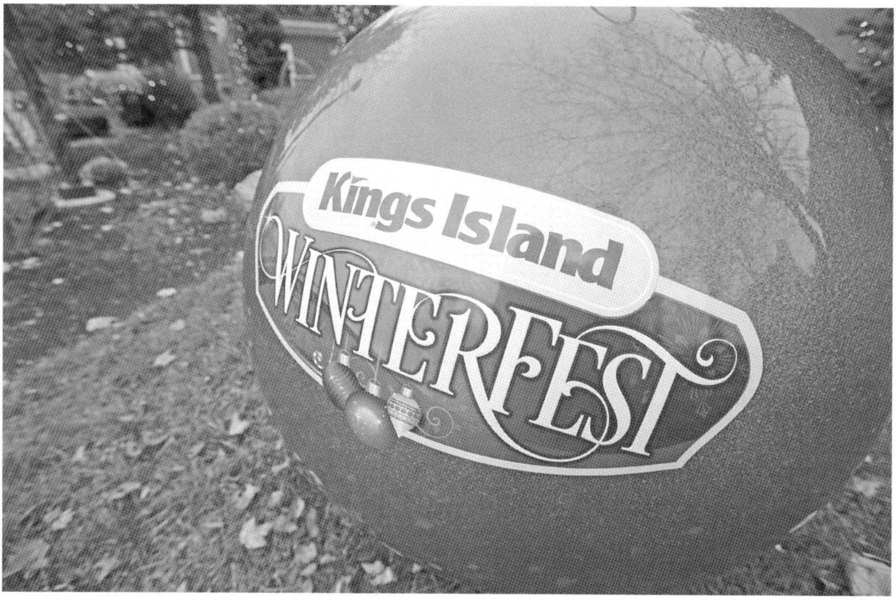

A giant Christmas tree ornament with the WinterFest logo welcomes people to Kings Island, November 24, 2017. Cincinnati Enquirer/*Sam Greene*.

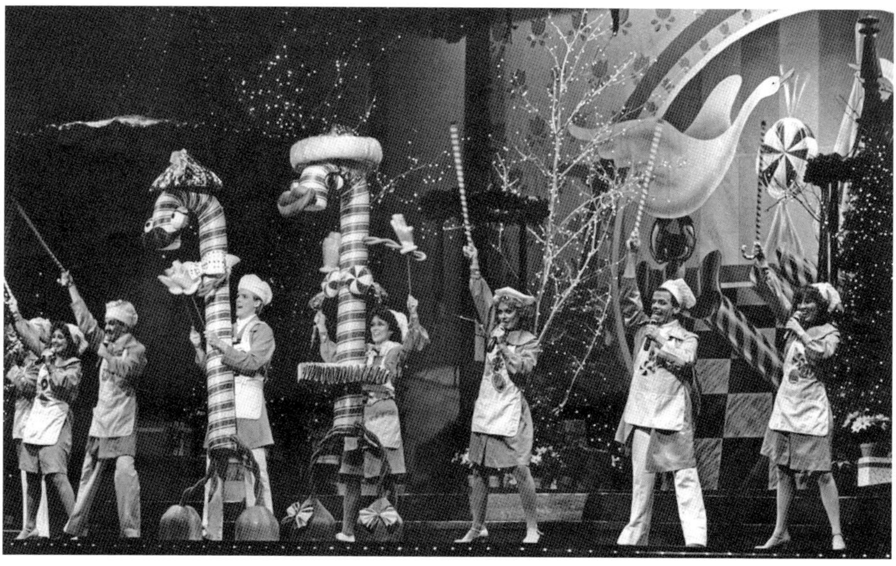

Canes on Parade: Candy canes of all sizes are part of the World of Christmas show presented at the Festhaus at Kings Island's Winterfest, 1984. Cincinnati Enquirer *photo*.

falling on the audience members. Even Top Cats, the swings, the castle and the carousel were operating, decorated with bows and garland.[92]

The guests at WinterFest enjoyed themselves, but they were dismayed with the price. Admission for adults and children over three would be $24.99, a drastic change from 1982, but discounted tickets were available if they were purchased ahead of time for a specific day. Season pass holders could buy tickets for $16.99 each. Ice skating cost $7.00 to skate and $3.00 to rent skates. A Paramount's Kings Island spokesperson, Maureen Kaiser, said that 2005 was the highest-rated event in park history, with thousands of visitors each day. This was not quite the case: WinterFest was not profitable.

WinterFest went dark. Despite 2005's enthusiastic pronouncements, WinterFest did not return. After various acquisitions, mergers and splits, in 2006, CBS found itself owning amusement parks, which was not part of its vision. So, in 2006, Kings Island (along with other park properties, including Kings Dominion in Virginia and Carowinds in North Carolina) was sold to Cedar Fair, which already owned Cedar Point Amusement Park in Sandusky, Ohio. On July 24, 2006, Kings Island and Cedar Fair, the new parent company, made the decision to focus on summer and fall, not winter. Spokesperson Kaiser noted in 2006 that WinterFest was popular but didn't make sense from a "numbers" standpoint, adding that many people had complained about the admission price.[93]

Each time WinterFest stopped, it was not because of a lack of visitors or the absence of an enjoyable product. It was because of corporate turmoil. In 2005, Paramount Kings Island marketing manager Jeffrey Siebert said that the 1992 cancellation came because the park had just extended its season through Halloween and couldn't turn it around in time. Kings Island still focuses on its spring, summer and fall activities, but the park uses a combination of park workers and outside contractors to transform from a Halloween to a Happy Holiday theme.[94]

Now, firmly in the twenty-first century, Kings Island as a whole has more than one hundred attractions, fourteen roller coasters and a 33-acre water park, all on 364 acres of land. In 2018, the park entertained 3,486,000 visitors. Kings Island started focusing on reviving WinterFest. More than 180 acres (more than half the park) would be open to visitors. A welcome return was the International Restaurant above the main entrance. For the first time, some of the park's roller coasters (such as Mystic Timbers) would be open during WinterFest. Altogether, seventeen rides would be running in Rivertown, Coney Island, Planet Snoopy and the Action Zone. These attractions included some old favorites, like Dodgem, Zephyr and Scrambler, as well as the Grand

and Character carousels. Nine "wonderlands" were created for WinterFest: Action Ice Zone, Artisan Village, Candy Cane Lane, Charlie Brown's Christmas Town, Coca-Cola Polar Bear Plaza, Coney Elf Village, Rivertown Wonderland, WinterFest Way and (of course) International Street. WinterFest had now become an amusement park that was open in the winter and not just a sparkly place to drink hot chocolate. Commensurate with this change, the price went up. In 2017, WinterFest re-opened with an adult admission fee of thirty-five dollars (lower rates for seniors and children).[95]

In 2018, the same areas were open with the addition of Tinsel Town in the back of Coney Mall and cookie decorating with Mrs. Claus. A variety of ticket prices was available, especially for people who planned ahead. This year, guests with Kings Island gold passes and those with Cedar Fair platinum passes could get in for free.[96] For 2019, more than twenty-one refreshment areas were available. As Mrs. Claus said, "Nobody likes a skinny Santa!"[97] That must go for WinterFest visitors, too!

THE BEACH WATERPARK

The Beach Waterpark and Kings Island have taken turns having troubles with maintaining a winter festival, even including its name. Kings Island's Winterfest/WinterFest ran from 1982 through 1991, then 2005, then 2017 and 2018. The Beach Waterpark's Holiday Fest ran from 1999 through 2009, then came back to life as Beach Mountain from 2014 through 2017.[98]

For $6.95 at Holiday Fest (with reduced rates for military members, seniors and children; toddlers were free), visitors enjoyed a 7,500-square-foot ice rink, toboggan races down water slides, carriage rides, live entertainment and a live Nativity and petting zoo. The animals could be seen from I-71, behind a large slide. In 2000, three lambs got in the spirit of the season and were born in the North Pole petting corral. By 2004, pony rides had been added and the ice rink had been shrunk. A $5.00 "day skate" was added for people who wanted to just skate during the daytime.

By now, the park itself was having problems. It had been a family operation since its opening in 1985, but it was finally announced in March 2012 that the family was closing the park and was looking for a new buyer. Adventure Holdings LLC purchased the park and opened it in 2013 as the Beach at Adventure Landing. The following winter, it opened Beach Mountain.[99]

Beach Mountain featured a forty-foot-high, four-hundred-foot-long, ten-lane snow tubing hill. A major carpet lift carried tubes back to the top of the hill, but riders had to walk. There was also an area for playing in the snow and a concession stand. Admission ranged from seventeen to twenty-five dollars; children under three were not allowed. With the increased price and decreased attractions, Beach Mountain was on thin ice, literally. When my youngest son and a friend planned to go tubing, they found on their arrival that the employees had decided to close the park that day. The Beach closed in 2019.

4

Things to Hear

Concerts

Cincinnati's Germans brought a singing tradition with them, forming what was called "Sängerfest" or "Sängerbunds" and creating the first municipal Sängerfest (Anglicized to Saengerfest) in the United States in 1849. These singing festivals eventually attracted thousands of audience members from across the country, as well as nearly a thousand singers in more than sixty choirs. The Saengerfest tradition has dwindled but is reprised on various occasions, such as celebrating Cincinnati's bicentennial in 1988.[100]

Cincinnati is blessed with the oldest continuous choral tradition in the United States: the May Festival Chorus. (There is disagreement as to whether the May Festival Chorus came out of the Saengerfest tradition or if it competed with the Saengerfest.) It was for the May Festival that Music Hall was built in 1878. The May Festival Chorus is the official chorus of the Cincinnati Symphony and Pops Orchestras. As such, the chorus has often performed under the direction of many talented directors. The chorus is composed mostly of nonprofessional singers, although many of them work in related fields, such as teaching music. One of May Festival's chorus members was a mayor.

Mayor Russell Wilson, who was described as a "barytone [*sic*]" who "formerly sang in the May Festival Chorus," accepted the invitation to take part in the *Times-Star*'s Christmas carol singing party on Fountain Square

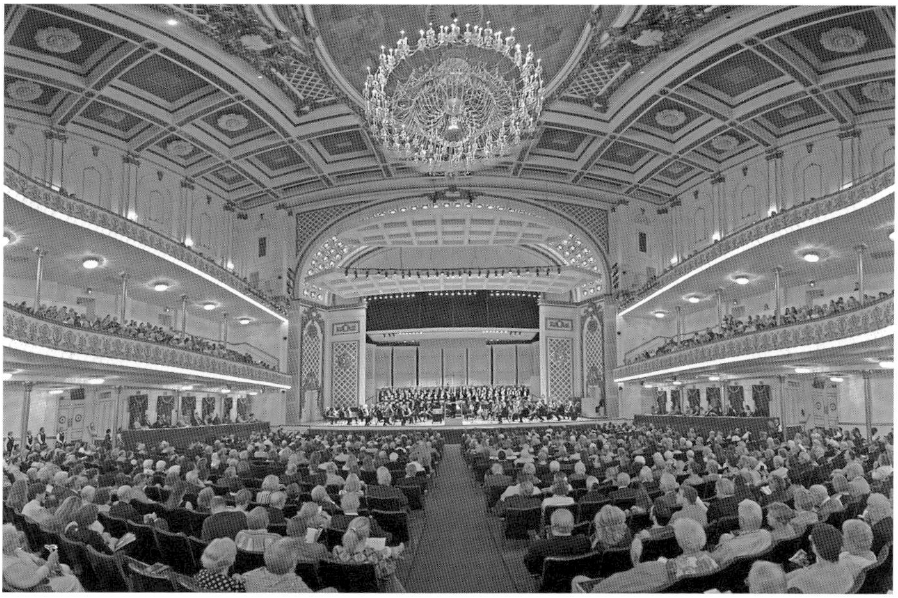

The Cincinnati Symphony Orchestra and May Festival Chorus in Music Hall, 2016. *Photo by Philip Groshong. May Festival Chorus.*

on Christmas Eve. Alfred Hartzel, chorus master of the May Festival Chorus, was to conduct the rehearsal and the performance on Christmas Eve.[101] The day before the festive gathering, the *Times-Star* published an editorial cartoon titled "The Spirit of Christmas." The Genius of Water, commonly called "the Lady," was looking down at a crowd of people, one of whom held a baton. She is thinking, "It's been worth standing here all these years just to hear this!" One of the figures below her adds, "I always knew Cincinnatians could sing."[102]

Cincinnatians love choral music, especially when the audiences can participate. Betsa Marsh wrote in the *Cincinnati Enquirer* in 1982 that the most festive Christmas outings were Carolfest at Music Hall and the Feast of Carols at the University of Cincinnati's College-Conservatory of Music (CCM). "Both are dedicated to the uplifting joy of song, whether the tune is carried expertly by a pro or high-spiritedly by an amateur."

A family favorite for many years was Carolfest (later called "A May Festival Christmas"), which featured the chorus. The Cincinnati Pops Christmas concerts also featured the chorus and often included dancers, a children's choir and a musical guest. A few stray characters frequently showed up as well, such as Santa and Mrs. Claus or Rudolph the Red-

Nosed Reindeer. In 1982, the chorus was joined by the Queen City Brass, the Cincinnati BoyChoir, pianist Vincent Schmithorst, organist Bob Muckenfuss and emcee Rob Reider.

Sometimes the May Festival Chorus is involved in so many concerts that it has to forego one. In 2011, for example, the entire chorus sang in Happy Holidays with the Pops, while the smaller chamber group sang the Christmas portion of Handel's *Messiah*, so there was no May Festival Christmas that year.

Another favorite choral concert is that presented by CCM. Its annual Feast of Carols features UC's undergraduate and graduate music students in a variety of musical settings. In 1982, for example, participating groups were the UC Men's and Women's Glee Clubs, the Chorale-Motet Choir, the Chamber Choir, the Cincinnati University Singers, the Brass Choir and the CCM Children's Choir, as well as the choirs from Colerain and Walnut Hills High Schools. Interspersed between the performances were sing-along selections for the wannabe professional singers in the audience.[103]

Cincinnati has many venues that offer some Christmas music, like Music Hall and the Aronoff Center. Other groups change venues throughout the city, so as to give a wider range of people a chance to hear the performance. Here are some examples from prior years:

- Holiday Pops, Christmas with the Pops and The Snowman with the Pops, performed at Taft Theatre by the Cincinnati Pops Orchestra (during the renovation of Music Hall)
- Sing Me a Story: How the Grinch Stole Christmas, performed at the Aronoff Center for the Arts by the Cincinnati Boychoir and guests Bob Herzog and Kathy Wade
- Westside Community Band Christmas Concert, performed at Mount St. Joseph University (bring a toy to donate)
- Making Spirits Bright, performed at Seton High School
- A Very Merry Christmas Concert, performed at the Carnegie
- Cincinnati Children's Choir Concert, performed at the University of Cincinnati Corbett Auditorium at CCM
- Cincinnati Civic Orchestra's Holiday Concert, performed at the Colerain Township Senior & Community Center
- The Ghost of Christmas Eve, performed by the Trans-Siberian Orchestra at US Bank Arena (now Heritage Bank Arena)[104]

A CCM music education major named Lynette Ranck gave reporter Marsh some tips for people who wanted to go out on their own for caroling. Here are Ranck's tips:

- Start by humming to warm up the vocal cords.
- Start with a song you know well and sing it lightly without worrying about technique.
- Avoid eating for half an hour before singing, especially milk or chocolate. (So much for the hot cocoa.)
- Wear a warm scarf around your neck and keep your extremities warm.
- Don't breathe through your mouth; it dries out the throat.
- Take your time between houses and breathe slowly through your nose.
- Invest in a pitch pipe to keep the group in tune.
- Get in the spirit![105]

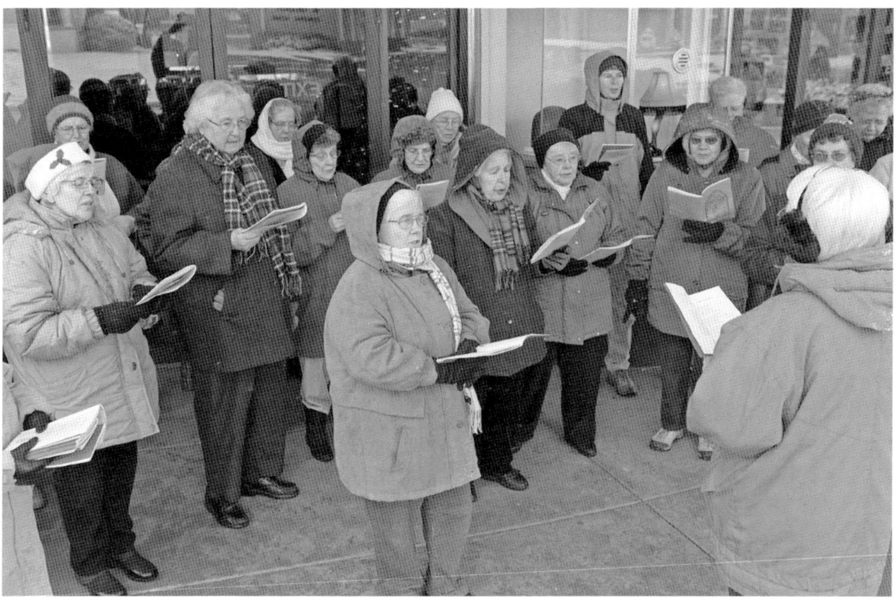

The Sisters of Charity from Mount St. Joseph came to sing Christmas carols in front of the Covedale Performing Arts Center, all part of "Holiday on the Hill," a Price Hill/Covedale holiday program, December 4, 2010. Cincinnati Enquirer/*Tony Jones*.

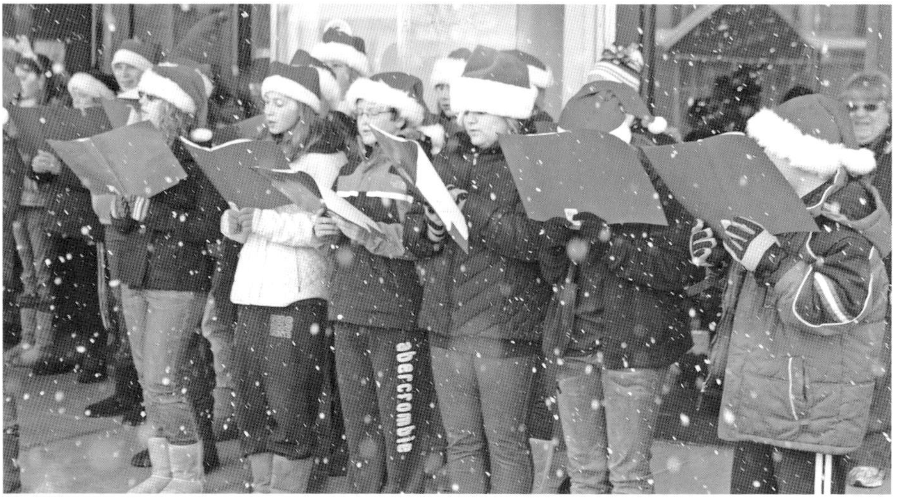

Members of the Black Hawk Singers, the seventh- and eighth-grade choirs from St. Dominic, part of "Holiday on the Hill," December 4, 2010. Cincinnati Enquirer/*Tony Jones*.

TRANS-SIBERIAN ORCHESTRA

In 2019, *Cincinnati Enquirer* reporter Luann Gibbs wrote, "You know the holiday season has arrived when Trans-Siberian Orchestra rolls into town."[106] TSO is not a Cincinnati creation, but it certainly is a Cincinnati tradition. Many Cincinnatians feel the Christmas holiday isn't complete without attending a TSO concert. TSO had not missed a concert in Cincinnati in almost twenty years, until the 2020 tour had to be canceled due to the coronavirus.

TSO has had a long tradition of visiting Cincinnati in December. However, it has slipped into town at other times of the year as well. In October 2010, TSO's Mark Woods worked with Oak Hills High School's orchestra for a concert called Orchestra Rocks. Woods was joined on stage by his son on drums and his vocalist wife. The *Today Show* even stopped by to tape a rehearsal.[107]

The TSO has been referred to as a "Holiday Hit Machine," and it is.[108] It was an idea born of hard-rock producer Paul O'Neill and record executive Jason Flom. Flom had signed a metal group called Savatage that had gotten some positive response at first, but their record sales were not doing well. Their label dropped them. Flom called O'Neill for some assistance, and the rest is rock history. With O'Neill as producer, Savatage released some records that got good play and even wrote a rock opera called *Streets*. The title of their 1987 album *Hall of the Mountain King* is familiar to any fan of Edvard Grieg. The record took Grieg's *Peer Gynt* and added metal. Savatage found an audience in Europe but still hadn't found their groove. Two setbacks took the wind out of them: the lead guitarist, Criss Oliva, was killed in a car crash in 1993, and his brother Jon Oliva got burned out.

The story might have stopped there but for a radio station in Florida, where the band had started. A program director started playing one song from their 1995 flop, *Dead Winter Dead*, which was about the Bosnian War. Then he contacted a friend of his, Scott Shannon, at a New York City radio station to sample the record. He played "Christmas Eve (Sarajevo 12/24)," a metal medley of "God Rest Ye Merry, Gentlemen" and "Carol of the Bells." It became an immediate hit. The rest is history. O'Neill renamed the group Trans-Siberian Orchestra after a real railroad in Siberia as a sign of hope in a harsh, unforgiving land.

The group began touring in the late 1990s and soon found out that the demand quickly exceeded their physical ability to satisfy all the requests. The concert typically lasts two and a half hours, with no intermission. Wanting to keep the focus on the holidays, the band kept the tour limited to the holiday season but created two touring teams. One heads west and the other heads east. Altogether, the band has 240 singers, musicians and technicians. About 140 local stagehands are enlisted in each concert city.

Not every city can host a TSO concert. The shows are limited to facilities that can hold the number of musicians on stage and the electrical demands backstage. The band has been known to blow out the power in some venues.

Despite their success, TSO has maintained their focus on the common people. Their ticket prices are low compared to other rock concerts. There is no VIP seating, and even when VIP performers join them on stage, they don't mention that ahead of time. Over the years, TSO has been joined by heavyweights such as Steven Tyler of Aerosmith and Roger Daltrey of the Who.

Blogger Amy Harris interviewed TSO guitarist Al Pitrelli in 2014 about their Cincinnati experience. Pitrelli, who lives in Pennsylvania, appreciated what his neighboring state had to offer. "I just know that it's especially a great town," Pitrelli said. "The state of Ohio has been so wonderful to us the past 16 or 17 years."

Trans-Siberian Orchestra touring started in the central Ohio area. Pitrelli noted that it felt as if he was back home when he played in Ohio. "That whole center of the country is terrific and the people are wonderful," he said. "I guess it has been since 1999 when we first started coming through

Ohio. Not too long after that, Cincinnati was probably in 2000. It is just one of the most important areas that we have played."

Pitrelli acknowledged that Cincinnati was as much a tradition for TSO as TSO was for Cincinnati. He said that the people here had embraced the band as part of their holiday tradition.[109]

"We want to make sure we come back here and do the best show possible year after year after year by making the band better, making material better, and making more and more production."

Trans-Siberian Orchestra concerts are unusual. They have been referred to as "Nutcracker on metal." Filled with flashing lights, explosions and a "hard rock/metallic" sound, they also make sure that the sound levels don't exceed the safe decibel limit. They also make sure the content is not offensive to the most senior or the smallest audience member. The theme of the first half is usually a small play featuring a young girl who is trying to find her way home for Christmas. The second half is an exciting performance of holiday favorites.[110]

"It is certainly good for families," guitarist Pitrelli agreed. "One of the things I am most proud of is that I can look out in the audience and see a 10-year-old kid sitting with his mom and his grandma, and they are all having the greatest time of their life." Pitrelli noted that the family dynamic in this country is a little fragmented and that he enjoyed seeing whole families at their concerts. "When I am playing Mozart's 24th Symphony and people are enjoying the music and then the stage is lit on fire and trusses moving to the shapes of spaceships and fire breathing dragons and getting everybody's attention, there is a different dynamic. It is a rock-n-roll show. There is no doubt about it. It is one of the greatest rock shows on the planet."[111]

If you want to get pumped up about the holiday, TSO is for you.

Church Music

Besides having a large variety of places to worship in, another benefit to having so many churches in the city is the myriad musical opportunities, especially at Christmas. Some churches, like St. Peter in Chains, offer concerts year-round with professional entertainers such as Chanticleer. Others, like Knox Presbyterian, Westwood First Presbyterian and St. Catharine of Siena, offer concert series composed of both professional and volunteer musicians.

Knox has been acknowledged as having the best music in the city. Westwood First has hosted the concert series since 1981.

Of course, due to COVID-19, many concerts were canceled in 2020. However, here is a smattering of previous concerts, with the hope that they bear hints of what future concerts will be like.

- Barnabas Episcopal Church: Remembering the Holidays: A Concert of Carols and Lullabies by the Ursuline Academy A Cappella Choir and the Cincinnati Collaborative Ringing Project
- Chapel of the Resurrection: My Brother's Keeper
- Christ Church Cathedral: Christmas on the Rocks by Cincinnati Men's Chorus, Handel's Messiah by Collegium Cincinnati, Festival of Nine Lessons and Carols
- Compass Christian Church: German Carol Festival, French Christmas Suite, Fantasia on Greensleeves, Waltz of the Flowers from Nutcracker Suite, A Charlie Brown Christmas performed by the Cincinnati Civic Orchestra
- Episcopal Church of the Redeemer: Musica Sacra
- Knox Presbyterian: Christmas Miniatures
- Mason United Methodist Church: Christmas in Warren County
- Montgomery Assembly of God: Blue Ash Montgomery Symphony
- Old St. Mary's Church: Musical Oratory of Advent
- Shiloh United Methodist: Bethany Van Meter
- St. Boniface: A Candlelit Christmas by Vocal Arts Ensemble
- St. Francis de Sales: A Candlelit Christmas by Vocal Arts Ensemble
- St. Peter in Chains: Advent Festival of Lessons and Carols
- St. Thomas Episcopal: Handel's *Messiah* Sing-Along
- Timothy's Episcopal Church: Remembering the Holidays: A Concert of Carols and Lullabies by the Anderson High School Combined Women's Treble Choir and the Cincinnati Collaborative Ringing Project[112]
- Westwood First Presbyterian Church: *Messiah*

CARILLONS

Sometimes, especially at Christmas, when you're walking around Cincinnati, you will hear the lovely sound of bells ringing in the air. You are probably not hearing silver bells, but rather bronze bells. They might be ringing in a church tower, or you might be hearing a carillon. Since 1842, Cincinnatians have been treated to the sound of bronze bells cast by the Verdin Company. Verdin has cast bells for fifty-five thousand installations around the world, including bells right here in Cincinnati. As its website describes, "Bells provide Westminster chimes and time strikes across college campuses and local communities; ring joyously to mark new beginnings; call people to prayer; chime in reverence; and toll in remembrance."[113]

The Verdin Company, led by president Tim Verdin after six generations of Verdins (and the oldest family-run company in Ohio), created the world's largest swinging bell, the World Peace Bell, installed in Newport, Kentucky, on December 31, 1999, to be rung for the first time on January 1, 2000. (Created by Verdin in Nantes, France, it weighs sixty-six thousand pounds and rings every day at noon.)[114]

Today, the company creates church towers, clock towers and carillons, and repairs or replaces bells. The "bells" in the carillon might not even be real bells, but rather digital ones. The company itself can be found in the former St. Paul's Church in Over-the-Rhine, built in 1850 adjacent to St. Mary's. (When St. Paul's Church closed, the territory reverted to Old St. Mary's Parish.)[115]

Old St. Mary's, the oldest standing church in the downtown environs, is what brought the two Verdin brothers from their home in France: to install a tower clock in the church.[116] However, the church was not known as "Old St. Mary's" then, as it had been dedicated to God on July 3 of that same year. The Verdin brothers were installing a new tower clock in a new, 170-foot tower, which was at the time part of the largest church erected west of the Mississippi Valley.[117] On July 5, 1992, a special Mass was celebrated in honor of St. Mary's 150th anniversary. Mass was celebrated in three languages: English, Latin and German. A carillon was donated by the Verdin Company, the Over-the-Rhine Chamber of Commerce and Star Bank.[118]

One of the best places in Cincinnati to hear a carillon playing during the Christmas season is in Mariemont, on the east side of Cincinnati. Mariemont was created by Mary Emery, one of Cincinnati's leading ladies, and is thought of as one of the first planned communities in the United States.[119] Commissioned by Mary Emery's sister, Isabel Hopkins, the one-hundred-foot tall "Mary M. Emery Memorial Carillon" was installed in 1929 to encourage patriotism in Mariemont's youth. For that reason, national holidays feature patriotic music, especially "Lindbergh's Day," celebrating Charles Lindbergh's achievement of the first successful solo transatlantic flight, which had occurred just two years before the carillon's installation. Today, the daily "Westminster Chimes" and "Vesper Hymns" are played by computer program; but you can still hear the human carillonneur playing the bells on Sundays and holidays.[120]

5
Things to See

Sports

Cincinnati is a sports town, with three professional major-league sports teams (Reds, Bengals and FC Cincinnati), a handful of minor-league teams and a few colleges in the area that have competitive sports. Of those, four are NCAA Division I teams (Miami University, Northern Kentucky University, the University of Cincinnati and Xavier University).

In the winter, of course, sports are generally limited to indoor contests of strength and will. We have had a number of hockey teams at different levels. Our only pro basketball team, the Cincinnati Royals, left town in 1971. Despite having the NBA Most Valuable Player (Oscar Robertson) and Rookie of the Year (Jerry Lucas) in 1964, as well as hosting the NBA All-Star Game in 1966, Cincinnati never won an NBA title.[121]

Luckily for sports fans, some of the local colleges have historic rivalries that are frequently seen around Christmastime. One such rivalry is in football, between the UC Bearcats and the Miami Redhawks. The "Battle for the Victory Bell" is the fifth-oldest Division I FBS rivalry, beginning in 1888.[122] As of this writing, UC has been on a winning streak since 2006. Both teams are considered contenders at the national level and have had players go on to play in the NFL (Ben Roethlisberger, Travis and Jason Kelce, Brent Celek, Kevin Huber, Trent Cole, Haruki Nakamura, Mardy Gilyard, Connor Barwin, Isaiah Pead and many more). This rivalry has provided great memories for players and spectators alike.

One game's memories are more painful. In 1923, while playing in the traditional Thanksgiving football game between Miami University and the University of Cincinnati, James Gamble Nippert was injured. Jimmy was the offspring of two of Cincinnati's greatest families, the Nipperts and the Gambles. Son of Judge Alfred K. and Maud Gamble Nippert, he had graduated from Culver Military Academy in Indiana and had returned to UC for a law degree after serving in the army at the end of World War I. He played football for a while but then left the team to focus on his law studies. His cleats were then filled by his younger brother Louis, but never quite as well, so Jimmy came back to the team at center. The team was just beginning to win more games when they went into their final game of the season against their local rivals at Miami University.

After a pregame chicken race that Thanksgiving Day, the game began. In the third quarter, Jimmy Nippert was stepped on by one of the Miami players, but he stayed in the game. Despite Nippert's injury, the nasty, sloppy field and the rainy weather, UC won, 23–0. However, Nippert's wound got worse, turning septic—some say perhaps as a result of the chicken droppings on the field.

In December, Jimmy was taken from his home, the Gamble Mansion in Westwood, to Christ Hospital. (Louis Nippert had been born in that house on Christmas Eve, a much happier holiday occasion. Ironically, Jimmy's grandfather had founded Christ Hospital in honor of his great-grandmother Elizabeth Gamble.)

For twelve days, Jimmy's mother did not leave his side. Maud Nippert sent a message to the UC students, and it was published in the *News Record*, the student newspaper. She said that Jimmy thanked them for their deep interest and knew that the whole campus wished him well. But it was to no avail.

On Christmas morning, Nippert uttered, "Five more yards to go, then drop"—the last words he had spoken during the game—and then died in his mother's arms. He was twenty-three years old.

In Jimmy's memory, Nippert's grandfather James N. Gamble (a partner at the Procter and Gamble Company) donated the funds to build a new stadium. Dedicated on September 27, 1924, Nippert Stadium is currently the fifth-oldest venue in college football.[123]

Commercial Club

Louis Nippert went on to become one of Cincinnati's great citizens. As an adult, he served as president of the Christ Hospital board for twenty-three years. In 1971, he was elected to the position of treasurer of the Commercial Club.[124]

The Commercial Club of Cincinnati was organized in 1880 to promote the business, civic and cultural interests of greater Cincinnati. Throughout its existence, the club has been led by Cincinnati's greatest civic and business leaders. It has also garnered the attention of national leaders. In fact, President William McKinley was the focal point of a meeting in 1897. After his train arrived at the Torrance Station and was met by a twenty-one-gun salute, he was taken to the home of J.G. Schmidlapp for entertainment and a brief rest. He was then taken downtown to the chamber of commerce, where he addressed the members of the Commercial Club. A public program was held in the evening.[125]

The meetings were most frequently held at the Queen City Club, such as the eighth-anniversary celebration on November 22, 1888. The *Cincinnati Enquirer* declared the annual dinner a "fitting climax to its laborers in the city's welfare." The celebration was described as being "like all of its famous predecessors…a grand feast of delicacies, reason, and wit." The club was said to have carried out "very effective work, quietly and without blow, in promoting the growth of the city and of improving and reforming its affairs." The chef outdid himself in preparing the menu, which included oysters, consommé royal, bass with "Holland sauce," lamb chop American style, terrapin from Maryland, canvas-back duck and coffee.[126]

Some of the wit referenced by the *Enquirer* article was on exhibit in the Christmas 1964 celebration. A book was made from the proceedings, with "'As You Like It' or 'So Shall Our City Be'" in gilt letters on the cover. The play, written by Frederick Geier, was performed by the members and relived historic moments in Cincinnati's (supposed) history. "William Shakespeare" and "Cincinnatus" were joined by various Cincinnatians on a journey through Cincinnati events and places. "Shakespeare" had the last word, fittingly:

God speed ye, worthy Gentlemen
Let nothing you dismay
Hold fast to your appointed task
To build a better day

For the fair city that you love
And serve in many a way.
Oh, tidings of comfort and every success
For your worthy efforts, may heaven you bless.

The members then joined in singing one verse of "God Rest Ye Merry, Gentlemen" and "Deck the Halls."[127] By all accounts, much fun was had by all.

Boar's Head and Yuletide Festival

Right in sync with Cincinnati's Porkopolis past is a favorite Christmas production, held at the Christ Church Cathedral downtown: the Boar's Head and Yuletide Festival. This popular celebration, which is held between Christmas and Epiphany, began at Queen's College, Oxford, England, in 1340. Tradition holds that a scholar was walking through a forest while reading a book on Aristotle. Suddenly, a wild boar viciously attacked him. Having nothing else with which to protect himself, the scholar rammed the metal-bound leather book down the boar's throat, killing it. The boar was then served at a celebration feast while everyone sang "Behold the King of Bliss!"

Historically, the festivity was celebrated in various places in England until it was brought to the New World by a persecuted French Huguenot family, the Boutons. They settled in Troy, New York, where the festival became a tradition. The festival was celebrated for the first time in Cincinnati at Christ Church on its 600th anniversary after the Reverend Nelson Burroughs was called to be the rector in 1939. Prior to this, the festival had typically been celebrated in schools. Burroughs gave it a church setting.

Many changes have taken place over the years, such as having a minimal celebration during World War II and allowing women to participate in the ceremony beginning in 1973. However, some things remain the same. The costumes and setting must be faithful to the fourteenth century, and the dean of the church must be involved. Best of all, the food must be homemade: a huge mince pie and plum puddings are enjoyed by the cast after the last performance. Although pigs have a long history in Cincinnati (and some of them fly in May during the Flying Pig Marathon), there are few wild boars roaming around, much less any attacking scholars! These days, a pig's head is roasted and garnished but not eaten.

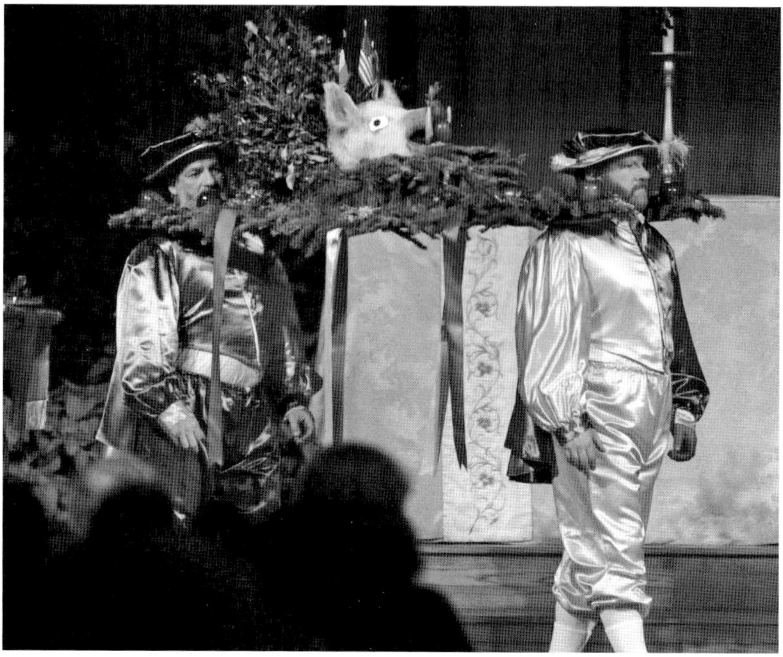

Joseph Leist (*left*) and Brad Frye carry in a boar's head in a scene during the Boar's Head and Yule Log Festival held at Christ Church Cathedral on December 28, 2002. Cincinnati Enquirer/*Brandi Stafford*.

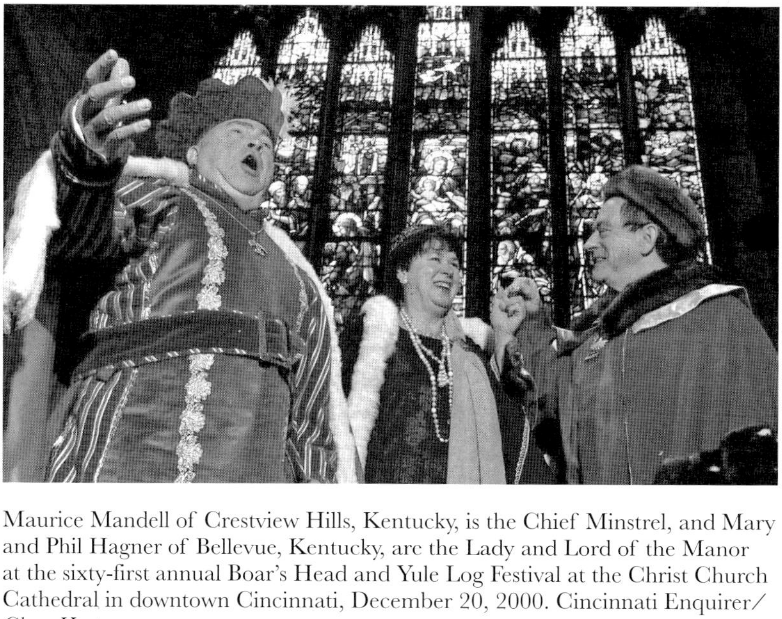

Maurice Mandell of Crestview Hills, Kentucky, is the Chief Minstrel, and Mary and Phil Hagner of Bellevue, Kentucky, are the Lady and Lord of the Manor at the sixty-first annual Boar's Head and Yule Log Festival at the Christ Church Cathedral in downtown Cincinnati, December 20, 2000. Cincinnati Enquirer/ *Glenn Hartong*.

As in the past, in twenty-first-century festival celebrations, a yule log crackles and burns, lit by the embers of the previous year's celebration. The boar is "carried in state" (brought in on a stretcher) and is, as the "Boar's Head Carol" describes, "bedecked with bay and rosemary." The boar is also surrounded by sprigs of evergreen and holly. The participants boisterously sing the "Boar's Head Carol" as they process in.

The festival is carried out by more than 150 volunteers, both performers and persons behind the scenes. The orchestra is made up primarily of professional musicians.

Beware! This is a very popular event and tickets go fast.[128]

NUTCRACKER

A favorite way to hear beautiful music and watch some spectacular dancing is Tchaikovsky's *The Nutcracker*. Since 1974, Cincinnatians have flocked to Cincinnati Ballet Company's "Nutcracker" (now known as "Frisch's Big Boy Presents the Nutcracker," although Frisch's has been a major sponsor since

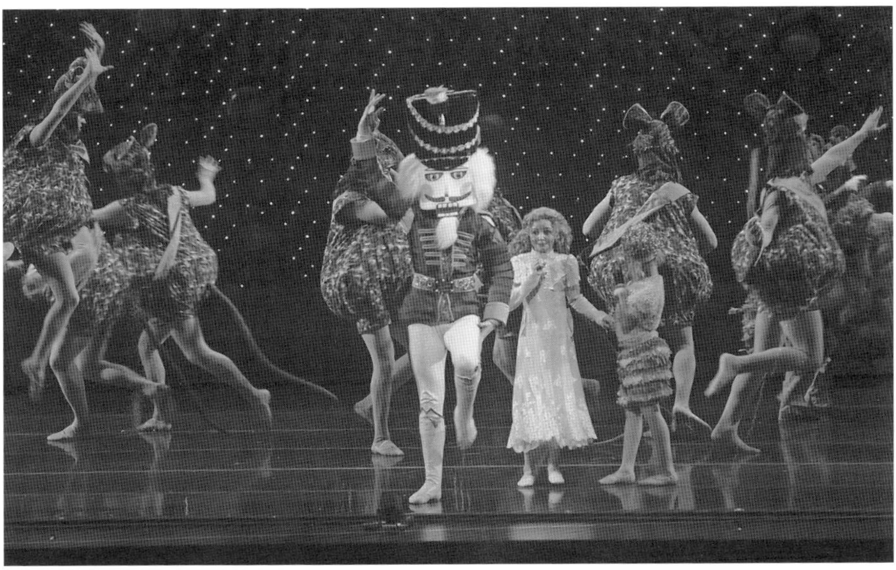

The Cincinnati Ballet brings the annual "Frisch's Big Boy Presents *The Nutcracker*" to the Aronoff Center for the Arts, December 22, 2011. Cincinnati Enquirer/*Leigh Taylor*.

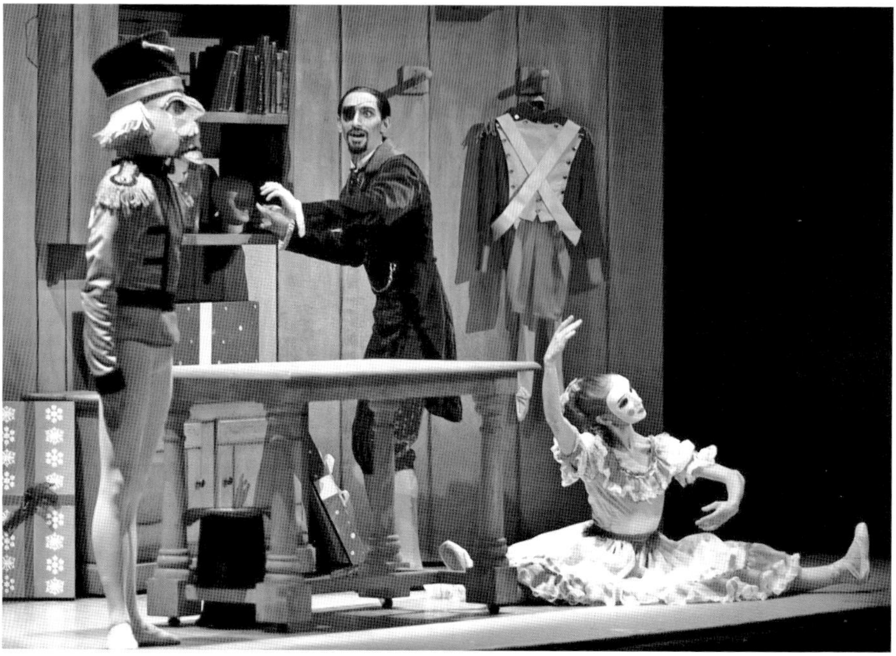

Members of the Cincinnati Ballet perform during the opening night of their production of *The Nutcracker* at Music Hall, December 18, 2002. Cincinnati Enquirer/*Brandi Stafford*.

the beginning). At the same time as that first performance in Cincinnati, the role of Clara was being danced in Salt Lake City by twelve-year-old Victoria Morgan, now the artistic director and CEO of the Cincinnati Ballet Company. Contrary to popular rumor, Sarah Jessica Parker was never a member of the company. However, like many children through the years, she did have a couple of small roles. The most notable of these was as a mouse that did a headstand at the center of the stage and clapped her feet in time to a grandfather clock as it chimed. This usually stirred up gentle chuckles from the audience.[129] Winners of a contest sponsored by Frisch's have been allowed walk-on, nondancing parts in past productions.

From 1974 to 2007, the ballet was performed in Cincinnati's Music Hall. Then the ballet moved to the Aronoff Center for the Arts until it returned to Music Hall in 2017. Six different versions of *The Nutcracker* have been staged in Cincinnati, and in its first season, three different choreographers were involved: Frederic Franklin, Moscelyne Larkin and Roman Jasinski.[130] For more than fifty years, the ballet orchestra has been conducted by the accomplished and beloved Carmon de Leone.

In 2020, the CBC could not perform the ballet for a live audience, so it recorded an "edited" version of the performance and presented it on the NBC affiliate, WLWT-TV.

Amahl and the Night Visitors

The Cincinnati Ballet's recent *Nutcracker* was not the first Christmas production on NBC. One popular production is the one-act *Amahl and the Night Visitors*. *Amahl* is considered the first made-for-TV (non-soap) opera. The music and libretto for *Amahl* were both created by composer Gian Carlo Menotti. Reflecting the stories of his childhood in Italy, the play focuses on the tale of the wise men searching for the baby Jesus. It first aired on NBC on live television on Christmas Eve 1951.[131]

Cincinnati has a special connection to *Amahl* by way of retired orthopedic surgeon James Sammarco. His involvement with *Amahl* goes back to when he was a ten-year-old boy in New Jersey.

"I was a boarding student at the Columbus Boychoir School in Princeton NJ for four years," Sammarco recalls. The school was originally formed in Columbus, Ohio, and moved to the Lambert Estate in Princeton in 1950. During that time, Sammarco commuted by train to Princeton. "We were associated with, but not part of, Westminster Choir College under John Findley Williamson, founder and president (the Godfather of choral singing throughout the Country), during my four years with the CBS. Four of us unchanged[132] were brought as an exhibit every Friday afternoon to the college and used in demonstrations in Master Classes for unchanged voice training, solo and ensemble. They loved us."[133]

Two weeks after Sammarco started at the school, Gian Carlo Menotti visited, looking for boy soloists. Menotti had been commissioned by the National Broadcasting Company (NBC) to compose an opera to entice people to turn from their radios to the new phenomenon of television. Sammarco, although he could not read music, was one of three boys chosen. One, Chet Allen, sang the part for the broadcast, with the others as understudies standing by on stage, dressed as shepherds, in case something unexpected happened and one of them had to step in.[134]

Sammarco later starred in the lead role for tours. After his voice changed, he left his professional singing career. And he was, indeed, a professional. "I was paid for singing at the Boychoir school, on TV, in special performances and for *Amahl*. The income was applied to my scholarship at CBS,"

Sammarco says. Music is still very much a part of his life, however. "I sang in choruses until I entered medical school. During the summer, I sang in New York at Radio City Music Hall. I still hear music in my head pretty much throughout the day."

After medical school, Sammarco opened his practice in Cincinnati in 1972, where he again became involved in *Amahl* as a consultant and supporter. He and his wife sponsor a scholarship for lessons and coaching for whoever sings the role of the Amahl character. After each season, he gives the boy a pin designed after the Christmas star that guided the three wise men to Bethlehem. The Cincinnati performances of *Amahl* are a joint production of the Cincinnati Chamber Orchestra and Madcap Puppets, colorful bigger-than-life puppets.

A Christmas Carol

While Cincinnatians listened to the new bells in the tower of St. Mary Church of the Annunciation in 1843, Charles Dickens worked for six weeks on his novella *A Christmas Carol. Prose. Being a Ghost Story of Christmas*. A little more than 115 years later, the Cincinnati Playhouse in the Park was created.

Cincinnati Playhouse in the Park was another theater venue affected by the COVID-19 pandemic in 2020. The season was canceled—but what about the local favorite, *A Christmas Carol*? For a solution, not only did the Playhouse go from the stage to the airwaves, but it also turned the play into a one-man show. (Cast and crew typically number in the forties for the production.) Thanks to the sponsorship of Macy's, Cincinnati Playhouse in the Park was able to join up with Cincinnati Public Radio and air *A Christmas Carol: A Radio Play* on December 23 and 24, 2020, on WVXU and WMUB.

Bruce Cromer has played the role of Ebenezer Scrooge since 2004 at Cincinnati Playhouse in the Park (and he played Bob Cratchit for eight years before that).[135] However, this was the first time he played all the roles himself. "Bruce [Cromer] is beloved as Scrooge," Blake Robison, the artistic director at the playhouse, observed, "and now we'll get to experience his immense talent and this holiday favorite in an imaginative new way."[136]

Another Cincinnati fan favorite as Scrooge was Joneal Joplin, who played the lead role at the Playhouse in the Park for eight seasons before Cromer. (Four men have played the lead since the playhouse's first production in 1991, with Cromer having the longest tenure.) For Joplin's final two years as

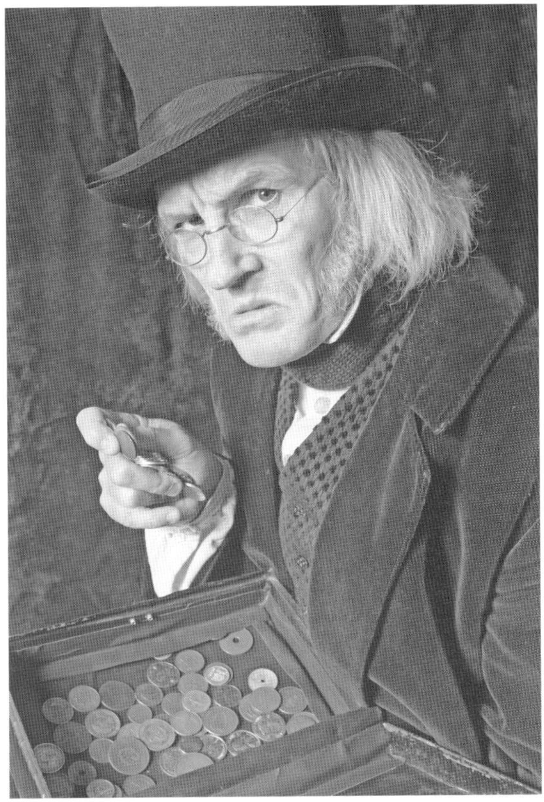

Right: Bruce Cromer playing Scrooge in the Cincinnati Playhouse in the Park production of *A Christmas Carol*. Cin Weekly/ *David Sorcher*.

Below: Children of all ages gather on Fountain Square to view the annual Christmas pantomime on the glass-covered balcony of Mabley & Carew in this 1895 photograph. *Public Library of Cincinnati and Hamilton County*.

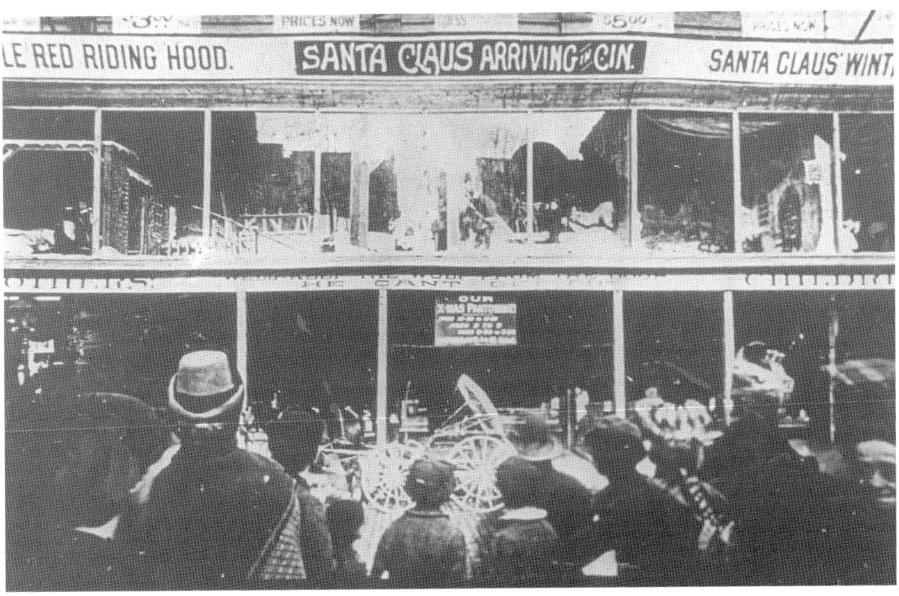

Scrooge, he was joined on the stage by his son Jared as the younger Ebenezer Scrooge. In similar fashion, Cromer has been joined recently by his son Charlie playing the younger Scrooge.[137]

Dickens wrote *A Christmas Carol* to draw attention to the disparity between the lives of the rich and the lives of the poor in England. In keeping with the spirit of the "reborn" Ebenezer Scrooge, the playhouse holds an annual Cratchit Family Food Drive to support the Freestore Foodbank. The playhouse has also partnered with the University of Cincinnati's Hoxworth Blood Center to run a November blood drive, where donors can get their tickets at half price.

Other Cincinnati entertainment venues and companies to check out each year at Christmastime include Children's Theater, OTRimprov, Cincinnati Shakespeare Company, Know Theatre and Ensemble Theatre. One performance held long ago on Fountain Square at Christmastime was the "pantomime" that Mabley's put on each year in front of its department store. Spectators lined up in droves on the street to watch the plays, which were usually familiar stories, as well as a presentation from Santa Claus. The first, presented in 1890, was *Little Red Riding Hood*. In 1892, Cincinnati artist Joseph Henry Sharp was commissioned by Mabley & Carew to capture the crowd watching the pantomime that year.[138] (The painting hangs in the Cincinnati Wing of the Cincinnati Art Museum in Eden Park.) *The Cincinnati Enquirer* described the scene:

> *Packed like sardines, every inch of available space covered with little toddlers' feet, or those of adults who held them aloft....They were of all sizes and ranks. The scion of wealth fought for his point of vantage with the ragamuffin, and when the first curtain was raised, and there displayed to view was the familiar form of Santa Claus, a shout went to heaven and down through alleys and streets from a thousand throats which told plainer than words that the old fellow was still king.*[139]

The last pantomime was held in 1923.

FOUNTAIN SQUARE

Fountain Square as we know it today is not how our predecessors saw it. Around 1815, what is now known as Fountain Square was a public market. At that point, twenty-seven years after the first white families came down the river on flatboats, Fifth Street was the northern border of downtown Cincinnati. The street was lined with meat stalls. It was not a pretty sight—or smell.

> *By the 1860s, the Fifth Street Market was occupied almost entirely by butchers and almost everyone agreed it was pretty disgusting. When Cincinnati decided to build Fountain Square on the site, the butchers sued and their case went all the way to the Ohio Supreme Court. The butchers lost and, three days later, the city sent an army of workmen, guarded by a battalion of police, to demolish the old market. The butchers claimed that an early deed mandated that the location was to be used as a market in perpetuity. The city obliged by installing a little metal cart for selling flowers. Every year, the mayor ceremonially bought one flower, for one cent, to maintain the terms of the deed.*[140]

A prominent fixture, the Tyler Davidson Fountain, was commissioned by Tyler Davidson's brother-in-law Henry Probasco. Called the "Genius of Water," it was also "a Temperance fountain," built to provide water to both thirsty humans and animals. At that time, the only place people could get a drink of water was in a bar or a saloon. Until the 1980s, some of the little bronze cups could still be found chained to the four drinking fountains.[141] The fountain was dedicated to the people of Cincinnati on October 6, 1871.

At that time, Fifth Street was just a parkway or esplanade. Over the next century or so, the block was redesigned a few times. What's known as "Core Block A" is today's Fountain Square, bordered by Fifth, Vine, Walnut and Sixth Streets.[142] In 1970, the fountain was moved toward the south end of the block, away from car traffic. The fountain was renovated in 2000 and again in 2006. These renovations included cleaning the fountain and modernizing the pipes that conveyed the water. The parking garage below the fountain no longer had a (somewhat unwelcome) fountain of its own.[143] Each winter, the Tyler Davidson Fountain is decked out with lights that sparkle in place of the running water.

The buildings around Fountain Square have changed, as well. One of the first structures to be built in proximity to the fountain was the Fountain Square Building. It was heralded as "one of the outstanding showplaces of the city" by the *Daily Commercial*. It was, indeed, the tallest building in the neighborhood at eighteen stories, but the lot the builders were able to procure was only thirty-three feet deep with a frontage of one hundred feet on Walnut Street[144] (near where Government Square "Area D" is now). The building was half of its intended magnificence.

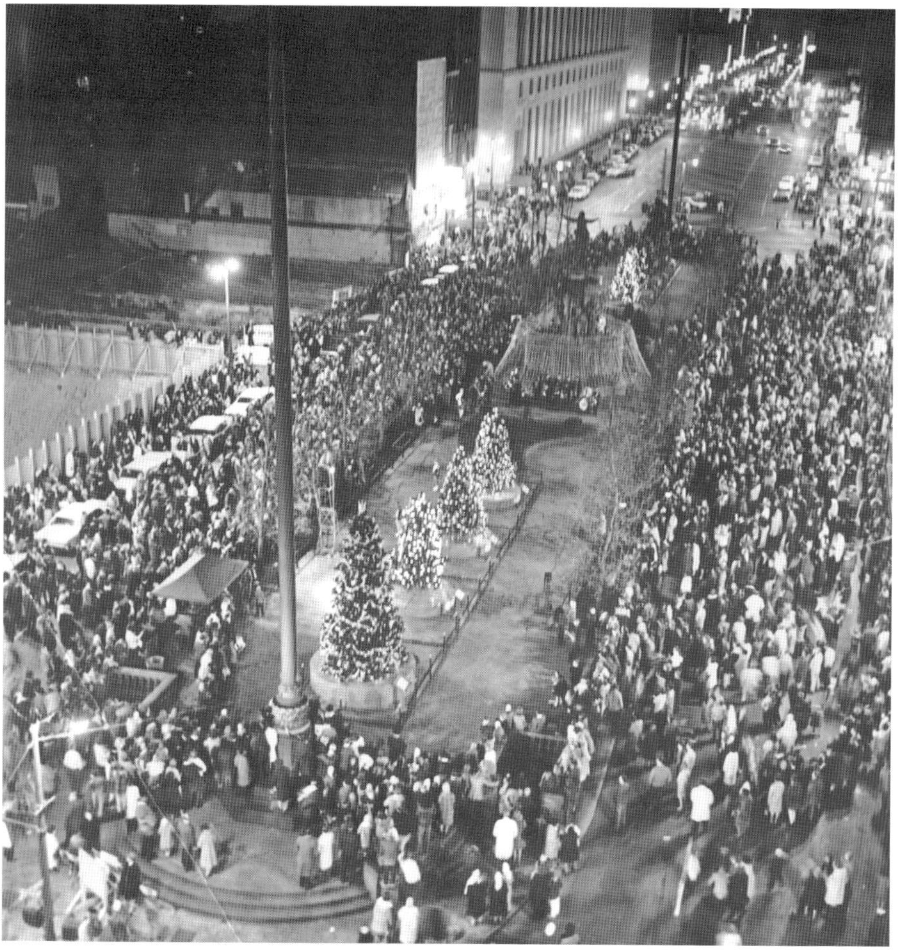

In 1850, the Fraternal Order of Eagles acquired the land, then the building, promising that there would be no changes to the building for its tenants, who enjoyed a unique "one-floor-one-tenant" plan. In 1865, the city spent $1 million to purchase the entire block of Core Block A. Eventually, all existing buildings were leveled to enable the construction of the Fifth Third Bank Center. As a result, the existing businesses had to relocate. The Maisonette and La Normandie moved one block north to Sixth Street.

The northwest corner of the intersection of Fifth and Vine has had many incarnations. It was here that Isaac Rollman first sold dry goods in 1867. The building on this corner grew through the years. In 1952, under the ownership of Mabley & Carew, it underwent a multimillion-dollar renovation. Finally, under the ownership of Elder-Beerman, the building was razed in 1991.

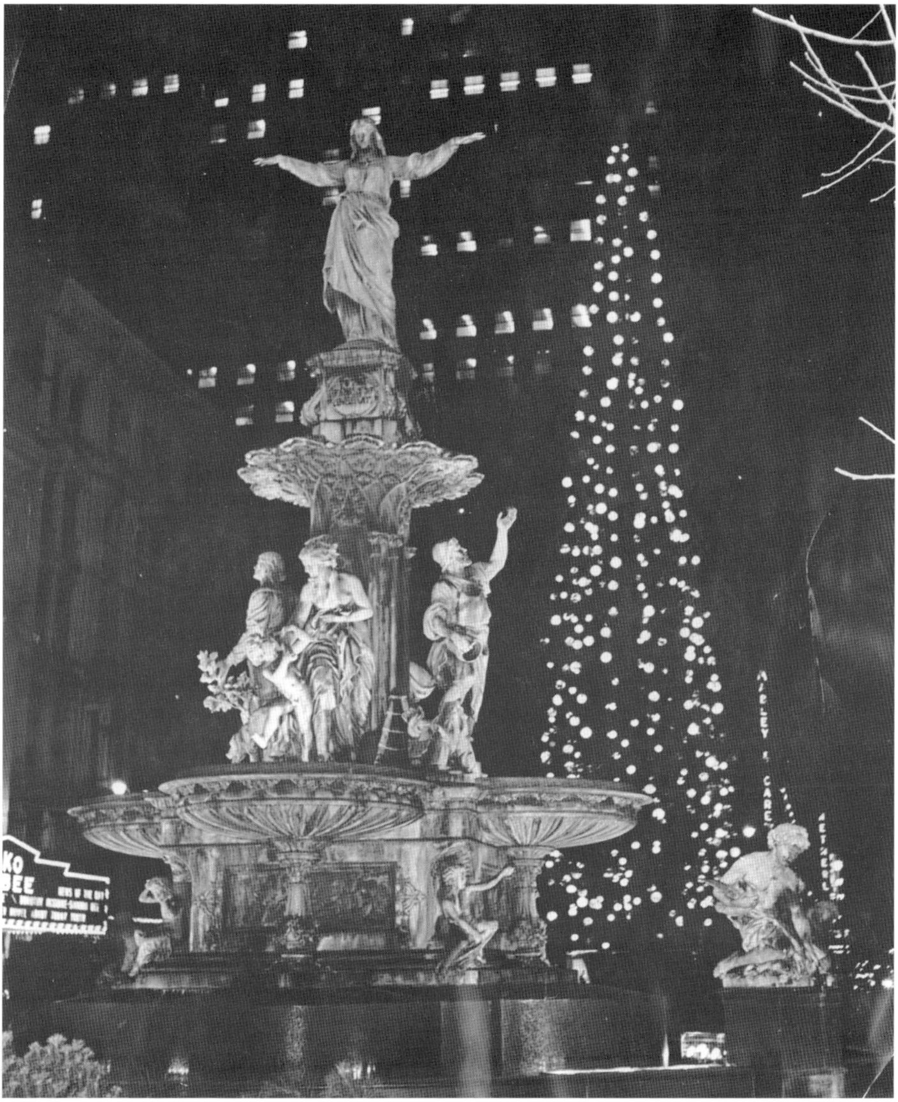

Opposite: Crowds jam Fountain Square for tree lighting, November 25, 1965. *Cincinnati Enquirer* photographer Fred Straub took this shot from the sixth floor of the Carew Tower. Cincinnati Enquirer *photo*.

Above: The Tyler-Davidson "Genius of Water" gets her Christmas trimmings." On December 1, 1959, trees were aglow once again on Fountain Square as Tommy Maler, six, and his sister, Amy, seven, pulled the light switch with Vice Mayor William Cody Kelly on two 100-foot Christmas trees. Cincinnati Enquirer *photo*.

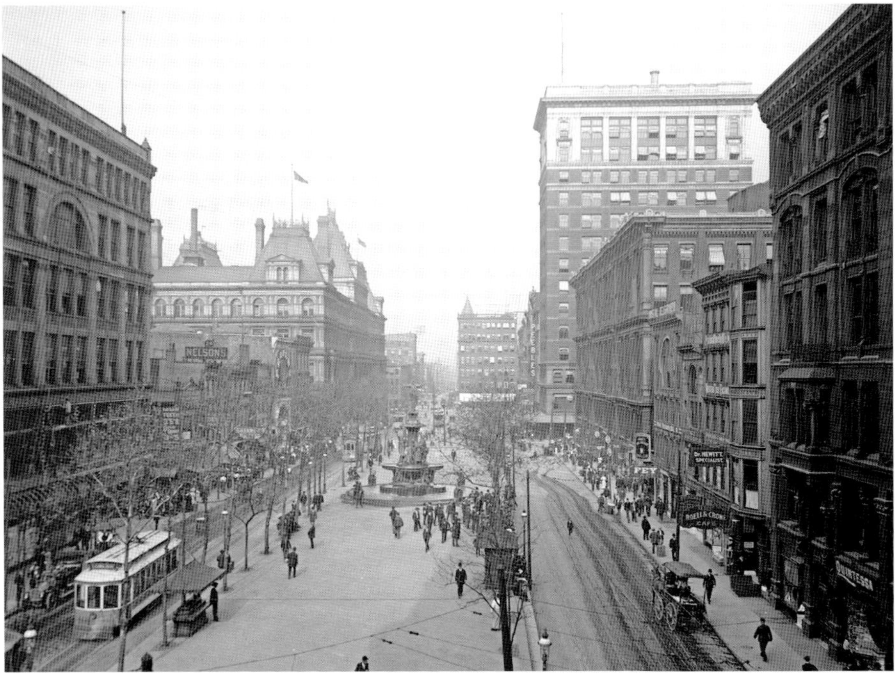

The 1907 version of Fountain Square. *Library of Congress.*

Eventually, the new "Fountain Place" building took its place to the west of Fountain Square, with frontage on Fifth and Vine. For many years it housed Lazarus/Macy's, Tiffany & Company, Brooks Brothers and Palomino Euro Bistro, but these are gone as of this writing. In their place will be "The Foundry," a mix of office and retail space.[145]

The southwest corner of Fifth and Vine now boasts the Carew Tower. For a long time, however, that corner was nothing to boast about. In the mid-1800s, it was known as "the Nasty Corner." It has been described as "a hotbed of drunkenness and carousing."[146] A *Cincinnati Enquirer* editor wrote on December 27 that Christmas Day 1850 had been quieter than usual, as "there was less of pistol firing and firing of crackers, which must be attributed to the Chief of Police."[147]

The corner was cleaned up when the first Carew Building was constructed in 1891. The Carew Tower was built in 1930 in a style described as art deco and Streamline Moderne. At forty-nine stories and 574 feet tall, it was the tallest building in the city for a long time—until the 2011 completion of the Great American Tower (which is about 90 feet taller). Some in Cincinnati challenge the status of the upstart that stole the crown (so to speak) from the Carew Tower, as the tallest part of the Great American Tower structure is non-occupiable. The Great American Tower has only forty-one stories, while the Carew has forty-nine. The Carew's roof is also almost 80 feet above Great American's. However, the best part of this two-tower story is that from the Carew Tower's observation deck, the view of the Great American Tower is spectacular—as is the view of the tri-state region, including Kentucky and Indiana.

Carew Tower was also the first building designed for mixed use (even before New York City's Rockefeller Center). Still today, the Carew Tower holds a treasure trove of goodies. It houses many offices in its upper floors. On the lower floors, you'll find Hathaway's Diner, which is like a trip back to the 1950s. Milkshakes are made by blending milk and ice cream and are served on a paper doily. Egg salad and tuna salad can be served on a plate or in a sandwich. If you're missing the '50s, stop in. In the Carew Tower Arcade in December, you might even find a beautifully decorated evergreen tree and a certain chubby gentleman in red.

Fountain Square and the Tyler Davidson Fountain form the center of the city, a great place for Cincinnatians and visitors to gather and celebrate,

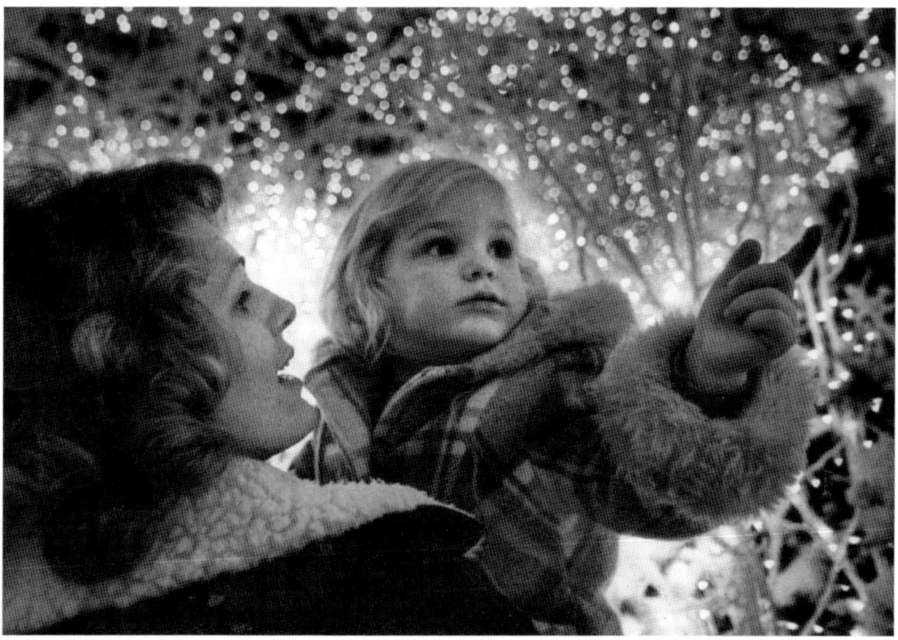

Debbie Wallingford of Milford is as entranced with her daughter, Tonya, two, as Tonya is with the Christmas decorations in the Carew Tower Arcade, November 24, 1977. Cincinnati Enquirer *photo*.

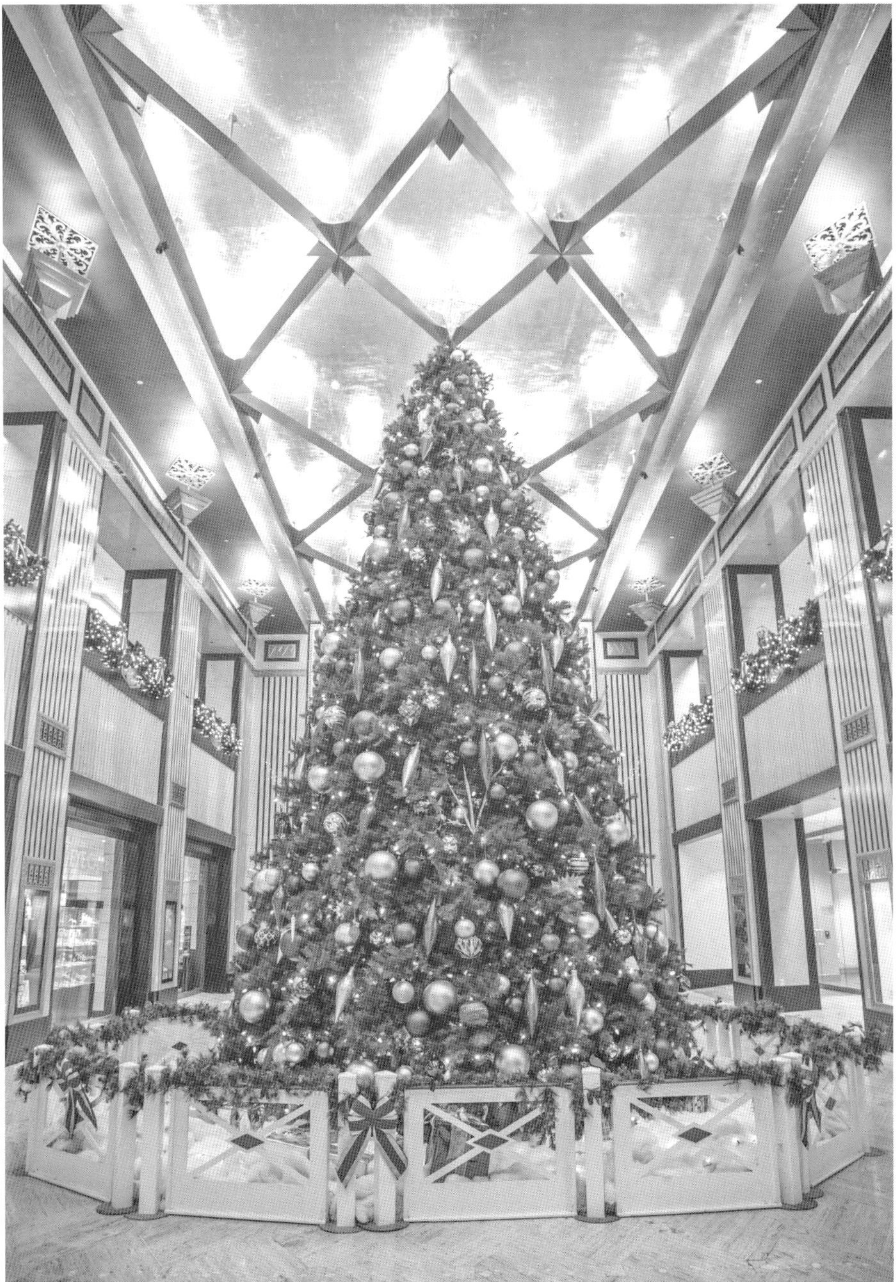

Underneath the Carew Tower is a beautiful arcade that has, at various times, housed shops and restaurants. Of course, at Christmastime, the arcade often boasts a beautiful tree and a jolly gentleman in red. Cincinnati Enquirer *photo.*

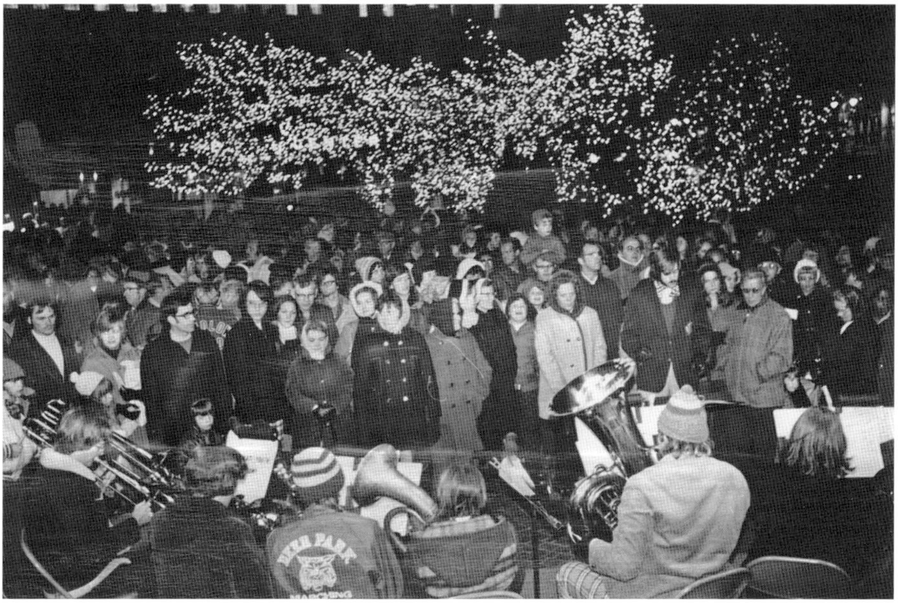

Mayor Theodore Berry proclaimed the month of December and the first two weeks of January a season for the celebration of Christmas and Hanukkah, then pressed a magic button that filled the trees with twinkling green and white lights. Onlookers welcomed the lights with a cheer, then they joined the May Festival Chorus and the Cincinnati Youth Symphony brass choir in singing "Joy to the World," November 29, 1974. Cincinnati Enquirer *photo.*

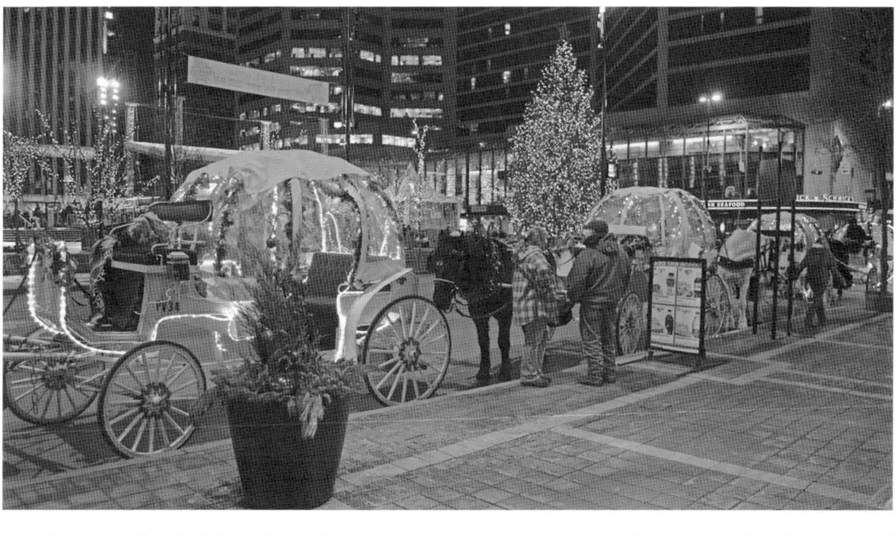

Carriages outlined with delicate lights await the brave passenger desiring a brisk ride around downtown Cincinnati. *Photo by Denny Gibson.*

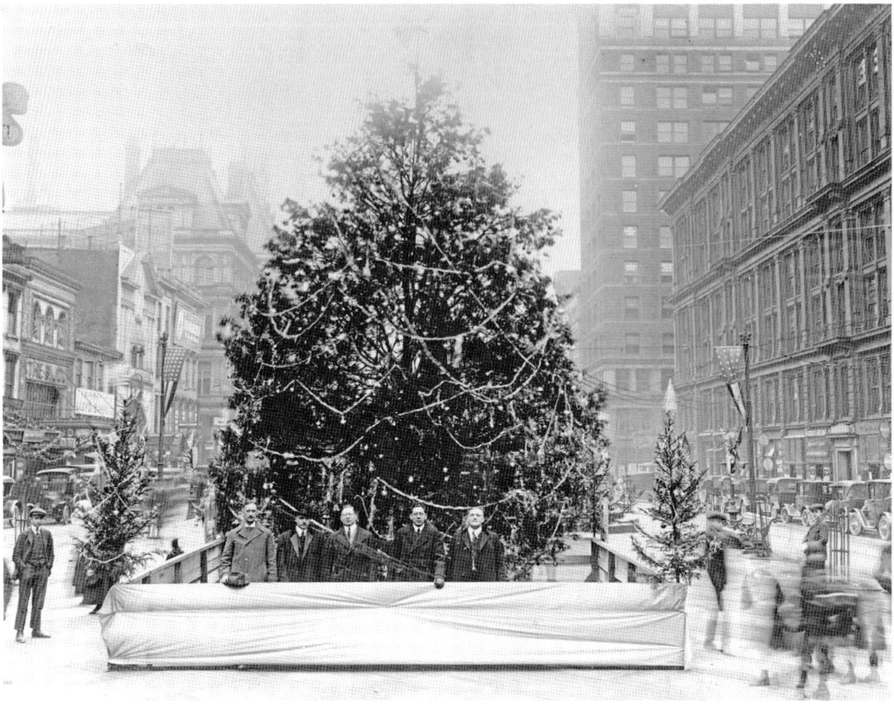

City officials gather for the lighting of the first municipal Christmas tree at Fountain Square in 1918. The community tree that year was donated by the B.P.O. Elks Lodge No. 5. *Cincinnati Historical Society*.

so it is a natural place to have a Christmas tree and lighting ceremony. The first tree that could be considered a "community" tree was erected in 1913, with the city taking it over and providing a municipal tree in 1918. That first tree, standing forty-five feet tall with two thousand electric lights, was sponsored by the Cincinnati Woman's Club, which still exists to this day (and celebrated its 125th anniversary in 2019).[148]

Although Fountain Square is a natural place for the community to gather to enjoy the city's Christmas trees, not all of those trees have been natural. The 1960s was a "mod" time in the United States. People were looking forward to what the future might bring. One way that this was manifested was in the department store decorations. Eleanor Bell wrote in the *Cincinnati Enquirer* that stores' Christmas themes were "more likely to be carried out in pink, blue or all-white than…in the traditional red and green."[149]

In 1960, as plastics like high-density polyester were taking off, Cincinnati's Fountain Square Decorating Committee decided it was time

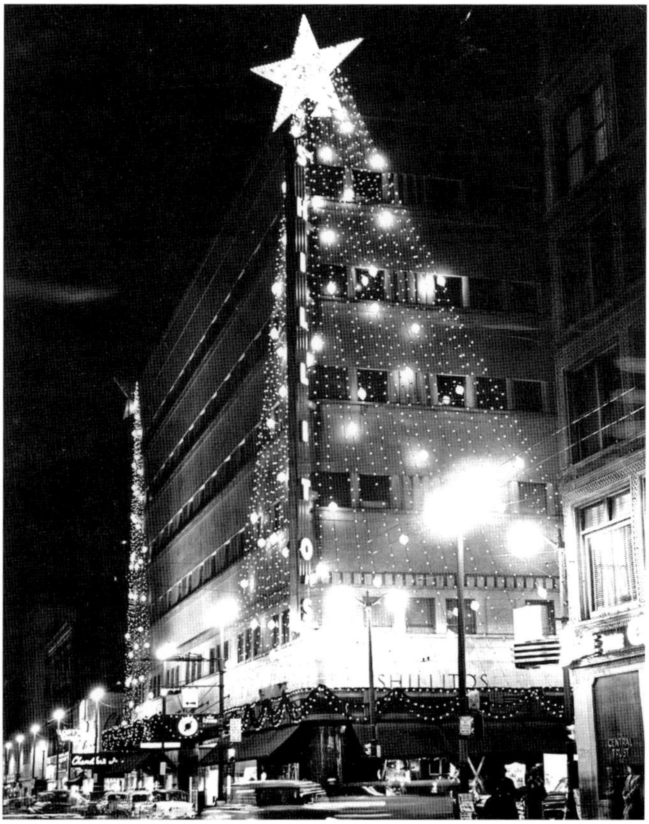

Shillito's department store at Seventh and Race Streets embraces the Christmas season with this display in 1960. Cincinnati Enquirer *photo*.

to "put new life into the downtown Christmas display." Instead of the two natural trees of 1959, twelve plastic trees would decorate the square, with four at each end of the square and two on each side. The trees were eleven feet tall and about four feet across at the fullest point. The lights were embedded inside the trees, creating sparkling near-perfect triangles in the night. What about the old ornaments from the trees of years before? They were donated or sold to various organizations. The committee assessed that the cost of the plastic trees was about the same as the two large natural trees. The committee planned for the plastic trees to be used for two years and then replaced.[150] The city reverted to having real trees at some point.

By 1962, Fountain Square had seven Christmas trees, one representing each country of France, Germany, Ireland, Italy, Mexico, Holland and America. The *Cincinnati Enquirer* article describing the lighting event did not specify if the trees were real or artificial.[151]

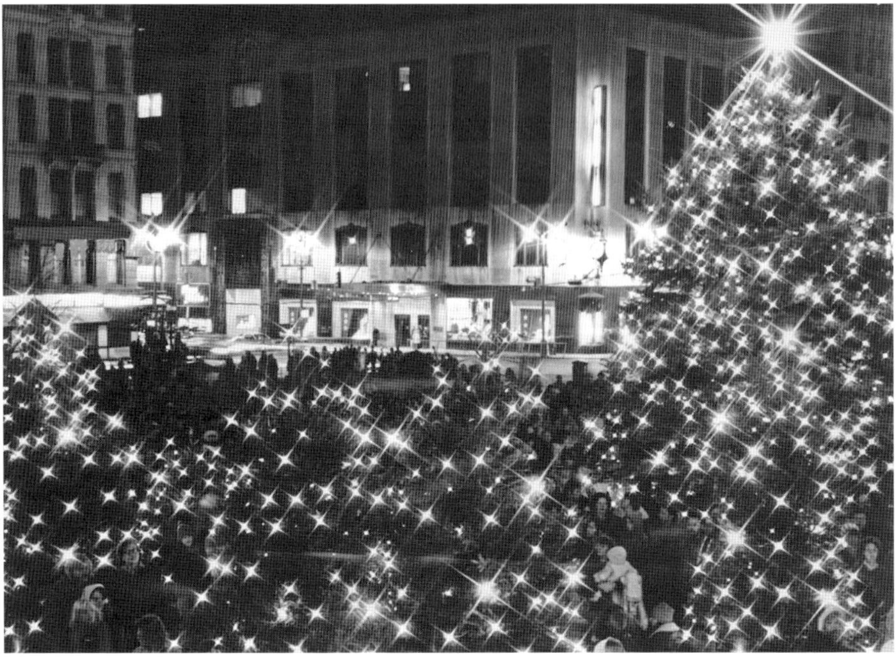

The official beginning to the yule season arrived as Mayor Theodore Berry, accompanied by several Cincinnati Council members, threw the official switch on November 18, 1975, lighting up the Christmas lights strung through the tree branches on Fountain Square. Cincinnati Enquirer *photo.*

A real tree caused Cincinnati to briefly become the laughingstock of the nation in 2020. Late-night host Stephen Colbert even made jokes at our expense on his TV show.[152] The Macy's Holiday Tree, a sixty-five-foot Norway spruce, arrived in Cincinnati after a long drive on a truck. Picture what trees on a Christmas tree lot look like after being stacked one on top of another. They need a little loving to reach their potential. *USA Today* declared, "It IS beginning to look a lot like Christmas—well at least, Christmas in 2020."[153] The tree defended itself on its own Twitter account with a bio of "Just a tree living in the city." Thousands of people followed the tree and were delighted at tweets like, "Like all of us, I'm just doing the best I can in these trying times."[154] One Twitter follower let the tree know it was loved no matter what: "Don't worry, Charlie Brown loves you."[155] After workers "fluffed up" the tree and decorated it, it was just as beautiful as those of previous years.

Throughout the years, gorgeous Christmas trees could be found inside downtown venues, of course, such as the tree that was often found inside

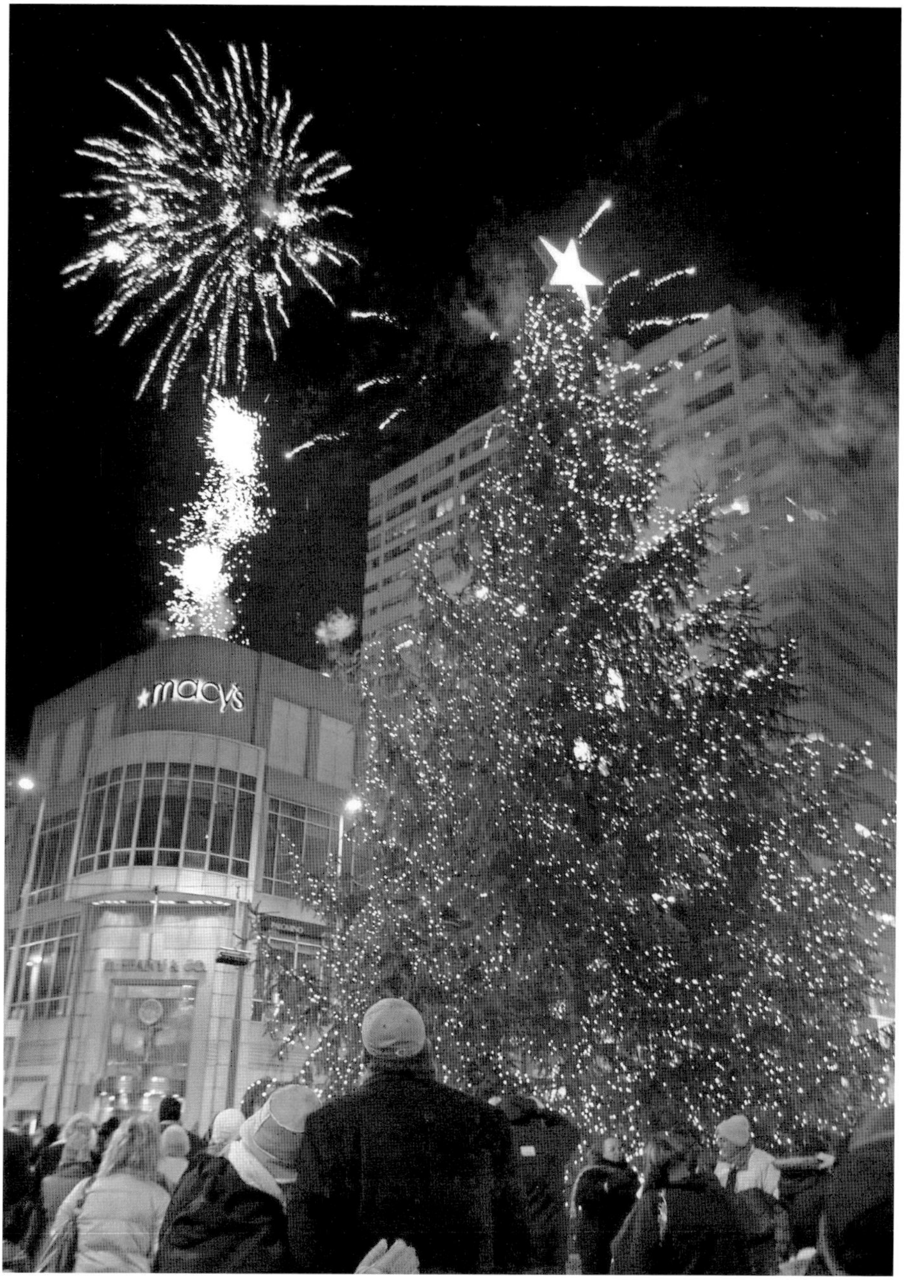

The crowd enjoys watching fireworks as they go off over the newly lit evergreen tree during ceremonies for the Annual Tree Lighting at Fountain Square on November 26, 2010, in downtown Cincinnati. The Norway spruce from Lloyd Hurst of Wooster, Ohio, stands about sixty feet tall. Cincinnati Enquirer/*Joseph Fuqua II*.

the Carew Tower Arcade. Not too far away, you could also get a boost to your Christmas spirit in what was then known as the Netherland Hilton. Starting in 1931, the Netherland began to offer a tree and other decorations for hotel guests as well as downtown workers and shoppers. In 1959, the choir from the Ninth Street Baptist Church sang Christmas carols against a background of poinsettias. This particular year, the twenty-seventh annual dedication of the Netherland's tree—the largest indoor tree in the city—attracted more than three hundred people. The tree shone with five hundred colored lights, which sparkled amid ten thousand ornaments. Hotel manager Harry Nolan commented that the turnout was vastly different from their first year, which didn't even have a dozen people in attendance. Nolan bought a drink for everyone there.

The original idea was for WLW to broadcast the festivities, but not many residents were feeling very festive in the midst of the Great Depression. So the WLW announcer began to fake the festive event. He brought the Restaurante Continentale's house band into the lobby and had it perform. Some of its musicians played, while others sang and were eventually joined by the few guests who showed up. It was broadcast on WLW's (then) 500 kilowatts. Manager Harry Nolan received enthusiastic mail from across the country and even from a fisherman in the Gulf of Mexico. Their success at "making spirits bright" that night encouraged them to make it an annual event.[156]

Professional Lights

Boy band 98 Degrees (whose members were from Cincinnati) had a hit in the 1990s with "If Every Day Could Be Christmas."

If every day could be Christmas
What a wonderful world this would be
We could carry this feeling within us
All through the year (All through the year)
If every day could be Christmas

Christmas lights up the city
Rooftops covered in snow
Lovers sharing a sleigh ride cuddle close
And their eyes seem to glow[157]

Cincinnatians love their Christmas lights. Our city streets, businesses and neighborhoods light up the night. In 1973, a national energy crisis dimmed some of the Christmas lights, but not our spirits. One writer referred to the crisis as "the most pressing problem of our current times," saying: "Warnings have been sounded from the top down. They come from President Nixon over the air waves of television and on the front pages of newspapers, and they have come from local leaders in every corner of the United States. Conserve your fuel at all costs."[158]

Public buildings had to set their thermostats lower in the winter and higher in the summer. With the holiday coming, store managers were scrambling to figure out a way to light up the holiday yet conserve energy.

Beechmont Mall, on the east side of town, followed a Pueblo Indian tradition to save energy. The tradition originated centuries ago in Mexico, was then brought to New Mexico and finally spread to the rest of the country. Mall officials created *las luminarias* (or *luminaria*) and placed them around the roof of the mall. These lights are sand-filled paper bags with a lit candle inside. Ray Penno, president of the Beechmont Mall Merchants Association, said that they would light more than 150 *luminaria* (if it wasn't too wet or windy out). Anderson High School students kept an eye on the lights and re-lit the candles when necessary.[159]

Beechmont was not the only mall to think outside the box. Western Hills Plaza didn't put all of its decorations into use, especially those that required lighting, like its twenty-five-foot candles, twenty-five-foot gold trees and a fifteen-foot elf. The plaza had one major holiday display instead of eight, with an unlit eighteen-foot Santa. Small birch bushes with twinkle lights were placed in the center of the mall surrounded by garlands and toy soldiers with no lights. Spotlights were directed at the Nativity scene, however. Going even further, Northgate Mall had no outside decorations; even its store signs were turned off after 11:00 p.m. Inside, its Christmas lighting was reduced by more than three hours daily. Western Hills Plaza Merchants Association president Carl Gray said that Cincinnati Gas & Electric had given them permission to light up many of their displays, "but we decided against it after the President issued his energy decree."[160]

Gray's comment was echoed by Bill Dickhoner, senior vice president of Cincinnati Gas & Electric: "There is no question about it. If all the traditional lights and displays were turned on, we could handle it. There is no energy crisis in Cincinnati. And, speaking personally, the Christmas season always has been one of gaiety and lights. It would be a shame if we could not have a little bit of this, this season."[161]

In a return to using living trees, Fountain Square's twelve Colorado blue spruces were unlit in 1973, so the city was ready for a change the following year. Once again, live trees were delivered by Ammon Nursery in Florence, Kentucky: a twenty-five-foot Norway spruce, a fifteen-foot "Winter King" hawthorn, a dozen hawthorns between ten and twelve feet tall and a dozen eight-foot "false" blue cypress. The larger trees in the center of the display had lights, as did the living trees around the perimeter. The previous year's living trees had been planted in French Park to replace those lost in a tornado. The living trees of 1974 were planted in Sayler Park to replace those lost in the April 3, 1974, tornado, part of the "Super Outbreak" of tornados in Ohio.[162]

Nowadays, we are cognizant of our energy use in terms of cost and climate damage. However, we have more energy-efficient lights and electric devices for our Christmas displays and everyday use.

Perhaps the most famous light display in Cincinnati is the PNC Festival of Lights at the Cincinnati Zoo & Botanical Garden. This celebration, which began in 1983, offers a magical atmosphere, with three million LED lights strung throughout the grounds. Some of the animal displays are also open for nighttime enjoyment. (Of course, the animals can also be seen during the day enjoying the holiday season.)

People who want to take it all in at their own pace can follow the lit paths that guide them through the sights and sounds of the zoo. For the more adventurous, the North Polar Express train ride offers a brisk view of the park.

If you're in the mood for more boisterous activities, enjoy the entertainment that the zoo provides. Enjoy the beautiful Christmas trees and Christmas carolers aglow with the lights and joy of the season. Visit with Santa and get a tasty treat at one of the S'mores-n-More stands.

As you walk through the zoo, you might run into some of our local Cincinnati celebrities. Even Fiona the hippopotamus and the Nutcracker have been seen while on break from the Cincinnati Ballet Company's performance of *The Nutcracker*. The ballet stars are not the only things shining brightly at the PNC Festival of Lights.

If you haven't gotten enough views of animals at Christmastime, take a drive up to Morrow, Ohio, to the Christmas Ranch, or to Sharon Woods's Heritage Village. Both of these allow combinations of driving, riding, walking and shopping. What could be better? The Holiday in Lights at Sharon Woods is even open on Christmas Eve and Christmas Day. The drive-through portion of the celebration features about a mile of one of

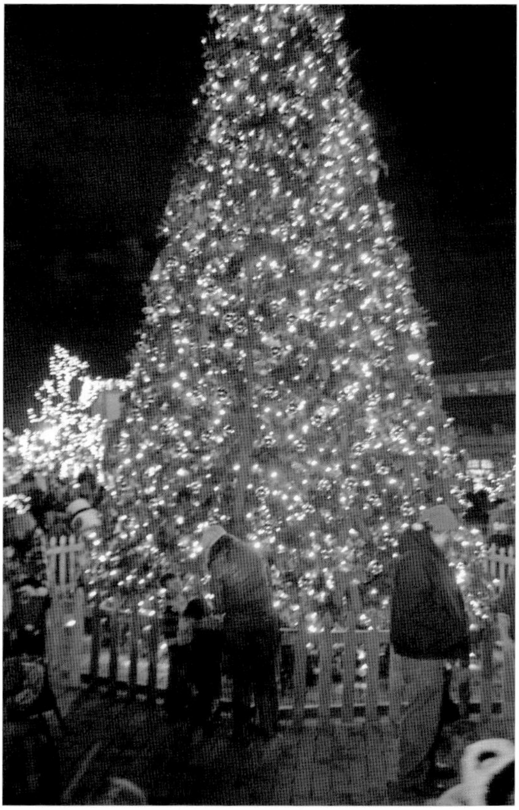

Left: The tree is lit at the Cincinnati Zoo & Botanical Garden's annual PNC Festival of Lights, November 23, 2014. Cincinnati Enquirer/*Tony Jones*.

Below: Lions at the Cincinnati Zoo & Botanical Garden check out a Christmas gift, December 23, 2016. Cincinnati Enquirer/*Cara Owsley*.

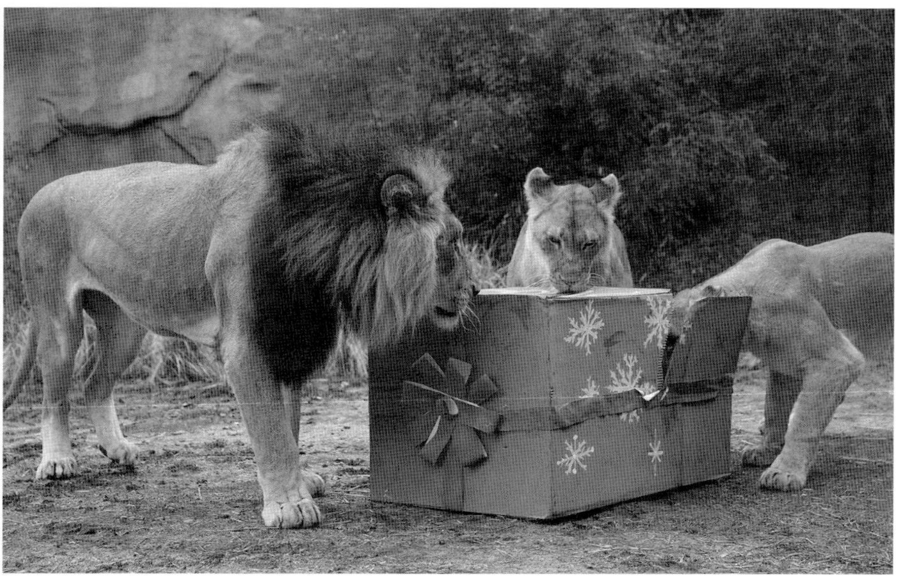

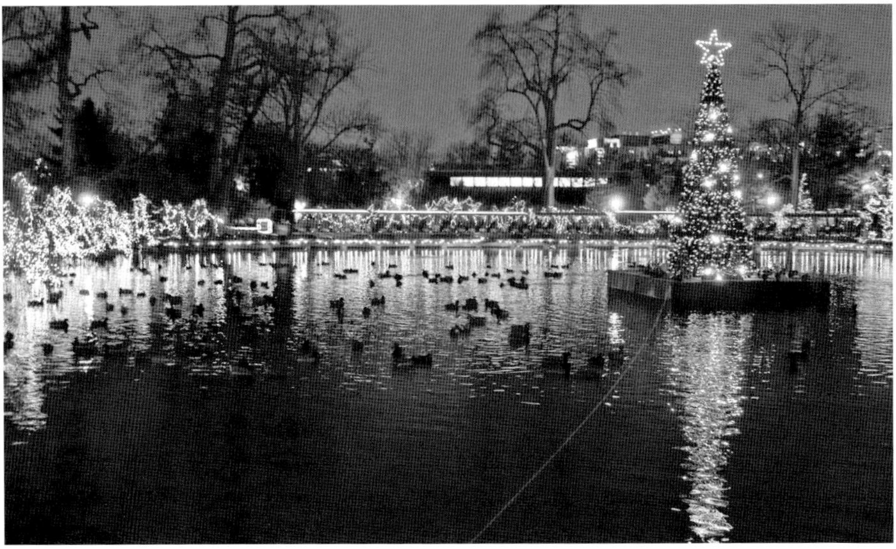

The Cincinnati Zoo & Botanical Garden most recently celebrated thirty-four years of the PNC Festival of Lights (which PNC has sponsored for twenty-five of those years), December 16, 2009. Cincinnati Enquirer/*Thomas E. Smith*.

Hamilton County's favorite parks. Tickets can be bought online; at the gate, tickets must be purchased by credit or debit card. During two nights, the drive-through is closed to vehicle traffic to allow visitors to walk the park. Dogs are welcome if kept on a leash.

The Christmas Ranch also requires purchasing tickets online (one ticket per car); at this time you can pre-order hot chocolate and chocolate cookies. These refreshments are also available at the welcome center. After checking in at the welcome center, you can drive through the ranch, or you can take the opportunity to park in the parking lot. From here, you can visit the Reindeer Room, visit with Santa, check out the gift shops or enjoy the Enchanted Forest.

For people who want to enjoy the sights of Christmas in a quiet, reflective mood, Cincinnati has several opportunities. One of those options is the Cincinnati Nature Center in Tealtown (near Milford), which has some beautiful light displays with nature as a backdrop. Light in the Forest is a new offering to reflect a theme of peace and tranquility, with the forest as a canvas. OBLSK, another BLINK participant, created three installations to softly illuminate the trees and paths. Besides the light display, visitors can also enjoy shopping, music and bonfires and can take in the historic decorations in Krippendorf Lodge and Abner Hollow Cabin.[163]

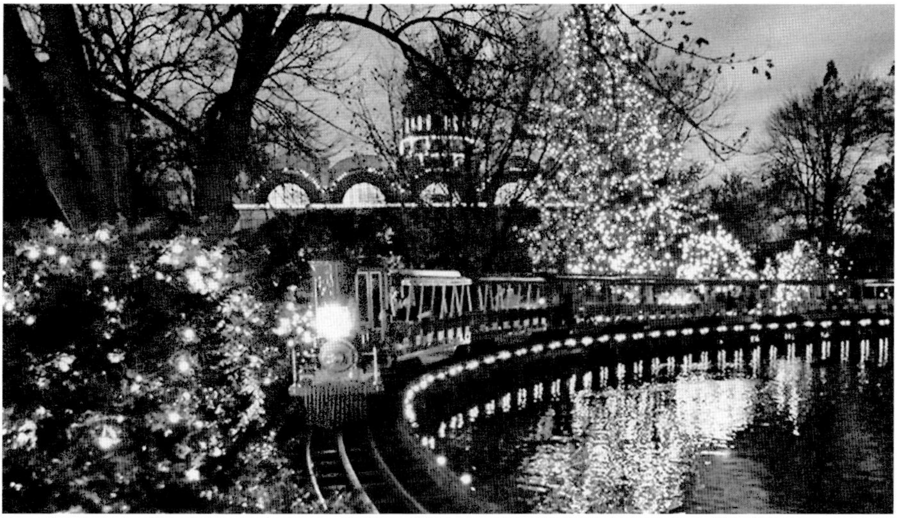

All aboard for the opening of the Festival of Lights, as the Cincinnati Zoo railway passes through the Cincinnati Zoo & Botanical Garden, November 17, 1995. The annual holiday festival, then in its fourteenth year, used 1.5 million bulbs strung throughout the sixty-seven-acre park and remained illuminated for seven weeks. *AP/*Cincinnati Enquirer*/Doug Cochran.*

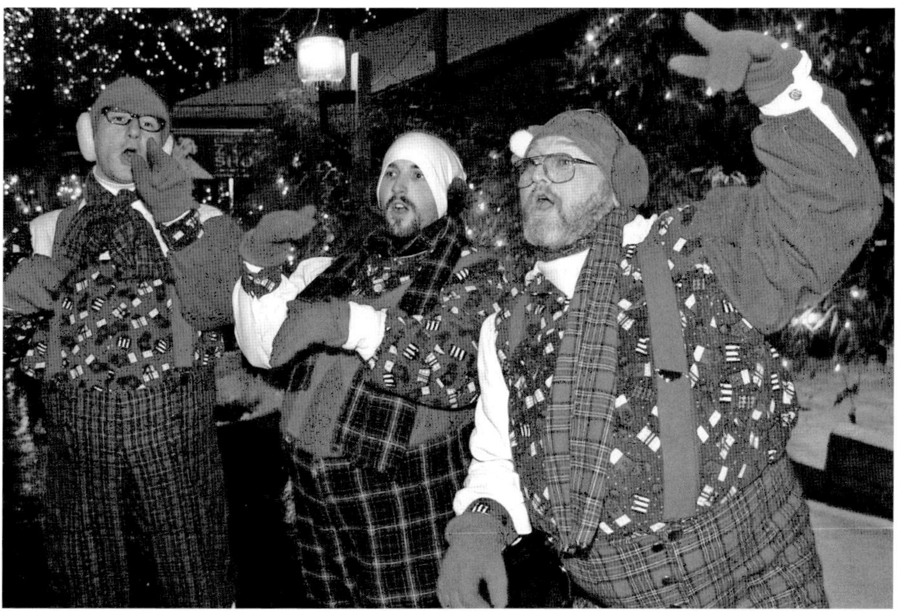

Denny B. Thomas (*right*), who plays "Lucky Dee Elf" at the Cincinnati Zoo Festival of Lights, sings an elf rap tune with fellow elves Zip (Mitchell D. Stallons) (*center*) and Bo (Jeff Shearer) as the trio works on a snowy and rainy night, December 13, 2000. Cincinnati Enquirer/*Craig Ruttle.*

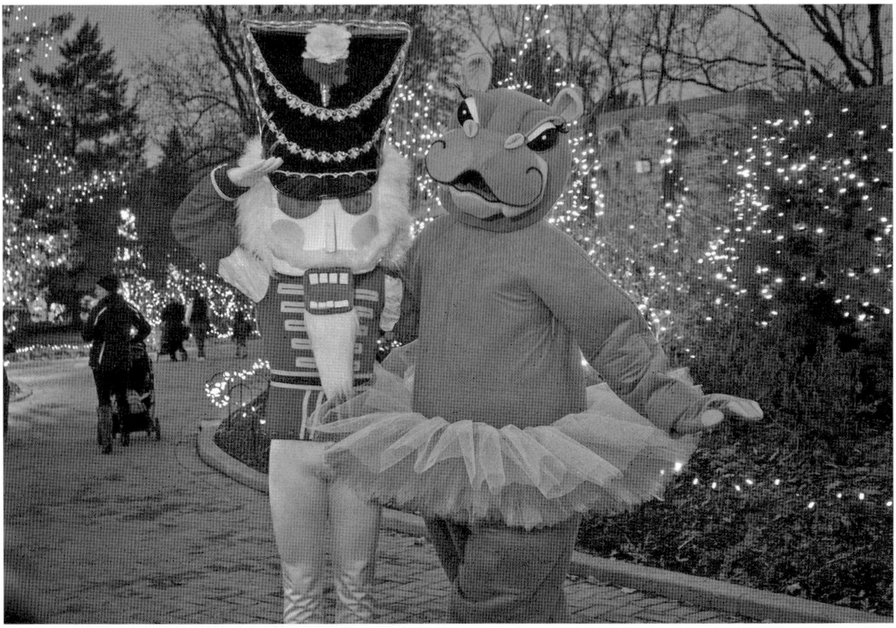

The Nutcracker and Fiona of the Cincinnati Ballet take photos with guests during the thirty-sixth annual Festival of Lights at the Cincinnati Zoo on December 15, 2018. Cincinnati Enquirer/*Shae Combs*.

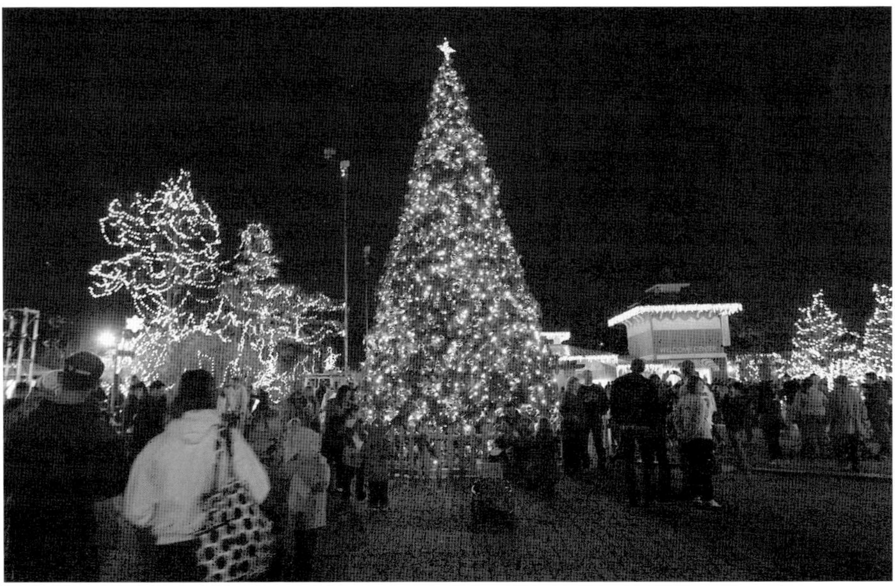

The giant Christmas tree was aglow during the Cincinnati Zoo & Botanical Garden's thirtieth annual PNC Festival of Lights, December 14, 2012. Cincinnati Enquirer/*Jeff Swinger*.

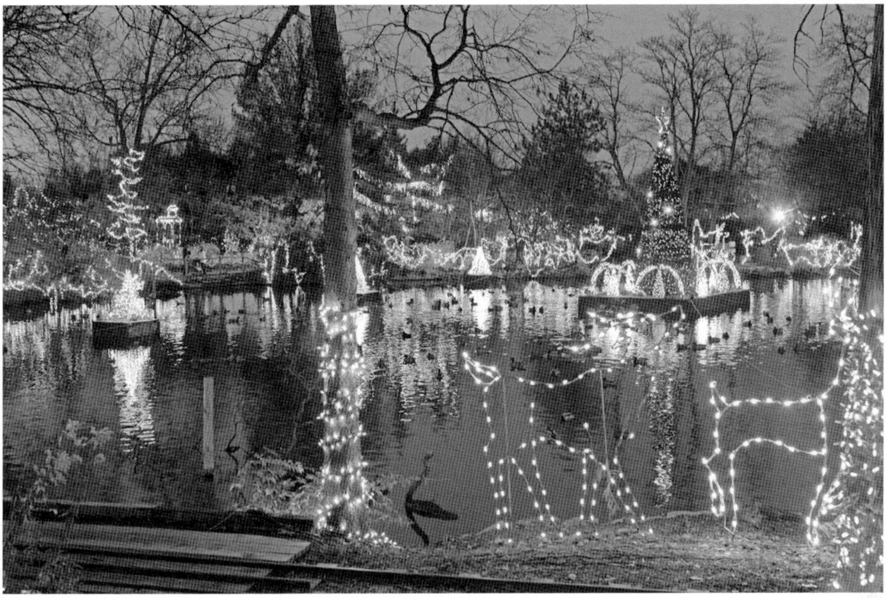

Swan Lake at the annual PNC Festival of Lights at the Cincinnati Zoo & Botanical Garden, November 22, 2014. Cincinnati Enquirer/*Tony Jones*.

For those of us who are a little less mobile, other facilities offer an *auto*-mobile experience. On the east side of Cincinnati, Coney Island Amusement Park offers its Christmas Nights of Lights. Buy your tickets online and enjoy driving through the two-and-a-half-mile route of lights accompanied by your favorite Christmas songs and carols. It is open from early November to early January, including Christmas Eve and Christmas Day, from dusk until 10:00 p.m.

On the northwest side of Cincinnati, Pyramid Hill has another auto opportunity through its sculptures and lights. In 2020, its presentation was called Journey Borealis. Brave Berlin, the designers of BLINK in Cincinnati, designed the light display, which is made up of more than one million lights. The experience is completely contactless. Check out the website before you purchase tickets. Music in the past has been provided by some Cincinnati greats, such as the Cincinnati Chamber Orchestra and the Cincinnati Boychoir.[164]

The Christmas Glow, in Middletown, features more than 3.8 million lights in its two-mile-long Christmas Around the World drive-through experience. If you want to get out of your car, you can visit Santa at the Christmas Village Santa Workshop, check out the gift shop and bond with the animals in the petting zoo. Bring a canned good and get two dollars off the admission price, with the collection going to the Hope House Mission of Middletown.[165]

If you have the car but not the money for admission, some of Cincinnati's churches (especially the Nazarene churches) usually offer live Nativity scenes to drive through.

NEIGHBORHOOD LIGHTS

A favorite activity of many, not just Cincinnatians, is driving through neighborhoods to see what families and friends have done to their houses. From brilliant, dazzling displays using lots of wattage choreographed to festive music, to simpler, quiet statements, Cincinnati neighborhoods have it all. If you're looking for a Nazarene church's live Nativity, try the Montana Church of the Nazarene in Westwood on the south side of Montana Avenue. As you drive up the Montana hill, check out the playful house display on the north side of the street at 2574 Montana. Keep driving west on Montana and turn left onto Epworth Avenue, just before the Westwood branch of the Public Library of Cincinnati and Hamilton County. Here you will find the Westwood neighborhood shining brightly in its neighborly approach to Christmas lights, for the street is lined on both sides with *luminaria* (lights made out of special bags or milk jugs with a candle set inside). The tradition is represented well on Epworth Avenue in Westwood.

Besides Westwood, many Cincinnati neighborhoods have their "stars" when it comes to house decorating. One such home was Nick Melisci's on Riddle Road in Clifton. For decades, Melisci created a "Yuletide extravaganza" with pinwheels, Santas, reindeer and signs. In 1975, in honor of the upcoming national bicentennial year, he added a sleigh with Santa and bicentennial angels.[166]

These neighborhood displays are often listed on the *Cincinnati Enquirer*'s website, Cincinnati.com, or on Facebook pages dedicated to Cincinnati's Christmas lights. A discussion of Christmas lights in Cincinnati would not be complete without talking about the Zapf family in North College Hill at 2032 Galbraith Road. For thirty-eight years, Bill Zapf Sr. decorated his house with lights, Santas, Mrs. Santas, reindeer, elves and just about anything you could think of when it comes to Christmas. Zapf Sr. passed away in 2008, but his Christmas traditions are well represented in the efforts of his son Bill Jr.[167]

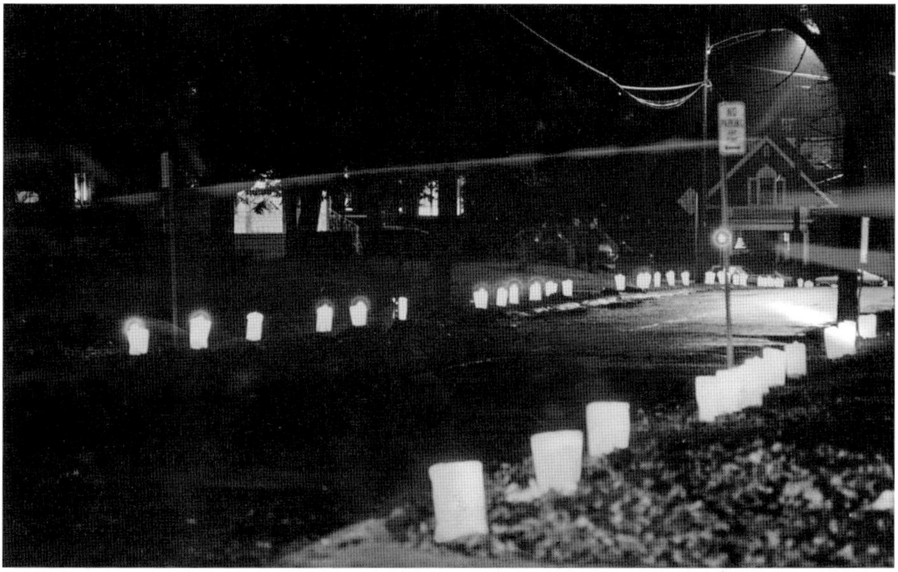

Luminaria light the way along Junietta and Epworth Avenues in Westwood, Christmas Eve 1973. About sixty residents placed candles in bags for outside decorations instead of Christmas lights requiring light bulbs. The idea springs from a tradition in Spain and Mexico in which soft lights burn at Christmastime along roads and walks to light the way to the Christ Child. Cincinnati Enquirer *photo*.

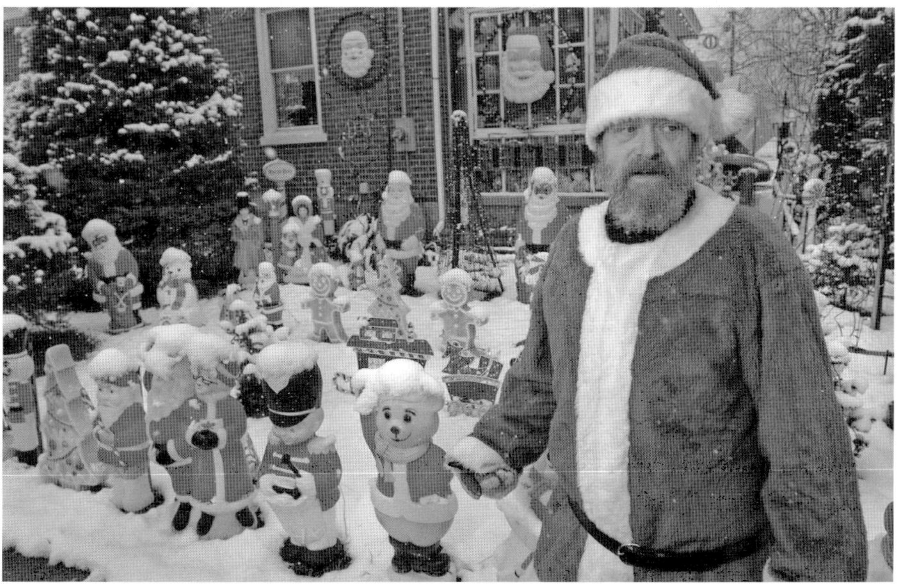

Billy Zapf carries on the tradition of his dad, the late Bill Zapf (1940–2008), who dressed as Santa each holiday season and decorated his North College Hill home with seventy thousand Christmas lights, December 19, 2009. Cincinnati Enquirer/*Tony Jones*.

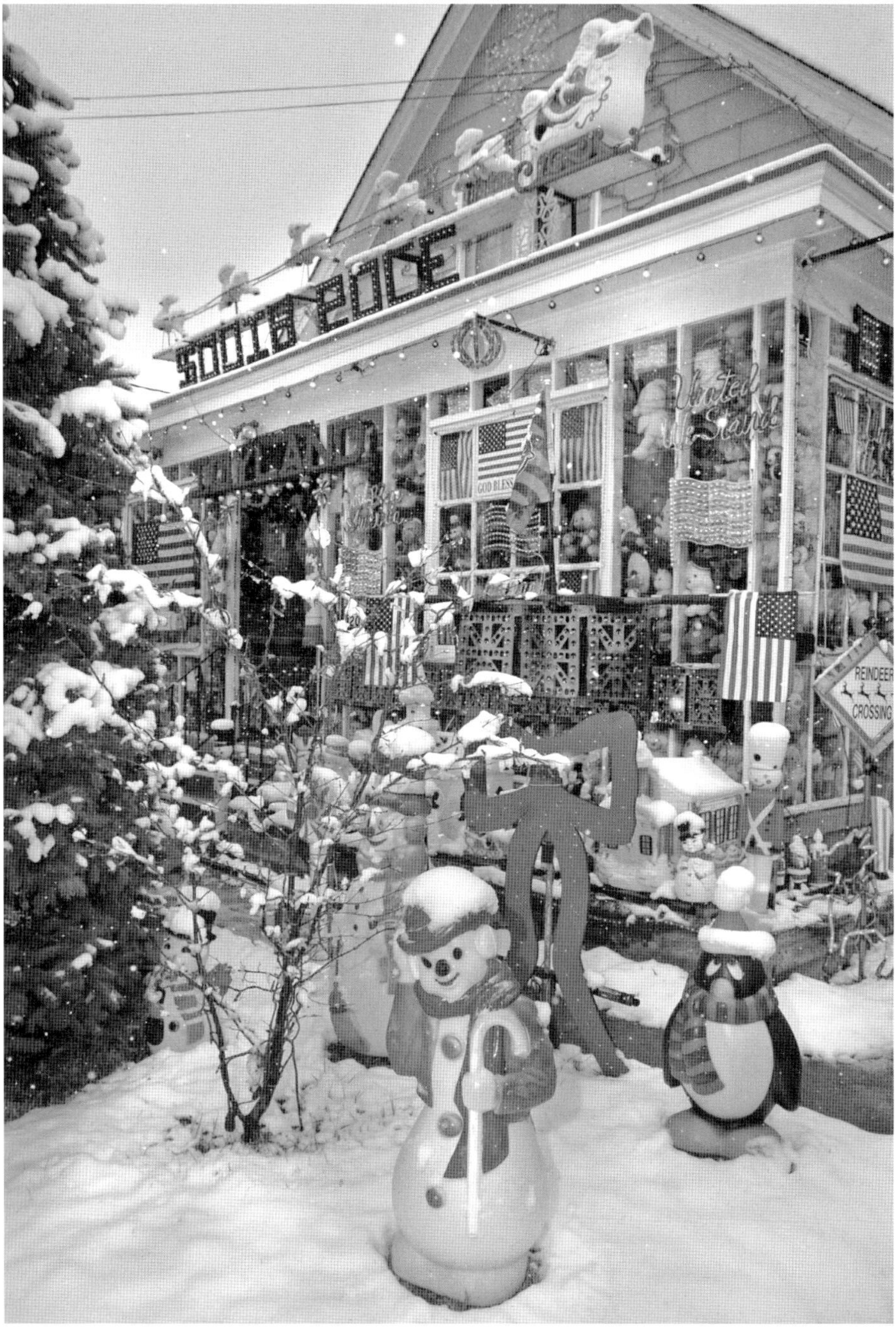

If you have ever been on the 2000 block of West Galbraith Road during the holidays, you noticed the lights and displays that Billy Zapf, here dressed as an elf, put up. The scene shown here is on December 19, 2009. Cincinnati Enquirer/*Tony Jones*.

NATIVITY SCENES

One neighborhood display focuses more on the Nativity itself and less on the lights and secular aspects of Christmas. Retired mail carrier Larry Buchanan and his wife, Martha, for decades have created a Nativity scene in the front yard of their Boudinot Avenue home. Larry started at home in Delhi in 1955, then continued after moving to Westwood. While in Delhi, they won two first-place awards and a second-place award for their displays. Larry completed a two-year course at the Gebhardt Art School of Cincinnati and was also art director for the Verona Fathers Missions. (For many years, they also owned Buchanan Studios in Cheviot.) All of the clothes that the mannequins wore were made by Larry and Martha. Children from Westwood Elementary often took a "field trip" to see the display.[168] Even St. James Day Care Center, down the street from the Buchanans' home, delighted their little wards each year as they loaded up the baby and toddler strollers and walked down to see the beautiful display. Christmas is their biggest display, but they also decorate the yard for St. Patrick's Day, Easter, Halloween and Thanksgiving. After sixty-six years, they're starting to downsize their display by giving their children and grandchildren some of the decorations.

EDEN PARK

Eden Park is a beautiful haven atop one of Cincinnati's tallest hills. Besides the Krohn Conservatory, it also boasts the Cincinnati Art Museum, the Murray Seasongood Pavilion and the Cincinnati Playhouse in the Park. Originally created for the purpose of building a reservoir for the city's water reserve, the two reservoirs have been co-opted for more modern use. The lower (east) basin was dismantled in the 1960s and turned into ball fields. The upper basin was partially filled in to become a reflecting pool named Mirror Lake, a favorite destination of dog walkers and nature watchers. Eden Park has a very interesting history.

By the mid-nineteenth century, Cincinnati had become America's fastest-growing city. In 1859, the city began acquiring land for what remains a jewel in the Cincinnati Parks' crown: Eden Park. A major portion of the land that became Eden Park came from one of Cincinnati's leading families, the Longworths, friends of the Lytles.

Patriarch Nicholas Longworth was known for being a lawyer, a dabbler in real estate and a home-grown vintner. One famous story about Nicholas arose when he defended an alleged horse thief. Longworth got the man acquitted, so the man was allowed to keep the horse he was accused of stealing. Grateful, the client offered Longworth his moonshine stills as payment. However, when Longworth went to collect his "payment," the stills were not available. Instead, the man offered him some "worthless" acreage along Western Row in downtown Cincinnati. Longworth snatched the property up. By 1859, the land was worth $750,000 (approximately $23,766,325 in 2021 dollars); the land's value soon shot into the millions. Longworth found much of his new land perfect for growing grapes. Nicholas Longworth, at this point of the nineteenth century, had more money, owned more land and produced more wine than anyone else in the country.

As good as Longworth's judgment of potential property was, his eye for flora and fauna was even better. Maryland botanist John Adlum, who gave Longworth his first grape vines, claimed that if Longworth were thrown into the Ohio River, he would bob to the surface clutching a rare species of fish in one hand and a freshwater pearl in the other.

Longworth developed an interest specifically in the native Catawba grape after a friend gave him a vine sample. At his vineyards' peak, his vines covered more than three thousand acres, producing almost 575,000 gallons of sparkling Catawba wine. Longworth's wine was a favorite of Henry Wadsworth Longfellow's and was often shipped to the poet by the crate.

Eventually, powder mildew and black rot started obliterating many vineyards. Nicholas Longworth spent his final days looking for a grape that might withstand the rot. His dying words involved asking if his vintner son-in-law, W.J. Flagg, had arrived. Just before slipping into unconsciousness, he said he wanted to tell Flagg of a new vine he had found that was resistant to mildew and rot.

Despite attempts to save them, Longworth's beloved vineyards died off. His son Joseph donated the land to the city of Cincinnati to become the foundation of Eden Park. (Joseph once noted that he felt people would only remember him as the son of his father, the first Nicholas, and the father of his son Nicholas II. To some extent, this is true, but his largesse is not forgotten.)[169]

Starting in 1900, the city decided it wanted the land for a park. By this time, the mansion needed repairs. One of the leading ladies of Cincinnati, Mary Emery, offered to step in and pay for the repairs, but the city council refused to allow it. Under continued pressure from the crooked administration of George "Boss" Cox, the family buckled and sold the land and the mansion to the city. The mansion was razed, and Lytle Park was created. A century and a half later, this square became the site for an annual Crib of the Nativity in 1939.

One of the city's favorite Nativity scenes goes by many names, depending on the speaker (similar to what the trains in the Cincinnati Museum Center are called). Its official name is the Western & Southern Crib of the Nativity, but it is also referred to locally as the Eden Park or the Krohn Conservatory Nativity scene, crib or crèche. (*La crèche* is French for "the crib" or "the manger.") All along, since its inception in 1939, this Nativity crib has been sponsored by Western & Southern Insurance Company and its founder, Charles Williams.

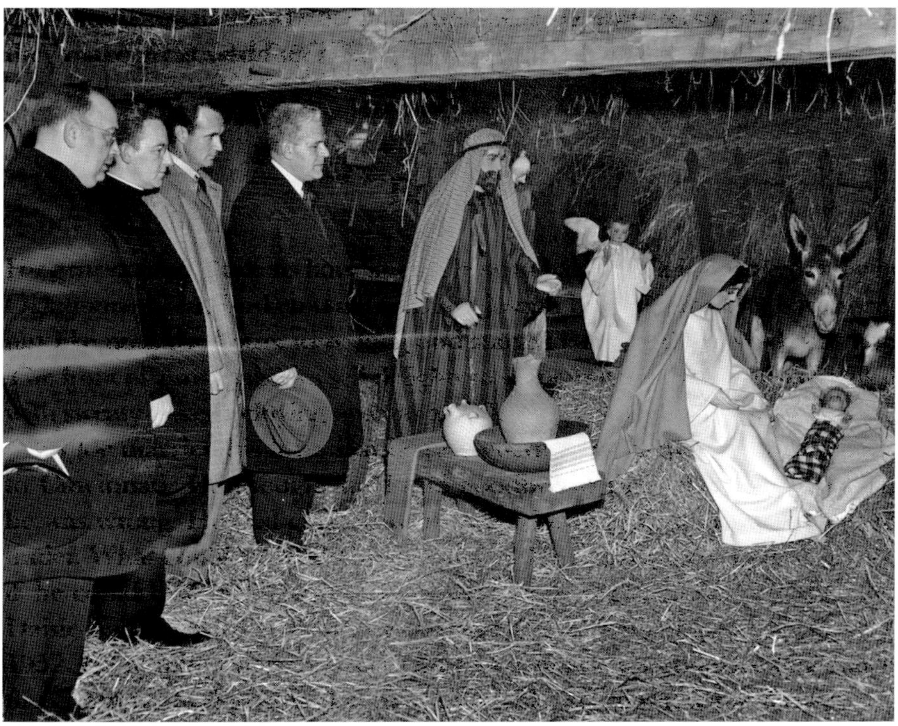

Cincinnati's famous Crib of the Nativity was dedicated for its tenth yuletide season on December 12, 1948, in Lytle Park. Conducting the dedication were (*left to right*): Senior Major Paul D. Seiler, Divisional Commander, Salvation Army, who presided; Reverend Watler C. Ahr, who offered the dedicatory prayer; James R. Williams, son of the founder, Charles F. Williams; and Mayor Albert D. Cash, who accepted the display for the city. Cincinnati Enquirer *photo*.

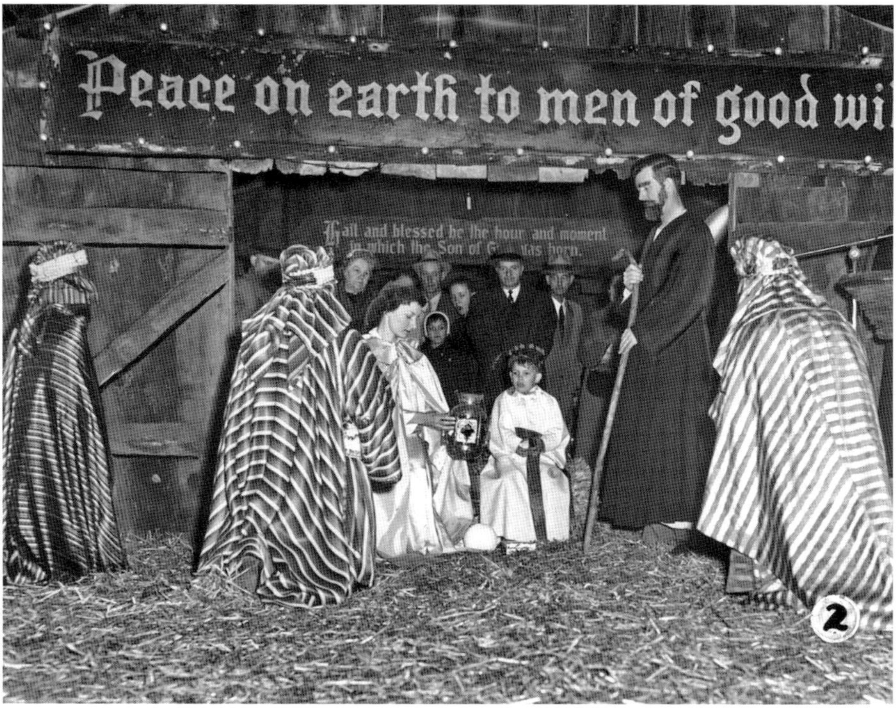

At Lytle Park, the twelfth day of the Christmas season was observed with a pageant recalling the visit of the Wise Men to the Christ Child. According to biblical historians, it was on the twelfth day of their travels that the baby Jesus was disclosed to the Wise Men. Playing the parts of Jesus, Mary and Joseph were, respectively, five-year-old Francis Niehaus, Carol Thomas and Henry Niehaus. These three Wise Men were Myron Kilgour, Joseph Diehl and Robert Niehaus. Cincinnati Enquirer *photo.*

Mr. A.L. Heger created the Nativity scene at his home in Lakeside Park. The scene has been moved four times. In 1939, Western & Southern Life Insurance Company's founder Charles F. Williams convinced Heger to allow them to move it to Lytle Park so that more people could enjoy it. There it stayed until 1945, when it was moved to Union Terminal, so that service members returning from World War II on trains could get an immediate glimpse of home and the holiday spirit. That year, Mayor James Stewart, Monsignor R. Marcellus Wagner and Chief of Police Eugene Weatherly dedicated the Nativity crib. Then it went back to Lytle Park.

The downtown mansion that General William Lytle had built on Fourth Street in the early 1800s was—according to General Lytle's will—to remain in the Lytle family in perpetuity. His grandson William Haines Lytle (who became Brigadier Gen. William Haines Lytle and a well-known

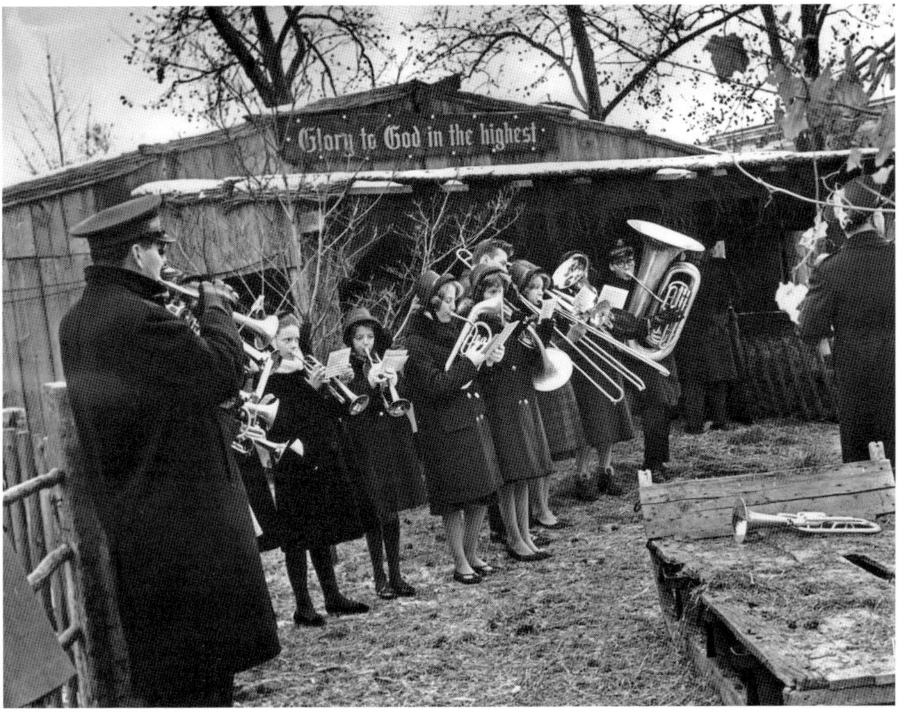

Lytle Park Crib of the Nativity, December 1963. Cincinnati Enquirer *photo.*

poet on both sides of the Mason-Dixon line) was born there in 1826. (In 1834, the Lytles even entertained President Andrew Jackson there during his only visit to Cincinnati.)

Unfortunately, Lytle Park faced a challenge when I-71 (the Northeast Expressway) was being constructed in the 1960s. In January 1959, Dean Ernest Pickering, the chair of the City Planning Commission, said the commission was basically considering three things: cutting through the park and taking down all the houses on the north side of Fourth Street; tunneling under the existing buildings; or selling air rights to business and building owners to build above the highway after their original facilities were razed.[170] The park itself had to be reduced in size to accommodate the highway.[171] The Nativity crib was therefore moved (the fourth and, we hope, final time) to Eden Park in 1967, next to the Krohn Conservatory.

Although the Crib of the Nativity is next to Krohn Conservatory, they are maintained by two different organizations. The Crib of the Nativity is under the auspices of the Cincinnati Christ in Christmas Committee. The opening of the crib each year is usually attended by prominent

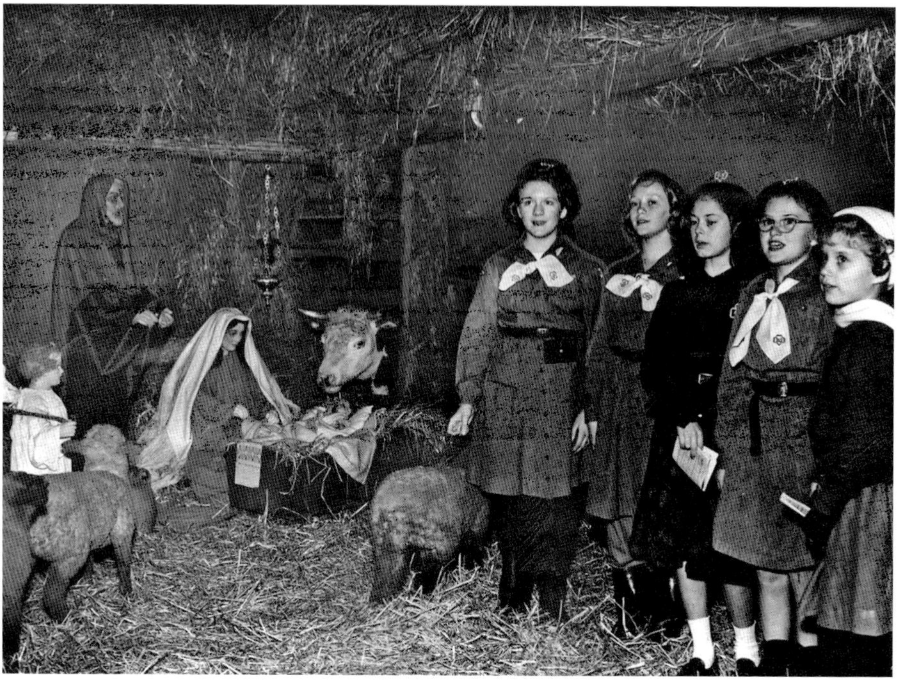

Lytle Park Crib of the Nativity, 1951. Cincinnati Enquirer *photo*.

Cincinnati civic, business and religious leaders. The Salvation Army has been a loyal supporter and often participates in the opening ceremonies. As the key sponsors of the crib, an official from Western & Southern Life Insurance always participates. The festivities usually start with an official proclamation by the mayor and a blessing from a local religious leader.

Mary, Joseph and the baby Jesus are made from wax, supplemented from time to time with live participants as shepherds. The animals for the live display are provided by local farmers.

The animals have had their ups and downs. Unfortunately, sometimes people don't behave, especially the younger ones among us. In January 1959, some youths aged approximately ten to fourteen were seen smoking around the back of the manger. They were quickly dispersed by Louis Hughbanks, one of the shepherds. However, the kids evidently returned, and the manger animals paid the price. A fire broke out during the night among the animals and all their hay. Although most of the sheep were saved, the cow—which, along with the donkey, belonged to dairyman Karl Foltz—died. Head shepherd Harry Pracht, who had played a shepherd for fourteen years, mourned its loss. Wiping away tears, seventy-five-year-old

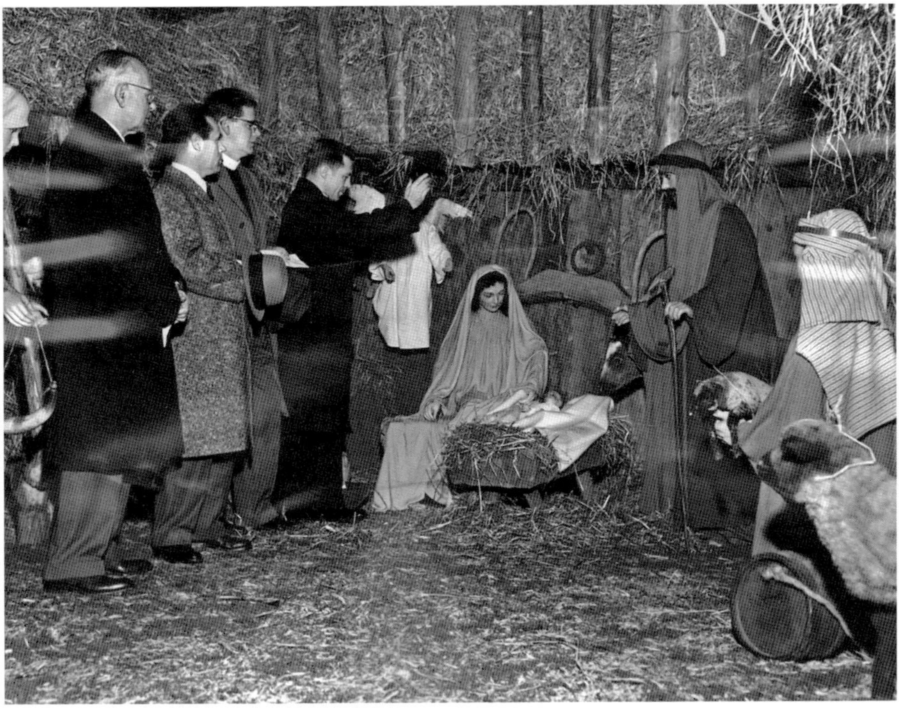

At the December 20, 1957, Crib of Nativity dedication in Lytle Park, Brigadier William E. Chamberlain of the Salvation Army gave the invocation, and Reverend Richard D. Isler, executive secretary of the Greater Cincinnati Council of Churches, pronounced the benediction. The Salvation Army Band and the Country Day School Flute Ensemble provided the music. Mayor Donald D. Clancy accepted the dedication of the crib, and Reverend Monsignor Henry J. Klocker, assistant national director of the Catholic Students' Mission Crusade, gave the speech of dedication. Cincinnati Enquirer *photo*.

Pracht told a reporter: "This is awful, awful. I tried to save the cow, but I couldn't get its rope untied." The donkey and several sheep were burned slightly. The Cincinnati Fire Department battalion chief William Teischer judged the crib a total loss and estimated the damage at $10,000. The wax figures were a total loss, but A.L. Heger's widow asserted that if Western & Southern wanted it rebuilt, that could happen. "We have other figures and costumes and can go ahead," she said. "But we'll have to hunt up a new barn."[172]

More joyful was 1956, when one of the sheep took the nativity idea to heart. On Christmas morning, she gave birth to a lamb, despite the cold weather. Harry Pracht was once again on hand to watch over the flock and promptly named the lamb "Merry Christmas."

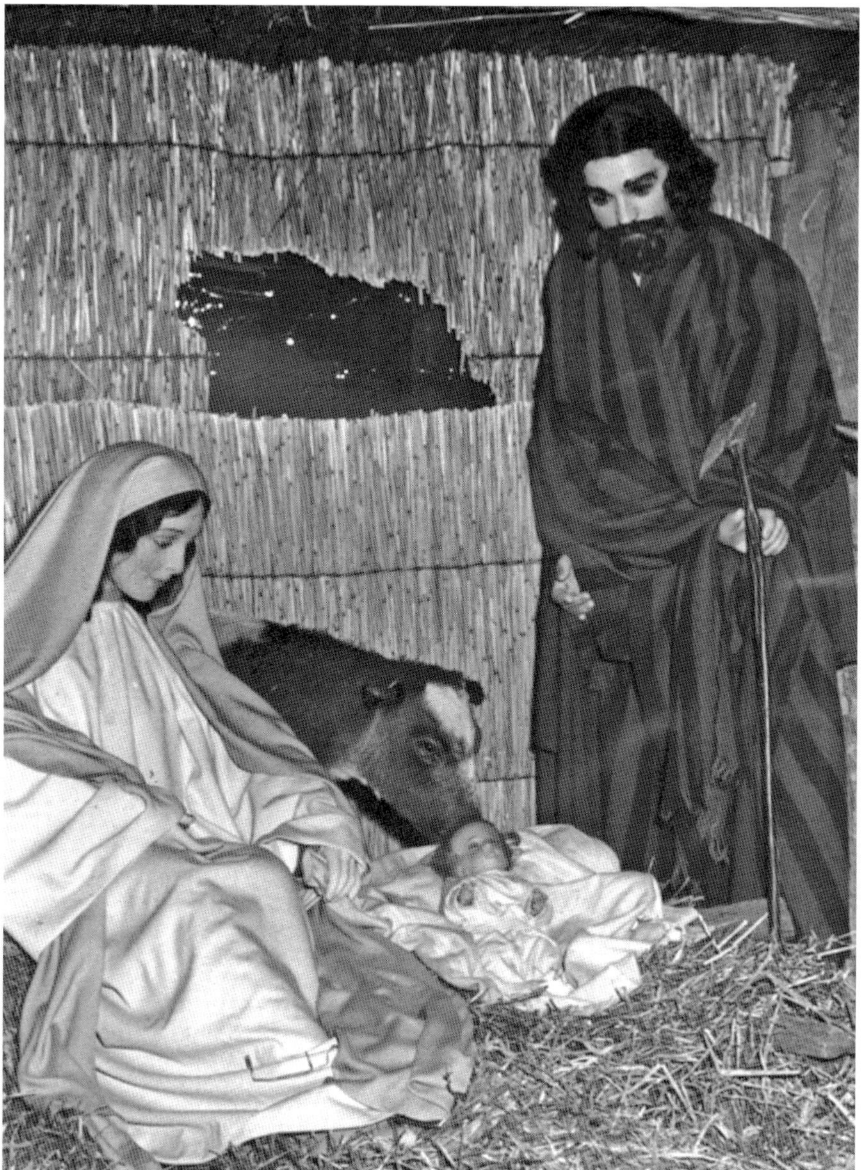

The Lytle Park Christmas Crib opened to the public on December 21, 1955, with special ceremonies at the scene. Captain William F. Carlson of the Salvation Army and Reverend E.L. Whalen, director of the Catholic Youth Organization, gave the invocation. Mayor Charles P. Taft accepted the crib for the City of Cincinnati. Also present were Lauren Schram, president of the Council of Churches and vice president of the Western & Southern Life Insurance Co.; Ferd Niehaus, food broker; and Raymond E. Clift, executive vice president of the Safety Council and chairman of the Christ in Christmas Committee. Cincinnati Enquirer *photo*.

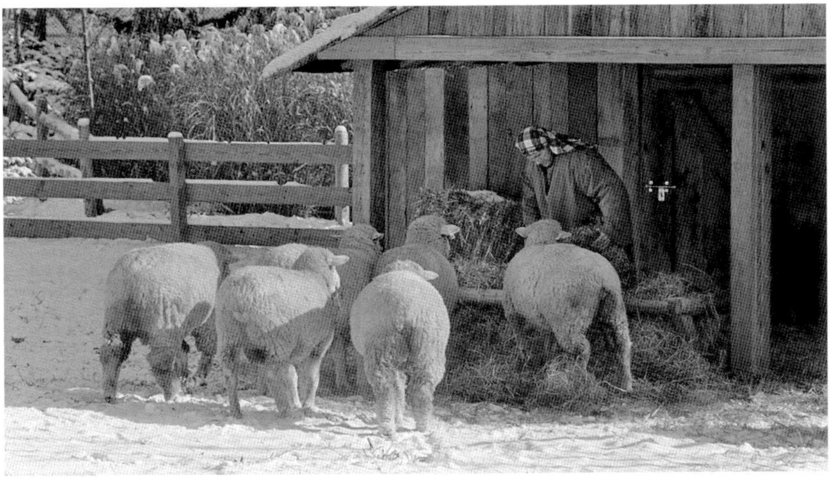

Jay Biedenharn of Crittenden, Kentucky, feeds the sheep at the Crib of the Nativity at Krohn Conservatory in Eden Park on Christmas Eve morning. The Biedenharn family built and has staffed the Nativity scene since 1954. Cincinnati Enquirer/*Tony Jones*.

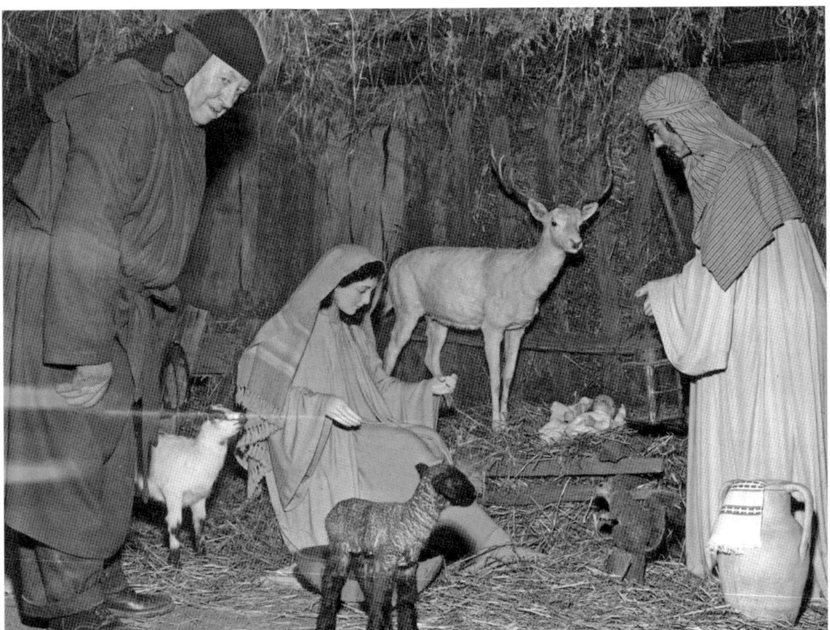

A lamb was born at the Lytle Park Nativity scene. The wobbly legged lamb provided extra realism to the manger scene in Lytle Park. Harry Pracht, caretaker of the Lytle Crib, watched the newborn lamb as it looked at the Nativity scene. The lamb is at the center of the crib, near the foot of the statue of Mary. Cincinnati Enquirer *photo*.

The Crib of the Nativity is just a few steps away from the Krohn Conservatory. They are two separate entities. A 1989 Supreme Court decision affected many of Cincinnati's displays—including Eden Park's—based on the recommendation of the city's solicitor. Two public holiday displays on city property in Pittsburgh, Pennsylvania, were challenged by the American Civil Liberties Union. One display was a Christian Nativity scene inside the Allegheny County Courthouse. The second was a large Hanukkah menorah, erected each year by the Chabad Jewish organization, outside the city-county building.

> *In a 5-to-4 decision, the* [Supreme] *Court held that the crèche inside the courthouse unmistakably endorsed Christianity in violation of the Establishment Clause. By prominently displaying the words "Glory to God for the birth of Jesus Christ," the county sent a clear message that it supported and promoted Christian orthodoxy. The Court also held, however, that not all religious celebrations on government property violated the Establishment Clause. Six of the justices concluded that the display involving the menorah was constitutionally legitimate given its "particular physical setting."*[173]

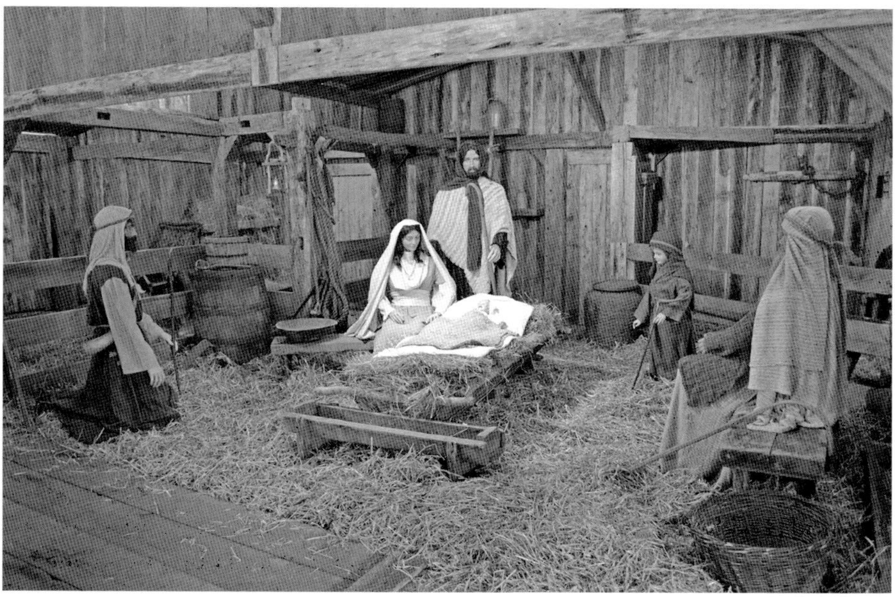

The Lytle Nativity scene has become part of the Christmas tradition for many families. *Courtesy of Denny Gibson.*

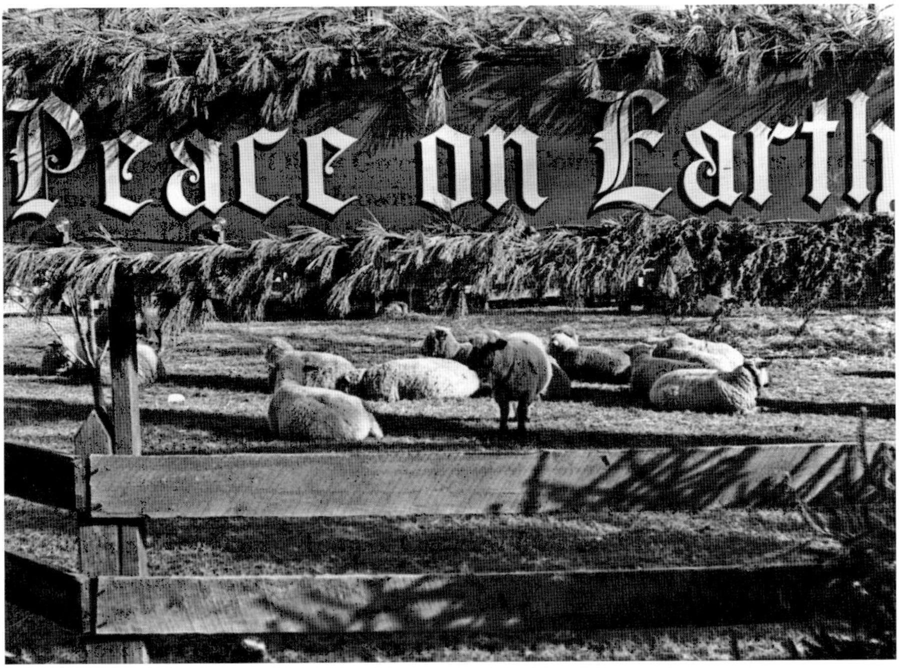

Sheep graze as the Nativity scene is dedicated for a twenty-eighth time. In a December 19, 1966, article, *Cincinnati Enquirer* reporter Paul Mason wrote of the scene, "At this Christmas season, an altar of prayer for the safety of men in Vietnam, and for world peace." At the ceremony in Lytle Park, Brigadier William H. Harvey, divisional commander of the Salvation Army in Cincinnati, observed that order must precede peace. "Bless those who serve the cause of freedom in Vietnam," he prayed. Cincinnati Enquirer *photo*.

The opinion of Cincinnati's city solicitor's office was not binding, but city leaders were reluctant to not follow it. Senior Assistant Solicitor Daniel J. Schlueter noted that perhaps secular displays in the conservatory might offset the religious message of the crèche. Park board member Marlene Holwadel expressed hope that Western & Southern would reapply. One of the options discussed was to move the Crib of the Nativity a little farther away from the conservatory.[174]

In September, the Western & Southern Nativity scene was allowed to remain after a few adjustments were made to make the display more secular. These adjustments included a Christmas tree, a "Season's Greetings" sign and a "Candy Cane Walk."[175]

Krohn Conservatory is actually a Cincinnati City Park. Mention "city parks," and trails, rivers and playgrounds might come to mind, but this Cincinnati City Park is a building. It was erected in 1933 and shows hints

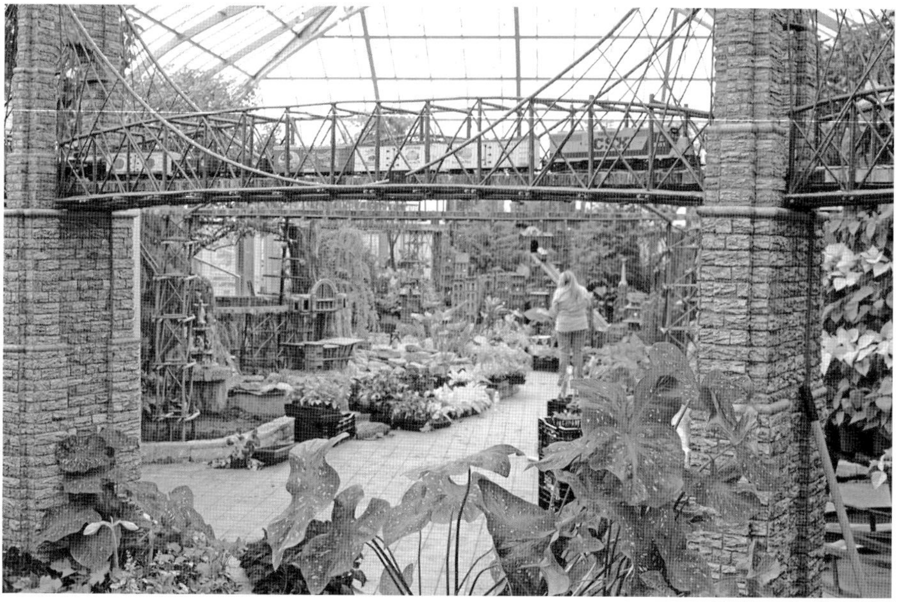

Krohn Conservatory was open from 10:00 a.m. to 2:00 p.m. on Christmas Day, 2018. *Community Press/Jennie Key.*

of the art deco movement that was so prevalent in Cincinnati at that time. The conservatory itself was originally a greenhouse, with aluminum and glass walls.

Exhibitions rotate through Krohn Conservatory, but two stand out. One is the annual holiday display, resplendent with poinsettias and other plants basking in tones of red and green. The Cincinnati Choo Choo Holiday Show was offered to visitors in the past. (Children four and under were free.) Family Nights Krohn by Candlelight has been another visitor favorite.

Each year in the spring, the conservatory also holds a spectacular butterfly show. Step into the conservatory, and you're instantly transported to a lush tropical environment (complete with an indoor waterfall) with thousands of plant species, including a special bonsai exhibit. Butterflies from all over the world delight adults and youth alike. One of the best treats is to sit still and see what butterflies alight.[176] The Krohn Conservatory is a model of innovation in conservation and displays thousands of varieties of international plant species.[177]

6
Things to Smell

Freshly Cut Trees

Not surprising, given Cincinnati's German heritage, Christmas trees are popular in Cincinnati. The first person to have a Christmas tree in Cincinnati is thought to be Ludwig (later changed to Louis) Rehfuss, a medical doctor and native of what is now known as Baden-Württemberg, Germany. Rehfuss came to Cincinnati in the 1830s and opened a wholesale and retail drug business.[178]

According to Don Heinrich Tolzmann, PhD, local expert on all things German, Rehfuss was a founding member of Cincinnati's Deutsche Gesellschaft (German society) and helped found a German newspaper, the *Cincinnati Volksblatt* ("folks' sheet"), in 1836. Tolzmann quotes Gustav Koerner, author of a German American history published in Cincinnati in 1880, who says that Rehfuss "contributed very much to the elevation and liveliness of social life in Cincinnati by means of his social talents as well as by means of his good fortune, which made his home a real social center."[179] No doubt he enjoyed showing his tree to his friends, especially the German ones.

Incidentally, Ohioans played an important role in the tradition of Christmas trees. President Benjamin Harrison's administration was the first to have a decorated Christmas tree at the White House. And millions of parents have been able to breathe a sigh of relief since Thomas Alva Edison invented the incandescent light bulb, thus replacing real candles on trees.

Modern Cincinnatians, like many Americans, debate the advantages of real Christmas trees versus "fake" trees. Whether they're described as "fiber optic," "slim," "pre-lit," "flocked" or "artificial," a fake tree by any other name isn't going to smell like Christmas (sorry, Mr. Shakespeare). (An online search provides descriptions of what artificial trees *do* look like and can smell like.)

We had a house fire two weeks before Christmas in 2010. Exhausted from the cleanup, my husband and I couldn't bear the thought of buying, erecting, decorating and dismantling a tree of any kind, but we didn't want the kids to experience an even drearier Christmas than it promised to be. We bought three little pre-lit trees, one for each boy, and plugged them in. The trees were green, but it was a blue Christmas. Even buying a "Charlie Brown tree" or decorating an outside tree might have been better. It was like pouring salt in the wound to have no live tree at all.

According to the American Christmas Tree Association, in 2020, about 80 percent of Americans planned to have a Christmas tree; about 80 percent of those would probably be fake.[180] The artificial trees are definitely easier to clean up after, whether you take your tree down on December 26, January 1, January 6 (Epiphany), January 13 (my birthday) or Valentine's Day. One downside is that you have to then store your tree until next Christmas season; but if you buy a pre-decorated tree, you don't have to store all those ornaments separately.

One of the arguments that lovers of fake trees make is that artificial trees are kinder to the environment and are more sustainable. This is not necessarily a strong argument. Sure, you most likely would buy fewer fake trees than real trees, the former usually being paid for with two or three live purchases. However, most Christmas trees are procured at Christmas tree farms, a sustainable (and important) form of agriculture. Those of us blessed with large properties or low morals might just wander out and chop a tree down, but that tends not to be the case these days. Dr. Sally Brown, a soil specialist at the University of Washington, said that almost all Christmas trees come from farms that wouldn't be able to stay in business without the holiday.

"It's actually a really nice, sustainable type of agriculture," Brown told Seattle's KING-5. "You're getting good land use and benefits to the soil from growing these trees, and it's a big source of income. So, the environmental impact of having acreage devoted to Christmas tree farms is pretty minimal." She noted that it was a toss-up between the two types of tree. A 2010 study by PE International, "Comparative Life Cycle Assessment of an Artificial Christmas Tree and a Natural Christmas Tree," found that driving to and from the tree farm had more of an impact.[181] If a real tree is still your pleasure, you can offset your car's carbon footprint by combining a few shopping trips or carpooling.

Those who want the fresh tree scent without the cleanup can usually obtain freshly cut evergreen branches from nurseries, online or Christmas tree stands. These boughs can be used in wreaths, garlands or to "spruce up" an artificial tree's fake foliage. (Yes, I did that on purpose.)

Whether looking for branches or a whole tree, Cincinnatians have many choices. Many shopping areas, nurseries and even stores like Home Depot have pre-cut trees for sale. Most, if not all, of these sellers will offer a fresh cut off the tree's trunk. Some even provide a net "wrap" on the tree that makes it easier to transport.

One lot tree seller was Frederick Geraci of Symmes Township. "Back in the day" he would drive to Quebec, cut the trees and bring them back to Cincinnati. He sold them in various lots that he rented near the intersection of Montgomery and Kenwood— an area that was a lot wilder than it is now. Unfortunately, suburban sprawl forced him to relocate frequently as more stores were built. When Mike Pulfer of the *Cincinnati Post* caught up with him in 1975, he was at 7850 Kenwood Road in an empty lot and was calling it quits. Besides having to relocate, Geraci's business was hurt by the popularity of artificial trees, which he referred to as "bottle washers." He said that tree shoppers started expecting a perfect tree. "Because of [artificial trees], they don't like the real ones when the bottom branches don't get needles." He recalled one man who had wandered around behind his wife for more than an hour in zero-degree weather as she examined Geraci's trees. Finally, the man had had enough. "He came over and pointed to a tree and said, 'We're taking that one, dammit. That's the way God grew it, and there's nothing you can do about it.'"[182]

If you're in for the whole ceremony of tree cutting, fill a thermos with hot chocolate, grab a saw and visit one of these fine farms. Many of them also have animals and gift shops filled with "Christmassy" items. (If you don't have a saw, one can usually be furnished, along with the lumberjack to do the sawing.) Before you go, call the farm to make sure it still has trees left. (This is key for people who wait until the last weekend before Christmas to get the tree. For those people, I have two words: Home Depot.) You might also want to stop at an ATM, as many farm stands don't take plastic.

Hamilton County:

- Shaker Tract Tree Farm (Harrison) offers cut-your-own trees, plus free hot chocolate and cookies in the gift shop, which has "Shaker-inspired" baskets and other wood products.

Butler County:

- Bartels Farm (Hamilton) has trees, wreaths, live animals and hot chocolate (so you can skip the Thermos—or use it on the way up).
- John T. Nieman Nursery (Hamilton) has cut-your-own trees, pre-cut trees and balled trees (in case you want to plant it later), as well as hot chocolate and cookies.
- Nieman Nursery & Landscaping (Hamilton) has cut-your-own, pre-cut and live trees and a craft shop.
- Koch Christmas Trees (Okeana) sold only wreaths in 2020, but check them out in 2021 for their selection of cut-your-own trees.
- Station Road Farm & Landscaping (West Chester) has a year-round presence and has a farmers' market that delivers!

Greene County:

- Spring Valley Tree Farm (Spring Valley) sold out early in 2020, so make sure you call first.
- Young's Dairy (Yellow Springs) has two restaurants, a food/gift shop, ice cream and goats. What more could you want? Young's Dairy cofounder, Carl Young, also founded the tree farm just to the south of the dairy. Now that Carl and Dorothy are both gone, Carl and Dorothy Young's Tree Farm is run by their son Ben.

Warren County:

- Timberwind Tree Farm (Lebanon) offers antique tractor and wagon rides. They sold out early in 2020, so call first.
- Berninger Christmas Trees and Wreaths (Lebanon) has been around since 1955, so they have lots of tall trees available. Enjoy the free hot chocolate and popcorn.
- Big Tree Plantation (Morrow) has trees, animals, a great gift shop and Santa.

Brown County:

- Corsi Christmas Tree Farm (Hamersville) charges the same price for all their trees (fifty-eight dollars in 2019) on their one hundred acres. Try their hot chocolate and Italian chili in the Broken Store Lodge, as well as their free petting zoo.

Clermont County:

- Dirr Nurseries (Goshen) have both pre-cut and cut-your-own trees.
- Nana and Pap's Christmas Tree Farm (Felicity) has cut trees as well as live trees for planting. Enjoy their tractor rides and petting zoo.
- Rossman's Christmas Tree Farm (Blanchester) offers trees and handmade Christmas decorations, as well as free hot chocolate.

Campbell County (Kentucky):

- Tom Mitts Christmas Trees (Newport) offers free candy canes to the kids.

Franklin County (Indiana):

- Whitetail Acres (Brookville) encourages you to make a date with their reindeer before you choose your pre-cut, cut-your-own or living tree.[183]

One of the best "finds" if you're looking for a tree is not one specific farm. It's christmastreefarms.net. Warning! It's a time sponge. It might be my new favorite Christmas game. This website allows users to search by location, type of tree and species of tree. It also lists amenities that make the Christmas tree purchase real entertainment and not just a chore: animals, refreshments, gift shop, hay rides, tree balers and (drum roll, please) tree shakers. Who knew we needed one? (They shake the loose needles out of the tree.)

FAMILY DINNERS

What are your favorite smells of Christmas? Evergreens, perhaps. Maybe even the crystal-clear frosty fragrance that assaults your nose on a cold night. How about cookies baking with cinnamon, ginger, nutmeg? Or peppermint and chocolate? These are some of the universally liked smells of Christmas.

Some people's favorites are not so universally liked, however. One of the advantages (or disadvantages) of cooking your own family dinner, as opposed to going out to a restaurant, is that the smell of a meal that won't be served for hours permeates the house all day. By the time dinner rolls around, some people might not want to eat.

One German tradition, called *Viel Glück* (much luck), is gathering friends and family members to eat pork and sauerkraut on New Year's. The sauerkraut symbolizes wealth and prosperity, and the pork symbolizes well-being and good health. One year, being part German with German in-laws, I offered to jump the gun on New Year's and make roast pork and sauerkraut for our big Christmas Eve dinner. As I stood in the kitchen savoring the scent of the sauerkraut, one sister-in-law walked in the house and exclaimed, "What is that awful smell?!" Let's just say that sauerkraut isn't for everybody.

Another tradition was brought to the family by a Cuban American brother-in-law: *Noche Buena* ("good night") is one of the largest feasts of the season. Its centerpiece is *lechón* (suckling pig originally, pork shoulder more commonly in the United States), which is usually served with black beans (*frijoles negros*) and rice (*arroz*). Unlike the Germans' equivalent, the Latinos' tradition is not quite so pungent.

When I was a diversity communications consultant, I was hired by an advertising agency to help a local butcher with its annual ad campaign. One of their best products was chitterlings (sometimes spelled and always pronounced like "chitlins"). This is a popular food in African American communities. It is usually eaten between Thanksgiving and New Year's. The butcher shop was hoping to sell more of this product. The ways to do that would be (1) get existing customers to eat more; (2) get existing customers to buy them more often, outside of the holiday season; or (3) get new customers. Never had chitterlings? They are made by using the large intestine of a pig (sometimes cattle are used), which is cooked for hours, then served with greens, fried chicken, macaroni and cheese and other southern comfort foods.

Because of the organ that is being used, even though butcher shops clean the chitlins, they still need to be cleaned when the bucket is brought home from the butcher. A typical recipe calls for ten pounds of chitlins (which will lose approximately half its volume during cooking), bay leaves, garlic, onion and one or two potatoes. When I worked on this project, I asked an African American friend why one or two potatoes were used with ten pounds of meat. "To absorb the smell," she said, wincing a little. (By the way, that company's saving grace was the availability of online ordering.)

7
Things to Taste

Family Affairs

Foods we eat during the holidays often evoke strong feelings and memories. These might be special treats, such as the ribbon candy I loved as a child or the eggnog cookies I bake for my own family. My father had a special way with eggnog, which involved rum and bourbon. (We had a special eggnog jug for him that was marked with a skull and crossbones.) Other food memories might be from specific restaurants or dishes that were cooked by a family member. Historically, Cincinnati has had some glorious Christmas dinners that were prepared by a full cooking staff, no doubt.

An important, though perhaps invisible, person in throwing a great Christmas party is the housekeeper. Equally invisible, perhaps, is the lady of the house. In an 1882 *Penny Paper* (*Cincinnati Post*) advertisement (disguised as an article), "The Duties of the Housekeeper and the Pleasures of the Wife," the writer waxed eloquent about the joys of a home. "Then come the rooms and the old familiar spots, which make the place so sacred, and which will ever dwell and linger in the memory of man, and, finally, the advantages, the comforts, and the luxury which make our homes so sweet and familiar to all the members of the family."[184]

The piece went on to say that a housekeeper's most important item was the linen, "and the one which good and careful wives take great pride in. They know but too well that the husband, the brother or the son love to sit at a table that is clean, with a clean and neat table-cloth." (I shudder to think that last year's Christmas tablecloth in our home was plastic.) Finally, just slightly more important than the linen was the cuisine, for contributing "more to harmony and good feeling existing in a family than anything else." Luckily, Alms & Doepke had just the linen for the occasion.[185]

One *Cincinnati Enquirer* in December 1892 detailed a "grand affair" that took place at the Gaither home on Broadway. Not only was it a holiday celebration, but it was also a birthday party, celebrating the tenth birthday of Elizabeth Gaither Shillito (whose grandfather was John Shillito, founder of Shillito's Department Store). The article noted that it "seemed but yesterday that the sweet little maiden's beautiful mamma celebrated her own tenth birthday in the same parlor" surrounded with a "jolly set of girls and boys, now representative men and matrons in society." The "sweet little maiden" was surrounded by two hundred of her closest friends with last names of Taft, Burnet, Rhodes, Harrison and Groesbeck.[186]

In the same edition of the *Enquirer*, another "charming affair" was an afternoon reception at the home of Mrs. A.M. Dolph. The society page columnist observed that "Evans Place is noted for its pretty modern villas, those triumphs of modern architecture that are both handsome and convenient, and the Dolph residence is one of the prettiest and most hospitable in all Clifton." Guests represented the Gamble, Venable, Resor, Hosea, Hopple and Melish families. The names sound like a tour of streets in Clifton and Camp Washington.[187]

Christmas dinners often include a roasted pig, perhaps because of Cincinnati's "hog heaven" reputation. The city was known at one time as "Porkopolis" because of its being the top producer of hog products in the nation. (It is no coincidence that some of the country's oldest soap and candle manufacturers also got their start in Cincinnati. Besides meat, pigs also have a lot of fat.)

Both hogs (slower, more domesticated fatbacks) and razorbacks (larger, fiercer and more boar-like animals) were routinely brought en masse through downtown Cincinnati proper. The town's access to the Ohio River and canal system proved to be a boon to the meat market, preventing the animals from losing body weight while walking to market.

Cincinnati held the title of top pork producer until the Civil War, when the war lost the city access to the Mississippi River, hurting Cincinnati's shipping capabilities. Also, because of its wonderful waterways, Cincinnati had been late in jumping on the railroad bandwagon. Chicago, with its superior railroads, usurped Cincinnati's position as top hog. But in its heyday in the

1830s and '40s, Cincinnati was processing more than eighty-five thousand hogs a year in more than twenty-five meat plants.[188]

It's not surprising, then, that pigs played a prominent role in the Christmas festivities in mid-nineteenth-century Cincinnati. That role, however, was never played by the same pig twice, sadly. A few days before Christmas, according to historian Charles Cist, the pigs were decorated and paraded through the streets, accompanied by bands, crowds of people and the infantry. In *Sketches and Statistics, Cincinnati in 1851*, Cist wrote: "Christmas-day is the great gala day of the butchers of Cincinnati. The parade of stall-fed meat, on that day, for several years past, has been such as to excite the admiration and astonishment of every stranger in Cincinnati." After the parade, the pigs were then led to the slaughterhouses, of which Cincinnati had many, to be cut up and distributed among the stalls of the markets.[189]

On December 21, 1869, E.D. Mansfield (a friend of Dr. Daniel Drake's) published an essay in the *Cincinnati Daily Gazette*, "Christmas in 1826 and 1869—A Contrast and a Memory." (Mansfield wrote in the third person, as if he were not one of the two people he was talking about!) Mansfield discussed the availability of food in 1826's meat market.

> *You might go to market with 75 cents and come back with the best of Christmas dinners. But suppose you had no 75 cents; still there was no difficulty in getting a pretty good dinner for 25 cents. The pork houses, in those days, gave you pig's-feet and the back-bone for nothing! Lard, and flour, and eggs were very low, and you could get a pretty good dinner for 25 cents. Unless one was utterly paralyzed and in bed, there was no excuse for poverty—such poverty as we see now-a-days.*[190]

Mansfield noted that he didn't remember if a church was open on Christmas Day in 1826, but he concluded, "it was almost certain the Episcopal Church was. There was only one Episcopal, one Lutheran, and one Roman Catholic. The latter stood on Sycamore Street; and Bishop Fenwick occasionally preached there."[191]

A young pig called a "shoat" is one of the menu items featured in a Christmas dinner described by Pauline Rice Shields in the *Cincinnati Enquirer* of December 24, 1905, with recipes![192] Now, one might note that recipes on the twenty-fourth don't help much for the twenty-fifth, unless one happens to have the ingredients already in the larder. This is unlikely. Here are the highlights:

- Star Christmas Relish (made with blue-point oysters, anchovies, mushrooms and caviar)
- Cream of Tomato Soup (made from scratch, no Campbell's to the rescue!)
- Crabmeat Dewey (including mushrooms and truffles)
- Parker House Rolls
- Cider Cup (made with cider, Apollinaris water [naturally sparkling mineral water from Germany], curaçao and brandy)
- Young Shoat ("[T]his little suckling pig is seen in all Christmas meat displays.")
- Milk-fed Watertown Goose à la Tiny Tim (as in Charles Dickens's *Christmas Carol*, causing Tiny Tim to exclaim, "God bless us, every one!" Luckily, it uses the same stuffing as the pig.)
- Sweet Potato in Melon Form with Sprig of Holly
- Chestnuts and Raisins
- Star of Bethlehem Salad (hard-cooked eggs, pickled beets and peas with the egg whites cut into little baskets)
- Poinsettia Plum Pudding and Hard Sauce (stale bread crumbs, eggs, suet, brandy, citron, raisins and currants, in case you wondered)
- Individual Ice Cream in the Form of Christmas Candles (These could be bought for $1.50 a dozen.)
- Star Christmas Cakes

Shields suggests that the after-dinner snacks be consumed with this in mind: "With malice toward none, let all gather around the Christmas table and over the nuts, assorted fruits, bonbons, cheese, crackers, and coffee, plan how to lighten some less fortunate creature's burden and make of life all that is noble and pure."[193]

RESTAURANTS

What happens when you don't want to cook for Christmas, or if you don't have a full staff to do it for you? Cincinnati's variety of restaurants offers something for everyone, even on Christmas Day. Of course, many ethnic restaurants are open on Christmas Eve and Christmas Day, such as the Blue Gibbon on Tennessee Avenue. Some chains are also open. However, to really experience Christmas in Cincinnati, diners must try one of the distinctly Cincinnati eateries. Some of the classic restaurants offer special Christmastime meals, if not on Christmas Day itself: Arnold's Bar & Grill, the oldest continually operating tavern in Cincinnati;[194] Jeff Ruby's Precinct; and the National Exemplar's "Breakfast with Santa."

Some of the eateries that used to be open on Christmas have closed down in the recent past, even before the pandemic. A *Cincinnati Enquirer* article from December 21, 2012, listed some "Christmas Day Dining Options": the Restaurants at the Palm Court, La Petite France in Glendale (now closed), Ruth's Chris Steak House at the Banks, McCormick & Schmick's, the Blue Gibbon, Buca di Beppo, Benihana and Mitchell's Fish Market (closed). (Some of the closed restaurants are still listed in online reservation websites. The rule for the future is to call the restaurant directly and not rely on reservation websites to ask about Christmas reservations.)

Of course, as stated elsewhere in this book, the pandemic of 2020 changed a lot. Even restaurants that had been open in 2019 were not open in 2020 because of COVID-19. Thinking on their feet, however, many restaurants offered curbside pickup on Christmas Eve. Westwood's Ivory House (named for Ivory soap, in honor of Westwood's last mayor, James Gamble, of Procter & Gamble fame) offered a variety of holiday meals for curbside pickup, including meatloaf, pork loin, BBQ chicken, spaghetti and meatballs, chicken parmesan and vegetarian or beef lasagna, salad, dessert and cocktails. At the other end of the spectrum, Cracker Barrel offered pickup meals to take home and reheat on the holiday.

Some of Cincinnati's most historic restaurants offered Christmas dinner in the past, and many of us hope they do in the future. The Golden Lamb, in Lebanon, has been named over the years the most legendary, haunted, charming and historic restaurant in Ohio (among other titles). It was established by Jonas Seaman on December 23, 1803, when Cincinnati was only fifteen years old. In 2018, the holiday features included "*Frohe Weihnachten*" (Merry Christmas), seared venison; "Christmas Dinner at Mount Vernon," pork tenderloin and turkey breast; and "A Tribute to Cratchits' Christmas Dinner," roasted Indiana duck breast. During the holidays, diners were also treated to Lebanon's annual horse-drawn carriage parade, Sundays with Santa and Christmas carolers.

In 2020, the Golden Lamb's holiday menu was available for dining in or taking out, in what the restaurant called "Take & Bake." The Christmas Take & Bake was available for pickup on December 22 and served four to six adults. A special Christmas Eve menu was offered for dine-in eating.

Sometimes, Christmas meals focus on more than just "eat, drink and be merry!" In 2017, Washington Platform Saloon and Restaurant had a special "Feast of the Seven Fishes" on Saturday, December 23. This Italian American celebration arose from the Roman Catholic tradition of abstaining from meat on certain holidays, including Christmas. So, on Christmas Eve, fish was served. The dinner can be seven different types of seafood or just a couple of different types cooked seven different ways.

Other Christmas meals, such as that served by the Immaculate Heart of Mary Church, take place on Christmas itself. The church's Annual Christmas Dinner is offered free to anyone who has no one with whom to celebrate Christmas or has nowhere to eat. The parish gives rides to those who cannot make it on their own.

Candy and Ice Cream Parlors

Cincinnati has been blessed with excellent confectioneries offering candy, ice cream, old-fashioned soda[195] and more. A *Cincinnati Enquirer* article from 1900 put it in graphic terms.

> *The manufacture of candy in Cincinnati is an industry that few people know to be one of the lines in which this city stands well up in the list of candy-producing centers of the country. This is a fact, however, and there are but four or five other cities that stand ahead of Cincinnati in the amount of candy that is made by the large wholesale factories here. If the candy made in this city in the year 1899 could have all been saved until Christmas time and distributed to the inhabitants of Greater Cincinnati there would have been six pounds and a half to every man, woman and child. Or, in another way, if every inhabitant of the United States should claim an equal share of the candy made in Cincinnati in a year, and it were to be weighed out to all comers, they would get as their portion two fifths of a pound.*[196]

During this period, the cities "ahead" of us tended to focus more on wholesaling, that is, selling to stores or other manufacturers. These factories churned out more than a thousand pounds a day. Cincinnati, however, had a large group of retail manufacturers. This type of candy maker "makes candy upstairs and sells it in his store direct to the consumer at the rate of a hundred or a few hundred pounds a day." Cincinnati, at that time, had nine existing wholesale manufacturers and another one on the way. About 500,000 pounds was produced by Cincinnati's more than one hundred small wholesale candy makers.

Not only has Cincinnati been a leader in candy producing, but it has also been a leader in candy consuming. The candy shops' busiest holidays are usually Valentine's Day, Easter and Christmas. Which holiday is the best for business depends on their specialties. Doscher's Candy Company excels at Christmastime because of its fresh candy canes.

Doscher's Candy Company was founded in 1871 by Claus Doescher, a young German immigrant, who came to the United States when he was just nineteen. In Cincinnati, he learned about candy from his uncles, who were already in the sugar and candy business. (According to family legend, there were so many Doschers already in the confectionery business that Claus had to drop the first "e" from his name to set his candy apart from the others.) However, the uncles' company, the A&J Doescher Candy Company, didn't survive the Great Depression.[197]

Claus Doscher created the first Doscher's handcrafted candy cane with a process that involved using real peppermint oil, cooking small batches in copper kettles and working with his hands to roll, knead, stripe and hook the canes. After a few years, he formed Doscher Bros. Wholesale Confectioners with his brothers John and Heinrich on East Fifth Street between Broadway and Sycamore.

Claus didn't just make candy canes. He also developed the famous French Chew that continues to delight candy lovers everywhere. French Chew is a chewy, nougat-like candy that can be found in amazing flavors and shaped into either bars or individually wrapped mini pieces.

Christmas, of course, was the best season for Doscher's confectioners. A *Cincinnati Post* advertisement from December 1888 tempts the Christmas shopper with a "fine assortment of Pistache and Apricot Bonbons, all flavors of Buttercups and Chocolate Cream Drops, Hand-made Creams and others." They also had a "fine" mixture for Sunday school, as well as a variety of boxed candy and tree ornaments.[198]

Claus lived a short life, passing away at only thirty-seven. He left a wife, Sophia, two sons, John and Harry, and a daughter, Wilhelmina. Claus's brother John took the helm of the company and expanded its product lines to include cream candies, chewing gum, molded maple candies and Bon Ton chocolates. The company left retail to focus on the wholesale side of the business at its four-story factory on Central Parkway, formerly known as Canal Street.

Following their uncle's death in 1932, the second generation of Doscher brothers, Claus's sons John and Harry, ran the business. In 1939, John's "housekeeper," Nora Butler, died from a heart attack. After she passed, John revealed that Nora had actually been his wife of thirty years. He did not say why they had kept their relationship a secret all that time, although relatives did say they had suspected it.[199]

Sadly, John and Harry's partnership was short-lived: Harry passed away in 1939, followed in 1941 by John. Elsie Beck Doscher, Harry's widow, stepped in to lead the company while raising two small children, Harry and Marilyn. She even persevered in the difficult time following the Great Depression. (Elsie Doscher stayed active in the company until 1979. She died in March 1985 at the age of ninety-two.)

In 1945, the company moved to 24 West Court Street downtown. Elsie's son Harry III joined the business in 1953 following his graduation from the University of Cincinnati. His son Harry IV briefly worked with Harry in the late 1990s.

Harry decided to sell the business to Greg and Ronna Clark in 2003. Devoted to the company that his grandfather Claus had begun in 1871, Harry III worked with the Clarks until his death at eighty-one in 2009. Greg continued to make artisan candy canes and French Chew bars using the recipes, equipment and techniques that had been handed down for four generations of Doschers. Greg expanded the French Chew line by introducing seasonal flavors and bars to honor the Bengals and the Reds.

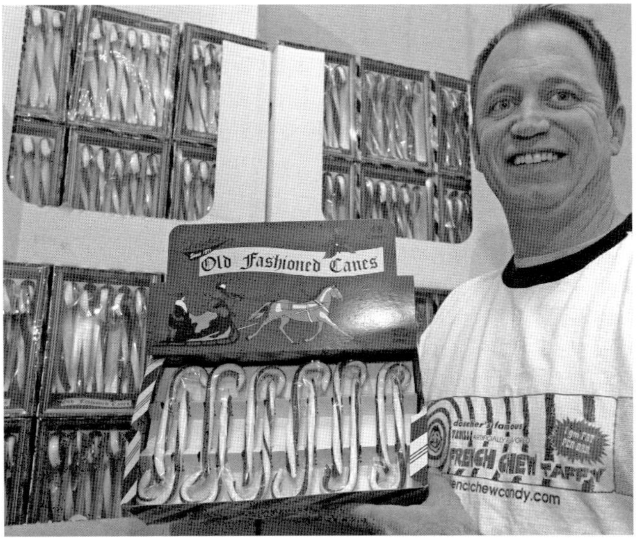

Greg Clark, president, holds a box of Doscher's Candy Canes at Doscher's Candies, 24 West Court Street, downtown, December 3, 2009. Cincinnati Enquirer/*Ed Reinke*.

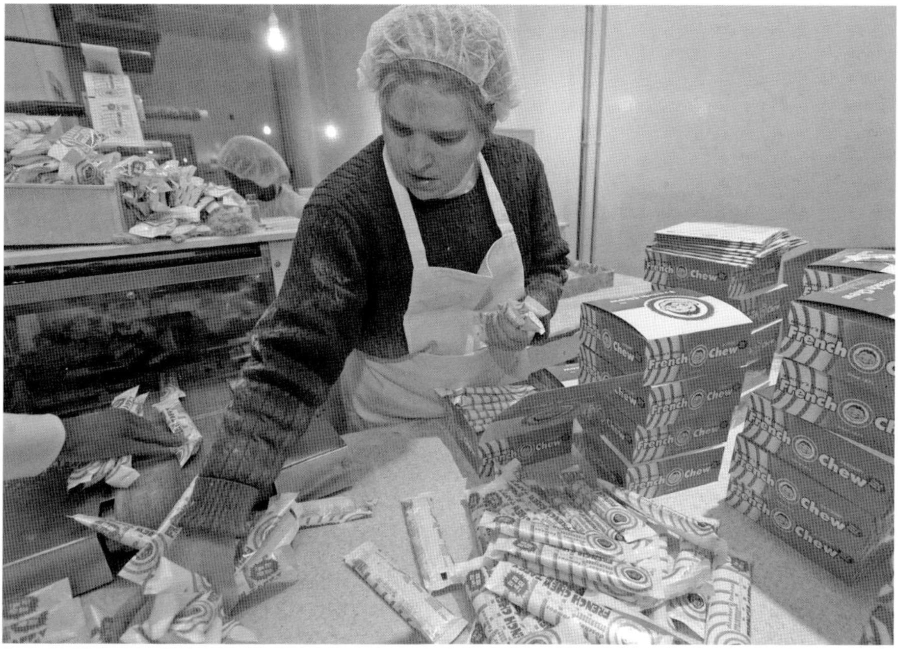

Ruth Harmeier packages Doscher's French Chews at Doscher's Candies, December 3, 2009. Cincinnati Enquirer/*Ed Reinke*.

In 2015, another Cincinnati family, Chip and Robin Nielsen and their daughter and son-in-law, Amy and Kevin Gilligan, joined the Clarks in the business. A new logo, fun packaging options, gourmet flavors and finding a new place to call home became Doscher Candy's focus for the next two years. The search for the perfect property ended with a farmhouse (built around 1835) in Newtown. It provides the ideal space for offices, retail space, a tearoom and a new candy production barn out back.

After 150 years, Doscher's is still using the same recipe to ensure that each candy cane is perfectly chewy and airy. They use the same copper kettles and time-honored techniques so that every candy cane is a one-of-a-kind piece of confectionery art.

In the mid-1880s, the Graeter family came to the United States from Germany (known then as Bavaria). As a teenager, Louis Charles "Charlie" Graeter worked in a market on Court Street at the foot of the Sycamore hill. One of his duties was to make ice cream. Back then, before refrigeration, he had to make it in small batches, putting rock salt and ice around the tub of cream and sugar to turn it into frozen ice cream. After he married Regina Berger, he opened a store of his own, and he applied what he had learned on Court Street. They established the first Graeter's store in 1870 in East Walnut Hills at 967 East McMillan. There, they made ice cream and candies in the back of the store, sold them in the front and lived upstairs.

Sadly, Louis Graeter's life was cut short by a streetcar accident in 1919. Regina not only continued to run the store, but she also made Graeter's the phenomenal success it is now. Regina opened a second store in Hyde Park, which is the oldest Graeter's store still operating today.

A fourth generation of Graeters runs the company now, with stores as far away as Columbus and Lexington. In 1934, Regina bought a location on Reading Road for expanded production capability. From there, the business is run by Charlie and Regina's great-grandsons, Richard, Bob and (wait for it) Chip. The dense, delicious ice cream is made the same way that Regina and Charlie made it—two gallons at a time.[200]

When he was just sixteen years old, Thomas Aglamesis left Sparta, Greece, and his many siblings to seek his fortune in the United States. His father had just died, and as the eldest son, he needed to ensure the welfare of his family. When his brother Nicholas joined him, they started working in downtown Cincinnati in the "Old Arcade," where they learned to make ice cream.

They saved up enough to open their own place and, in 1908, bought a store in Norwood, calling it "The Metropolitan." As the Graeters did, the Aglamesis brothers also churned all their ice cream by hand, using metal cylinders with rock salt and ice to freeze the cream mixture. They soon added candies to their offerings in the store.

They bought another store in Oakley, on Madison Avenue, in 1913, where in the back of the store they made chocolate candy from scratch. This store is the main store today and is a beauty to behold, with marble counters and tabletops from Portugal, as well as Tiffany lamps. In 1922, an ice-cream plant was added behind the store to expand production. Gleaming forty-gallon French copper kettles sit in the plant in which the ice cream is made.

When the Depression hit, Thomas and Nicholas sold the Metropolitan and changed the name of their company to Aglamesis Brothers. In the 1950s, Nicholas died and Thomas's health was failing, so Thomas's son James took over the company. (Another store was added later on in Montgomery.)[201]

At holiday time, the shop is festooned with evergreen garlands and shiny bows. Resting behind the glass display case are assorted chocolates: mixed chewy and creams, nuts and nutless, sugary and sugar-free, dark and milk chocolate, as well as turtles and chocolate-dipped pretzels and fruit—nonpareils like no other. And the pièce de résistance: opera creams. (Although they do contain plenty of cream, they are actually named for the process of creating these heavenly confections. The stirring of the fondant for the center is called "creaming.")

The *real* decorations are on the tables in the depths of the store, past the marble soda fountain counter. Follow the smell of the chocolate and you will find, amid the marble and metal tables and chairs, tablecloth-draped tables stacked with chocolate Santas and Christmas trees, boxes of mixed chocolates and other goodies. The dining area of the shop holds fifteen marble-topped tables (seating about four each). Three times a year, several of the round tables are taken out to make way for the stacks and stacks of mixed chocolates. Jim Aglamesis was usually at the center of it all, dressed in a white coat over his business attire, chocolate smudges on his elbow.

Their busiest season is Easter, followed by Christmas and then Valentine's Day, with their busiest two days each year traditionally being February 13 and 14, as errant husbands and boyfriends frantically stop by to pick up the forgotten present. There are about twenty-five employees in the "off"-

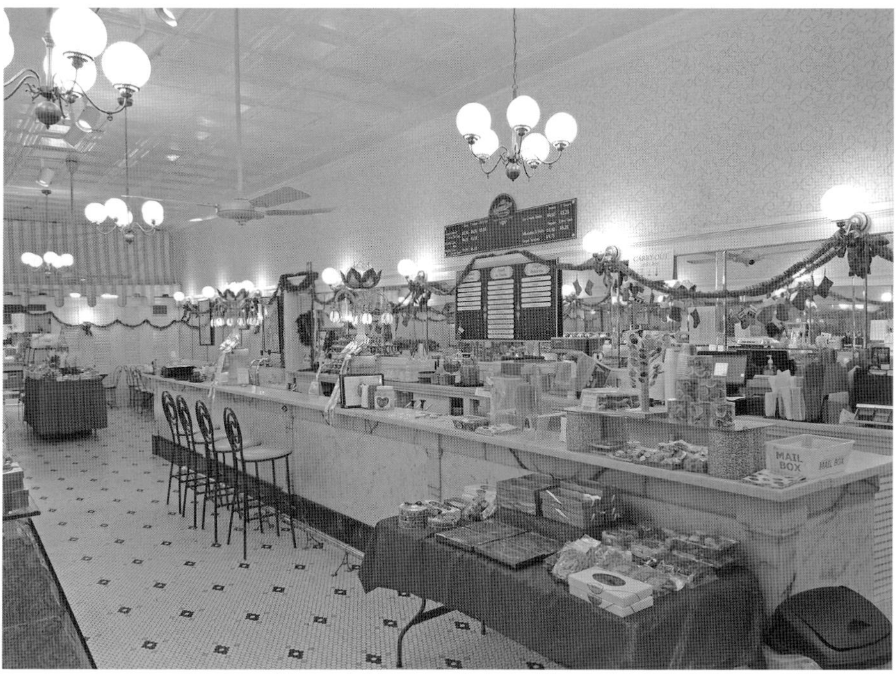

Aglamesis Bros.' Oakley store is all decked out for Christmas. *Photo provided by Randy Young, Aglamesis.*

season, with additional hires during the peak seasons of Valentine's Day, Easter and Christmas. Aglamesis Brothers has a national following; each year, they ship several thousand pounds of their assortments all over the country—golden-boxed messengers winging from Cincinnati.[202]

Jim Aglamesis died on January 23, 2021, at the age of ninety-three. Under the eye of his stepson Randy, the chocolate candies and ice cream are still made the "sincere" way in the Oakley store.

Many people in Cincinnati think Esther Price was a Cincinnatian. The company she founded in Dayton is now being run by a second generation of Cincinnatians, so it's worth a nod here. Esther Price was born in 1905 and died in 1994.

In a home economics class, her life was changed forever when she learned how to make fudge. Even when she graduated from school and got a job in retail, Esther continued to make candies for her friends and coworkers, especially at holiday times.

Finally, she gave in to her destiny and opened up her own candy store in 1926. She prided herself on using the finest butter and cream for her candies. At one point, she asked Jim Aglamesis for advice about making candy. She created a local favorite when she and the folks from Mike-Sells (now Mikesells) potato chips teamed up and created the chocolate-covered potato chip, available from October to March.

In 1976, Esther Price sold the company to four men from Cincinnati, including one named Jim Day. Although the company headquarters is still on Wayne Avenue in Dayton, the distinctive gold box can be found in dedicated Esther Price stores in Cincinnati as well as in many area Kroger stores. Today, Esther Price Candies sells its products in eighty-seven store locations in five states: Ohio, Indiana, Kentucky, Tennessee and Illinois.

Esther Price Candies once again became a family-owned business when Day became the sole owner in 2006. He was joined by his three daughters, sons-in-law and granddaughters. Day family members run the operations and serve on its board of directors. In 2009 and 2013, *Ohio Magazine* rated Esther Price the best chocolates in Ohio. Day died on September 18, 2020, at the age of ninety-two.[203]

Paul "Pep" Guenther returned from World War II in 1946 and—with his wife, Jean—opened up a candy store in Cheviot. Jean's Greek heritage helped shape the flavors that went into the sweets they created.

Since 1984, Fawn Candy has been owned by Jean and Pep's daughters Kathy, Jackie, Jean and Jane. They own two stores, one on Harrison Avenue in Green Township and a second in Rookwood Pavilion. They've now been joined by their children, nieces, nephews and grandchildren, making four generations of Fawns. The store is a good neighbor, often working with school and church fundraisers.

BAKERIES

Similar to Cincinnati's candy manufacturers, the stories of Cincinnati's bakers most frequently start with the baker arriving in Cincinnati in the late 1800s to make a better life for himself and his family. (And that baker usually came here from Germany.) Because of that connection, Cincinnati is blessed with an abundance of good bakeries. Some of these have expanded and can be found all over town, like Servatii's, Busken and Grote. However, when it comes to just the right pastry for that early-morning sugar fix, people often turn to Cincinnati's comfort food: the old-fashioned "scratch" bakeries. No preservatives and lots of butter, milk, eggs and cream. Everything is made from scratch, and nothing is better on your way to work. Most of them create beautiful, sumptuous wedding cakes, too: it would almost be worth your while to line up some more spouses.

ST. LAWRENCE

William Conrad Hartmann came to America in 1893 for a better life. He ended up in Cincinnati, as did many Germans about that time. He worked in a restaurant for several years, then returned to Germany to retrieve his sister. Bill Hartmann told a reporter that he still had his grandfather's papers with permission to leave from Kaiser Wilhelm II.

Conrad Hartmann opened the bakery in Over-the-Rhine. After serving in World War II, Conrad's son William came home and moved the bakery to St. Lawrence Avenue in Price Hill. "My father, Bill Hartmann Sr., started this bakery in this location in 1949, using the same recipes his father, Conrad Hartmann, used at his bakery on Western Avenue in 1901," Paul Hartmann said proudly.[204]

Bill Jr. worked in the bakery beginning at the age of twelve, working all the way through high school and college. He received a degree in education from the University of Cincinnati, but after trying his hand at teaching, he realized that the bakery was still calling him. Bill returned to the bakery, eventually taking it over in 1978 along with his brother Paul. Paul's son Nick also joined them in the business.

During an interview for *Cincinnati Magazine*, longtime employees Joan and Babs couldn't stop raving about the many specialties at Hartmann Brothers' St. Lawrence Bakery, including their creme horns, meringue cakes, butter doughnuts and chocolate twists. One of their most popular Christmas items was the chocolate bird's nest, made of small handmade cookies that are rolled in pecans and decorated with Swiss chocolate icing. Bill said they could barely keep up with all the bird's nest orders for Christmas.[205] Sadly, St. Lawrence Bakery closed its doors in 2021.

Bonomini

In 1970, the *Cincinnati Kurier* carried an ad for the old Blue Rock Bakery, telling consumers to "*Machen Sie schön jetzt Ihre Bestellung für Weihnachts—Stollen Kleingebäck und Kuchen bei* Blue Rock Bakery." (Make your order now for Christmas—Stollen Cookies and Cake by Blue Rock Bakery.)[206]

Joe and Rose Volz started the Volz Bakery on Virginia Avenue in 1926. When their building was torn down in 1974, they moved to the old Blue Rock Bakery on Blue Rock Street. Now owned by their grandsons, Bonomini Bakery has been baking for four generations and is going strong.

A 1969 help wanted ad in the *Cincinnati Enquirer* sought a baker, specifying an "experienced all around man" to work nights. They are still finding it challenging to find bakery workers. A "help wanted" sign hangs in the window. "It's hard work!" says Becky, a member of the Bonomini family. "Not everybody wants to do that."[207]

The atmosphere at Bonomini is like an old family neighborhood. One customer joins in a conversation. "I came here with my mother when I was a kid," he says as he takes his bag of cookies. "One time we came in her brand-new station wagon. As we were waiting, we looked outside, and it was going up in flames!" Luckily, that was the car and not the bakery.

Bonomini is still known for its old-fashioned rye bread, cakes, cookies, buns, fritters and doughnuts, filling the cases with seasonal treats like stollen at Christmastime and hot cross buns at Easter.

Another sign outside reads, "Enjoy the sweet things in life!" In Northside, most of the sweet things in life were probably baked that morning at Bonomini Bakery.[208]

VIRGINIA

Virginia Bakery was established in 1927 by William Thie and was then run by four generations of the Thie family. Tom and Maureen Thie, the last generation of owners, were there Tuesday through Saturday, creating the Thie family's signature schnecken and butterbits. (The latter came ready to eat or ready to bake.)

For the uninitiated, schnecken are large yeast rolls, with a touch of cinnamon and raisins, that are fairly dripping in butter. Each year around the winter holidays, the Virginia Bakery shipped out thousands of schnecken by UPS.

In December 1970, the *Cincinnati Kurier* ran an ad for Virginia Bakery, under "Wm. Thie, Konditor" (confectioner/pastry chef). It read, "*Deutscher Frucht-Stollen Óbst-Kuchen nach altem Rezept! Weinachtsgebäck & schön verzierte Torten. Reiche Auswahl an Plätzchen Hutzelbrot*" (German fruit stollen fruit cake following an old recipe! Christmas cookies and beautifully decorated cakes. Wide range of fruitcake cookies). *Hutzelbrot* was different from other fruitcakes in that it was moister and used nuts, as well as pears instead of citron and cherries.[209]

Virginia Bakery always had a steady stream of customers, but starting in early December, the line of customers would extend halfway to Skyline, and parking within two blocks of the bakery was impossible. Their other specialties were wedding cakes and bran muffins, which were "to die for," according to Sharonville resident Karen Zerbini, former publisher of *MD News Magazine*. "There's nothing I've had there that isn't absolutely the best in the city." "When people see the red and white string they know they're getting Virginia Bakery schnecken," Maureen Thie told a writer in early 2000.

The bakery closed in 2005. Originally, the Thies intended to open for the holidays to sell the old favorites, but that didn't happen. Maureen Thie said, similar to what Becky Bonomini said, that as their baking staff aged and retired, it was getting difficult to find younger workers who were willing to get up that early to bake.[210] (This is reminiscent of the old Dunkin' Donuts commercials in which the baker dragged himself out of bed in the dark, saying he had to make the doughnuts. Ironically, that actor died from diabetes complications.) According to *Virginia Bakery Remembered*, the demise of the bakery was exacerbated by an accident. (Tom fell off a ladder.)[211]

Schnecken fans in the Cincinnati area still have reason to hope. For one thing, some of the bakeries in town, such as Servatii's, make their own version of the Christmas treat. *Virginia Bakery Remembered* also has the Thies' recipe

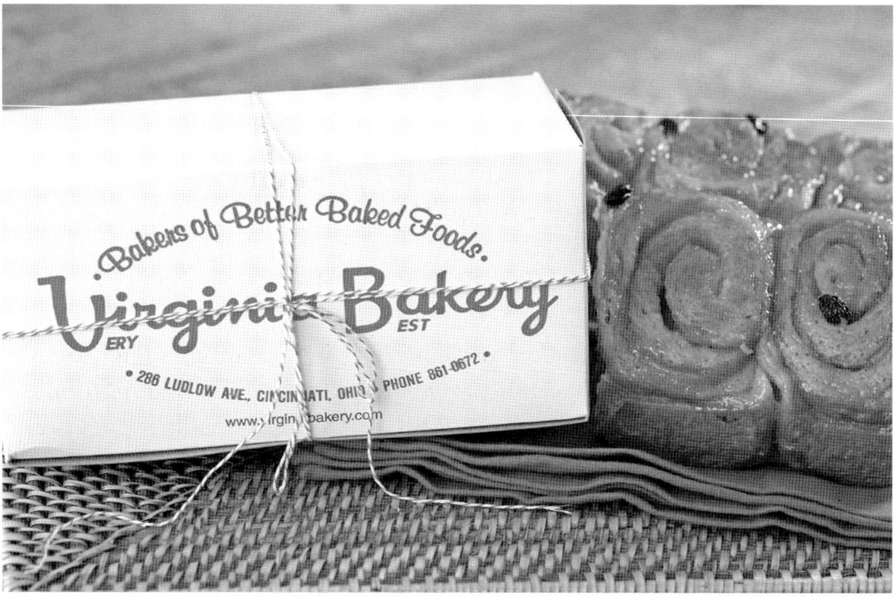

Virginia Bakery's red and white boxes stir up fond memories. *Photo by Kristin Ungerecht; provided by Virginia Bakery.*

for the Virginia Bakery version—for those of us who are willing to face the yeast. For those of us who can't seem to get a yeast dough to rise, never fear: Busken Bakery also has the rights to the Thies' schnecken recipe. Check out one of the four Busken locations to get your schnecken fix: Eastgate, Hyde Park, Highland Heights or Springdale.

Servatii's

German immigrant Wilhelm Gottenbusch opened his first bakery on Observatory Avenue in Hyde Park in 1963. Since then, for the past fifty-eight years, Wilhelm and his sons have grown their bakery and expanded their offerings.

Wilhelm brought with him the traditions of his father and grandfather (both named "George") over from Muenster, Germany. Wilhelm's father attended Germany's most recognized baking school and received his Konditor Meister (Master Pastry Chef) status. Wilhelm followed in his father's footsteps, earning his Master Baker status and starting his own business in Cincinnati. Wilhelm's sons Gary and Greg both apprenticed in Germany and earned their Journeyman status, Greg in pastry and Gary in baking. Gary continued in his father's and grandfather's footsteps by earning his Master Baker certification in 2001. In turn, the Gottenbusches have acquired some of the most talented bakers, decorators and pastry chefs in America. They work to uphold the values set forth by Wilhelm Gottenbusch fifty years ago. Today, Greg Gottenbusch runs the day-to-day business of Servatii's. Gary's son Paul is now the head night baker and is learning the family business.[212]

Servatii's Christmas offerings are legendary in Cincinnati. They are also very German, with tasty *adventsplätzchen* (advent cookies) like *pfeffernüssen* (spice cookies dusted with confectioners' sugar or glazed), butter drops, almond crescents (*kipfel*) and *springerle* (anise-flavored cookies), as well as gingerbread and stollen. They also offer yule logs, eggnog tortes and decorated brownies and cakes.[213] (And, speaking from personal experience, they make great wedding cakes.)

Busken

For generations, Buskens have known how to bake. Back in a little bakery in Oklahoma, Clem Busken taught his son Joseph how to bake. But back then, just like now, the hours were long and started early, and the work was hot. The front of most bakeries sell delights to savor, but the back is usually filled with sweaty bakers, cloying aromas and floating flour.

So Joe married his love, Daisie, said goodbye to his parents and moved to Cincinnati. He thought he'd said goodbye to the bakery life, too, but he was wrong. He had gone to work at a relative's cigar store, but it went under. What could Joe do? He could bake. He approached a grocer to see if he could bake in the back of his store; thus began an empire. Joe and Daisie had a son, Joe Jr., who also entered the family baking business in 1952. Eventually, the little bakery they were in was too small for how much the company had grown. Joe Sr. took a risk, borrowed some money and bought a failed grocery store at the intersection of Madison and Edwards Roads in Norwood. In 1970, Page joined his brother Joe Jr. in running the company. The rest is history.[214]

Busken cookies can be found all around town, all year round. These soft vanilla cookies with a subtle taste of almond are frequently in packages of

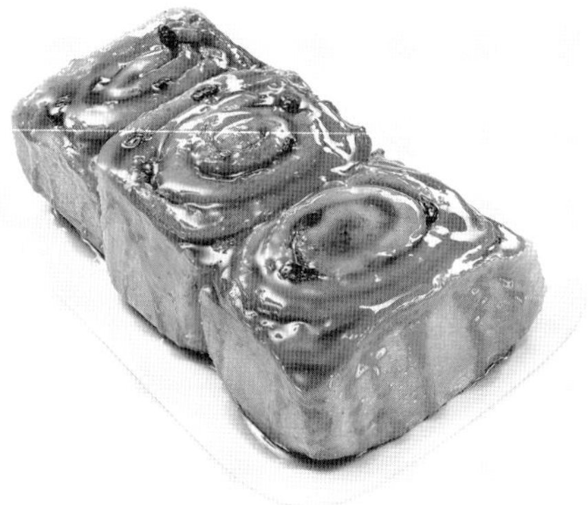

Schnecken bask in butter. *Photo provided by Busken Bakery.*

two, tempting shoppers from the counters in UDF stores and other locations. If you order "Luigi" cookies from LaRosa's, they're Busken cookies. Each presidential election year, they decorate cookies with the faces of the candidates and judge the winner by whose cookies sold the most.

At Christmastime, Busken has the baked treat for every holiday need: cookies, coffee cakes, decorated cakes (they even have a "Home Alone" cake!) and schnecken. When Virginia Bakery closed, they passed the Thie family recipe on to Busken. You'll want to buy them early and often, for after Christmas they're just a memory!

Afterword

Celebrating Christmas in Cincinnati is a gift of all the senses. We no longer march our hogs down Fifth Street, but we still enjoy our roast pork, wieners and wursts. The lights in our windows and on our trees are no longer real candles, and the trees themselves might not be real, either. But the warmth and light that our friends and families bask in is still as genuine. Our cards were not produced by Louis Prang or Gibson Greetings, and they might exist only in digital form, but the sentiment is the same of peace and goodwill to all people.

Merry Christmas!

Notes

Most newspaper articles were obtained via the following resources:
Cincinnati Public Library
NewsBank: America's Historical Newspapers
Reference and Research Services, Cincinnati History Library and Archives, Cincinnati Museum Center

Epigraph

1. Henry Wadsworth Longfellow, "Catawba Wine," Maine Historical Society Website, accessed April 6, 2021, https://www.hwlongfellow.org.

Chapter 1

2. *Cincinnati Enquirer*, December 27, 1850.
3. "NORAD Tracks Santa," North American Aerospace Defense Command, accessed March 15, 2021, https://www.norad.mil.
4. Beckman, *8 Wonders of Cincinnati*, 121–23.
5. "Tracing Hanukkah's U.S. Roots…to Cincinnati?" NPR, December 1, 2010, accessed March 22, 2021, https://www.npr.org.
6. Ibid.
7. Catherine Roma, *A City That Sings: Cincinnati's Choral Tradition 1800–2012* (Wilmington, OH: Orange Frazer Press, 2012).

8. Gregg Levoy, "As Cincinnati Sees Christmas, So Will the World—Next Year," *Cincinnati Enquirer*, November 18, 1977.
9. Sarah Brookbank, "Cincinnati One of the Best Places for Christmas Celebrations," *Cincinnati Enquirer*, December 20, 2018.

Chapter 2

10. "The First Christmas of Cincinnati's Pioneers," *Cincinnati Enquirer*, December 25, 1904.
11. Berten, *Cincinnati Christmas*, 4–5.
12. George Wartenberg, "Our Holiday Wasn't Always…," *Cincinnati Enquirer*, December 27, 1959.
13. Wartenberg, "Our Holiday."
14. Ibid.
15. Ibid.
16. Ibid.
17. Earle Cornelius, "In 1870, Congress Made Christmas Day a Federal Holiday. But Some Still Question Its Constitutionality," Lancaster Online, December 20, 2019, accessed March 22, 2021, https://lancasteronline.com.
18. Wartenberg, "Our Holiday."
19. Julie Irwin Zimmerman, "How Catholic Are We?" *Cincinnati Magazine*, April 2, 2016.
20. Zimmerman, "How Catholic Are We?"
21. Debra Mooney, PhD, and George Traub, SJ, "Xavier University: An Historical Perspective," *Xavier University*, no date, accessed March 14, 2021, https://www.xavier.edu.
22. "Parish History," St. Xavier Church, accessed March 14, 2021, http://www.stxchurch.org.
23. *Cincinnati Post*, November 23, 1882, 1.
24. "Chrismon" is a combination of "Christ" and "monogram." They are gold and white symbols of Christ that decorate Christmas trees in churches. Typical Chrismon ornaments are the Greek letters *alpha* and *omega*, fish, crowns and butterflies.
25. Herbert, *Old St. Mary's Church*, 116.
26. "Awaited," Crossroads Church, accessed March 13, 2021, https://www.crossroads.net.
27. Bill Cieslewicz, "Crossroads' Popular Christmas Show Is Coming Back," *Cincinnati Business Courier*, December 10, 2018.

Chapter 3

28. Dann Woellert, "Jets and Sharks and Aglamesis Ice Cream," dannwoellertthefoodetymologist, March 25, 2017, accessed March 27, 2017, https://dannwoellertthefoodetymologist.wordpress.com.
29. Julia Sweeten, "Fun Facts About 'White Christmas' and Its Connection to 'Holiday Inn,'" Hooked on Houses, December 3, 2019, accessed March 11, 2021, https://hookedonhouses.net.
30. "Cincinnati—Extreme Daily Snowfall for Each Year," Current Results, accessed March 12, 2021, https://www.currentresults.com.
31. "Timeline," Perfect North Slopes, accessed March 12, 2021, www.perfectnorth.com.
32. Ibid.
33. Beischel, *Lost Tea Rooms*, 7.
34. Ibid., 41.
35. Ibid., 31.
36. Ibid., 56.
37. Ibid., 15.
38. *Cincinnati Post*, December 21, 1882, 3.
39. *Cincinnati Post*, October 4, 1882, 4. Of note: this is one of the first pieces I found where "Christmas" was capitalized. After all, it hadn't become a national holiday until June 26, 1870.
40. *Cincinnati Post*, October 26, 1883, 3.
41. Jeff Suess, "A Look at Cincinnati's Lost Downtown Department Stores," *Cincinnati Enquirer*, January 5, 2018.
42. Wendy Hart Beckman, "The Lazarus Family: Sold on the City," *Cincinnati Magazine*, November 1, 2014.
43. "What Happened to the Shillito's Elves? Remembering a Cincinnati Christmas Tradition," WLWT-TV Digital Staff, November 20, 2020, accessed March 13, 2021, https://www.wlwt.com.
44. "Beyond Mere Windows," *(Cincinnati) Enquirer Magazine*, November 20, 1977.
45. Libby Lackman, "Animated Displays Delight Shoppers," *Cincinnati Enquirer*, December 2, 1959.
46. Beischel, *Tea Rooms*, 11.
47. "Beyond Mere Windows."
48. Beischel, *Tea Rooms*, 11.
49. Jeff Suess, "Our History: Old Gidding-Jenny Store Has Priceless Rookwood," Cincinnati.com, July 18, 2018, accessed March 13, 2021, https://www.cincinnati.com.

50. Katie Laur, "Letter from Katie: Blue Christmas," *Cincinnati Magazine*, December 11, 2011.
51. Suess, "A Look at Cincinnati's Lost Downtown Department Stores."
52. "Reinvention," Cincinnati Museum Center, accessed October 26, 2020, https://www.cincymuseum.org.
53. "About Christkindlmarkt," Germania Society, accessed December 17, 2020, https://germaniasociety.com.
54. Bridgett Raffenberg, "Christmas Markets and Holiday Craft Shows in Cincinnati [2020]," 365Cincinnati, October 19, 2020, https://365cincinnati.com.
55. Brian Mains, "Duke Energy Holiday Trains Display Taking Hiatus," WCPO Channel 9, October 7, 2016, accessed March 26, 2021, https://www.wcpo.com.
56. Mains, "Duke Energy Holiday Trains."
57. "Christmas Journey," EnterTRAINment Junction, 2016, https://entertrainmentjunction.com.
58. Eleanor Bell, "Stores Vie for Best Holiday Decorations," *Cincinnati Enquirer*, December 4, 1963.
59. Matthew S. Schwartz, "'I Vaccinated Santa Claus, Fauci Tells Kids," *Health*, NPR, December 19, 2020, accessed March 17, 2021, https://www.npr.org.
60. Phone interview with Dr. Roger Giesel, April 22, 2021.
61. Neediest Kids Of All. *1955–'56 Campaign Report for "Neediest Kids Of All,"* www.neediestkidsofall.com.
62. Ibid., *1954–'55 Campaign Report for "Neediest Kids Of All."*
63. Ibid., *1955–'56 Campaign Report for "Neediest Kids Of All."*
64. Neediest Kids of All, "Our Mission," accessed November 20, 2020, http://www.neediestkidsofall.com.
65. Dan Carroll, "Toy Team 9 Sets Record, Collects 10,613 Toys for Cincinnati-Area Kids at Christmas," Newsbreak, accessed November 20, 2020, https://www.newsbreak.com.
66. William Collins, "Union Central Adds to Joy: Chimes Feature Lyons' Tunes," *Cincinnati Enquirer*, November 20, 1958.
67. Garrison Hilliard, "Ruth Lyons Biography," Internet Movie Database, accessed March 17, 2021, https://www.imdb.com.
68. Beckman, *8 Wonders of Cincinnati*, 156.
69. Advertisement, *Cincinnati Enquirer*, November 1, 1882, Public Library of Cincinnati and Hamilton County Digital Library.
70. *Penny Paper/Cincinnati Post*, October 27, 1882, 1.
71. Advertisement, *Cincinnati Post*, December 1, 1883, Public Library of Cincinnati and Hamilton County Digital Library.

72. *Cincinnati Post*, December 22, 1939, 15.
73. "Louis Prang & Co. Prints," The Philadelphia Print Shop Ltd., accessed March 20, 2021, http://www.philaprintshop.com.
74. "Display Ad 2—no Title." *Cincinnati Enquirer*, November 27, 1880.
75. Brett Rosenstein, "Oldest Greeting Card Company," Ohiowins, accessed February 9, 2021, www.ohiowins.com.
76. George Elliston, "Old Santa Claus Is Conspicuous by Absence on Christmas Cards," *Cincinnati Times-Star*, November 29, 1940.
77. Rick Kennedy, "Gibson Refined Cole Idea," *Cincinnati Post*, December 25, 1984, 23.
78. "History of United States Postage," Wikipedia, accessed March 17, 2021, https://en.wikipedia.org.
79. "Gibson Greetings, Inc. History," Funding Universe, accessed February 9, 2021, http://www.fundinguniverse.com.
80. Gregg Levoy, "Kings Island Has 'Winterfest' Ready to Crown Season with New Tradition," Tempo, *Cincinnati Enquirer*, F1.
81. "Christmas? Already?" *Cincinnati Enquirer*, September 15, 1982, G1.
82. *Cincinnati Enquirer*, November 21, 1982, 80.
83. "Workers Prepare Kings Island Rink," *Cincinnati Enquirer*, October 25, 1982, C1.
84. "Hold the Cherry Syrup," *Cincinnati Enquirer*, November 25, 1982, G1.
85. "Winterfest: The Good News from Kings Island Is That the Off Season Is Canceled," *Cincinnati Enquirer,* November 1, 1982, A10.
86. "Kings Island Plans to Reopen Park for One-Month Winterfest," *Cincinnati Enquirer*, April 30, 1982, C3.
87. "Christmas? Already?"
88. Ponstingle, *Kings Island*, 116.
89. Ibid., 145.
90. Ibid., 173–74.
91. I was a Westinghouse stockholder, so I was a firsthand witness to these changes.
92. Jim Knippenberg, "How Holiday Magic Happens," *Cincinnati Enquirer*, November 20, 2005, D5.
93. Jessica Brown, "Winterfest Canceled; Attendance Blamed," *Cincinnati Enquirer*, July 25, 2006, B1.
94. Jim Knippenberg, "Winterfest Returning for Holidays," *Cincinnati Enquirer*, July 25, 2005, D1.
95. Chris Varias, "WinterFest Returns to Kings Island," *Cincinnati Enquirer*, November 24, 2017, 3D.
96. Jennie Key, "Brennaman to Help Open Kings Island WinterFest," *Cincinnati Enquirer*, November 22, 2018.

97. *Rudolph the Red-Nosed Reindeer*, Rankin/Bass Productions, 1964. She doesn't say this anymore: they edited the line.
98. Sue Kiesewetter, "Beach Hopes to Become a Destination for Winter," *Cincinnati Enquirer*, A22.
99. Ibid.

Chapter 4

100. *Cincinnati Enquirer*, May 1, 1988.
101. "Mayor to Add to Many Accomplishments; He Will Sing Carols on Fountain Square," *Cincinnati Times-Star*, December 17, 1935.
102. *Cincinnati Times-Star*, December 23, 1935.
103. Betsa Marsh, "Sing a Song of Christmas," *Cincinnati Enquirer*, December 2, 1982.
104. *Cincinnati Enquirer*, November 24, 2016, 7D.
105. Marsh, "Sing a Song of Christmas."
106. Luann Gibbs, "The Week Ahead," *Cincinnati Enquirer*, November 24, 2019, 8AA.
107. John Kiesewetter, "Trans-Electrifying: 'Today' to Feature Oak Hills Orchestra," October 1, 2010, C1.
108. Neil Shah, "How the Trans-Siberian Orchestra Became a Holiday Hit Machine," *Wall Street Journal*, December 3, 2015.
109. Amy Harris, "Trans-Siberian Orchestra Interview with Al Pitrelli," The First 3 Songs, 2014, accessed April 17, 2021, http://thefirst3songs.com.
110. Shah, "How the Trans-Siberian Orchestra Became a Holiday Hit Machine."
111. Harris, "Trans-Siberian Orchestra Interview."
112. *Cincinnati Enquirer*, November 24, 2016, 7D.
113. "The Power of Bells," The Verdin Company, 2021, accessed March 24, 2021, https://www.verdin.com/bells.
114. "World Peace Bell—Newport, KY, USA," Waymarking.com, accessed April 9, 2021, https://www.waymarking.com.
115. Herbert, *Old St. Mary's Church*, 104.
116. *Cincinnati Enquirer*, December 29, 2006.
117. "A History of Old St. Mary's," written in 1942 for the 1942 anniversary edition of *A History of Old St. Mary's*, accessed March 24, 2021, https://www.oldstmarys.org.
118. Herbert, *Old St. Mary's Church*, 50.
119. Beckman, *Founders and Famous Families of Cincinnati*.
120. Bebe Hodges, "Tradition Rings," *Cincinnati Magazine*, April 2021, 104.

Chapter 5

121. "Cincinnati Royals," Ohio History Central, accessed April 8, 2021, https://ohiohistorycentral.org.
122. Jeff Wallner, "Battle for the Victory Bell: Is the Miami-UC Rivalry Losing Its Luster?" WCPO, September 5, 2018, https://www.wcpo.com.
123. Beckman, *Founders and Famous Families of Cincinnati*, 99.
124. "Commercial Club Elects, Names Bullock Its Head," *Cincinnati Enquirer*, May 16, 1971, 2A.
125. "Visit: of President McKinley, Who Comes as the Guest of the Commercial Club. Public Reception on Change at One O'Clock. Will Be Banqueted at the Queen City Club in the Evening—The Programme Will Come on Change. The Troops Will Come Over. The Commercial Club." *Cincinnati Enquirer*, October 30, 1897.
126. "Eight Years: A Career of Usefulness and Pleasure Represented by the Commercial Club of This City. Its Annual Dinner Last Evening a Fitting Climax to Its Labors in the City's Welfare." *Cincinnati Enquirer*, November 23, 1888.
127. "The Commercial Club of Cincinnati Christmas Dinner," Queen City Club, December 19, 1964. Printer unknown, 50–51.
128. "The Boars Head and Yule Log Festival," Christ Church Cathedral, accessed March 16, 2021, https://cincinnaticathedral.com.
129. David Lyman, "Our Ballet's Biography: Cincinnati Ballet Has Graced Stages for 50 Years. Look Back on the Building Blocks of Its History," *Cincinnati Enquirer*, September 8, 2013, D4.
130. Lyman, "Our Ballet's Biography."
131. Janelle Gelfand, "Retired Surgeon Reflects on When He Sang in Made-for-TV Opera 'Amahl' in 1950s," *Cincinnati Business Courier*, December 14, 2018.
132. "Unchanged" refers to boy singers whose voices have not yet changed and are usually in the soprano range.
133. Email from Dr. Sammarco to author, March 23, 2021.
134. Gelfand, "Retired Surgeon Reflects."
135. Rob Bucher, "A Christmas Carol Review," Behind the Curtain Cincy, December 3, 2014, https://behindthecurtaincincy.com.
136. Rob Bucher, "Cincinnati Playhouse in the Park and Cincinnati Public Radio Bring a Christmas Carol to the Radio," Behind the Curtain Cincy, December 2, 2020, https://behindthecurtaincincy.com.
137. Bucher, "A Christmas Carol Review."
138. Jeff Suess, *Cincinnati Enquirer*, December 14, 2014, AA8.

139. "Delighted: Children That Gathered in Fountain Square Yesterday and Saw the Beautiful Tableau of Red Riding Hood and Santa Claus," *Cincinnati Enquirer*, December 7, 1890.
140. Greg Hand, "17 Curious Facts They Never Tell You About the Tyler Davidson Fountain: The Large Sculpture in Downtown's Fountain Square Has an Illustrious and Somewhat Mysterious History," April 21, 2017, accessed March 28, 2021, https://www.cincinnatimagazine.com.
141. Hand, "17 Curious Facts."
142. "The Ghosts of Fountain Square," *Cincinnati Magazine* 33, no. 8 (May 2000): 66.
143. "The History of Fountain Square," Fountain Square, accessed March 28, 2021, https://myfountainsquare.com.
144. "Ghosts of Fountain Square."
145. Evan Millward, "Changing Face of Downtown: A Look at the (Growing) Heart of Cincinnati," WCPO, March 9, 2021, accessed March 29, 2021, https://www.wcpo.com.
146. "Ghosts of Fountain Square."
147. *Cincinnati Enquirer,* December 27, 1850.
148. Jeff Suess, "The History of Our Favorite Cincinnati Holiday Traditions," *Cincinnati Enquirer*, November 26, 2020.
149. Bell, "Stores Vie for Best Holiday Decorations."
150. "Plastic Yule Trees for City," *Cincinnati Enquirer*, November 14, 1960.
151. Jim Golden, "Yule Season Lights Up Fountain Square on Thursday," *Cincinnati Enquirer*, November 18, 1962.
152. Sarah Brookbank, "Colbert Cracks Jokes About Our Fountain Square Christmas Tree," *Cincinnati Enquirer*, November 24, 2020.
153. Briana Rice, "This Christmas Tree Proves '2020 Has Been a Rough Year,'" *USA Today*, November 10, 2020. https://www.usatoday.com.
154. @TreeFountain, Twitter, November 10, 2020, www.twitter.com.
155. @DaveHollon, replying to @TreeFountain, Twitter, November 10, 2020, www.twitter.com.
156. Si Cornell, "Tradition in the Making," *Cincinnati Post & Times-Star*, December 16, 1959.
157. "98 Degrees—If Every Day Could Be Christmas," Song Lyrics: Know the Words, 2021, http://www.songlyrics.com.
158. Joe Minster, "Christmas with the Lights Out," *The News*, November 28, 1973.
159. "Mall Will Be Candle-Lit," *Cincinnati Enquirer*, November 22, 1973.
160. Minster, "Christmas with the Lights Out."
161. Marvin Beard, "Christmas Lighting Blackout Casts Cloud of Spiritual Darkness," *Cincinnati Enquirer*, December 4, 1973.

162. "Holiday Lights Returning," *Cincinnati Enquirer*, November 12, 1974.
163. Bridgett Raffenberg, "Drive Through Christmas Light Shows in Cincinnati, Perfect for 2020," 365Cincinnati, November 10, 2020, https://365cincinnati.com.
164. Ibid.
165. "Christmas Glow," Land of Illusion Amusement Park, accessed April 13, 2021, https://www.landofillusion.com.
166. "When Nick Melisci Decorates...All Clifton Knows About It," *Cincinnati Enquirer*, December 22, 1975.
167. Suess, "History of Our Favorite Holiday Traditions."
168. Ralph Gordon, "Westwood Postman Creates for Christmas," *Western Hills Press* and *Price Hill News*, December 6 and 7, 1972. Full disclosure: Martha Buchanan is my mother-in-law's first cousin.
169. Beckman, *Founders and Famous Families of Cincinnati*, 45.
170. Gilbert Sands, "Save Entire Lytle Park Area, Planning Chairman Urges," *Cincinnati Enquirer*, January 13, 1959.
171. Suess, "History of Our Favorite Cincinnati Holiday Traditions," 8E.
172. "Lytle Park Crib Destroyed by Fire," *Cincinnati Enquirer*, January 3, 1959.
173. "County of Allegheny v. American Civil Liberties Union, Greater Pittsburgh Chapter," Oyez, accessed April 20, 2021, https://www.oyez.org.
174. John Eckberg, "Board Denies Krohn: Constitutionality Questioned," *Cincinnati Enquirer*, August 29, 1989.
175. Ginny Hunter, "Nativity Scene Cleared for This Christmas," *Cincinnati Post*, September 14, 1989.
176. Beckman, *8 Wonders of Cincinnati*, 109.
177. "History & Master Plan," Cincinnati Parks, 2015–2018, accessed December 17, 2020, https://www.cincinnatiparks.com.

Chapter 6

178. Harlow, *Serene Cincinnatians*, 188.
179. Don Heinrich Tolzmann, "Our Rich History: The First Christmas Tree in Cincinnati, Thanks to German Immigrant, Dr. Rehfuss," *NKy Tribune*, December 19, 2016, accessed March 29, 2021, https://www.nkytribune.com.
180. Steve Bunin, "Verify: Is a Real or Fake Christmas Tree Better for the Environment?" KING-5, December 7, 2020, accessed March 29, 2021, https://www.king5.com.
181. Burin, "Verify."

182. Mike Pulfer, "Tree Selling Isn't What It Used to Be," *Cincinnati Post*, December 22, 1975.
183. Bridgett Raffenberg, "10+ Places to Cut Your Own Christmas Tree in Cincinnati (2020)," 365Cincinnati, November 8, 2020, https://365cincinnati.com.

Chapter 7

184. "The Duties of the Housekeeper and the Pleasures of the Wife," *Penny Paper/Cincinnati Post*, November 22, 1882, 4.
185. Ibid.
186. *Cincinnati Enquirer*, December 30, 1892, 5.
187. Ibid.
188. Beckman, *8 Wonders of Cincinnati*, 53.
189. Jeff Suess, "Christmas Past: Holiday Celebrations in Cincinnati Over the Years," *Cincinnati Enquirer*, December 14, 2014, AA8.
190. E.D. Mansfield, "Christmas in 1826 and in 1869—A Contrast and a Memory," *Cincinnati Gazette*, December 21, 1869.
191. Mansfield, "Christmas in 1826 and in 1869."
192. Pauline Rice Shields, "Christmas Dinner Menu: Menu. Recipes," *Cincinnati Enquirer,* December 24, 1905, B8.
193. Ibid.
194. Greg Hand, "Arnold's Bar & Grill Is Even Older than You Think," Cincinnati Curiosities, June 5, 2018, https://handeaux.tumblr.com.
195. At this point, my husband will be happy that I said "soda" instead of "ice cream soda." I did it for him, although the New Englander in me wanted to say the latter. He says "ice cream soda" is redundant. I tell him that soda comes in a can. He says that's "pop." We've had this exchange a few times a year for more than thirty-five years now.
196. "Candy: Making in Cincinnati Is One of Her Important Industries at This Time. The Business Shows a Wonderful Growth. Record for Purity of Product and Extensive Territory for Sales. Large Candy Centers. Retail Estimates. Cincinnati's Growth. Candy-Making Machinery," *Cincinnati Enquirer*, March 12, 1900.
197. Sarah Sturmon, *Cincinnati Post*, February 11, 1986, 35.
198. *Cincinnati Post*, December 21, 1887, 4.
199. Ibid., December 13, 1939, 17.
200. Beckman, *Founders and Famous Families of Cincinnati*, 112.
201. Ibid., 112–13.

202. Wendy Hart Beckman, "Candy Man," *Cincinnati Magazine*, February 2000.
203. "Jim Day, Co-owner of Esther Price Candies and Elder Graduate, Dies at 92," *Cincinnati Business Courier*, September 23, 2020, accessed March 18, 2021, https://www.bizjournals.com/cincinnati.
204. Beckman, "Mom and Popovers," *Cincinnati Magazine*, July 2000.
205. Grace Yek, "St. Lawrence Bakery Is Longtime Labor of Love for Hartmann Family," WCPO 9, accessed March 19, 2021, https://www.wcpo.com.
206. *Cincinnati Kurier*, December 18, 1970, 18. Translation by author.
207. Interview with author, March 20, 2021.
208. Beckman, "Mom and Popovers."
209. *Cincinnati Kurier*, December 18, 1970, 18. Translation by author.
210. Interview with author, February 2000.
211. Thie and Beischel, *Virginia Bakery Remembered*.
212. "About Us," Servatii Pastry Shop, accessed March 19, 2021, https://www.servatii.com.
213. Brian Planalp, "A Local Pastry Shop Makes German Holiday Treats so You Don't Have To," Cincinnati Refined, November 7, 2018, http://cincinnatirefined.com.
214. John Eckberg, "The Busken Story," Busken Bakery, 2017, http://busken.com.

Bibliography

Beckman, Wendy Hart. *8 Wonders of Cincinnati*. Charleston, SC: The History Press, 2017.

———. *Founders and Famous Families of Cincinnati*. Birmingham, AL: Clerisy Press, 2014.

Beischel, Cynthia. *Lost Tea Rooms of Downtown Cincinnati: Reflections & Recipes*. Charleston SC: The History Press, 2016.

Berten, Jinny Powers. *Cincinnati Christmas*. Wilmington, OH: Orange Frazer Press, 2011.

Dutka, Alan F. *Christmas in Cleveland*. Charlestown, SC: The History Press, 2020.

Harlow, Alvin. *The Serene Cincinnatians*. New York: E.P. Dutton and Company, 1950.

Herbert, Jeffrey G. *Old St. Mary's Church: Cincinnati, Ohio*. Milford, OH: Little Miami Publishing, 2006.

Ponstingle, Evan. *Kings Island: A Ride through Time*. Camp Hill, PA: Rivershore Creative, 2021.

Thie, Tom, and Cynthia Beischel. *Virginia Bakery Remembered*. Charleston, SC: Arcadia/The History Press, 2010.

Websites

Cincinnati Convention and Visitors Bureau. https://www.cincyusa.com.

Cincinnati Enquirer. https://www.cincinnati.com.

365Cincinnati. https://365cincinnati.com.

About the Author

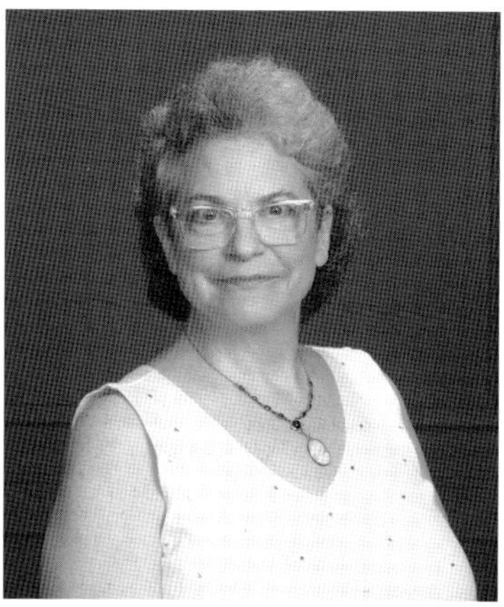

Wendy Hart Beckman is an award-winning freelance writer and editor. She has published about three hundred articles in both print and online publications and has received a baker's dozen of awards for her writing, editing and desktop publishing. Her last three books focused on the history of Cincinnati, where she has lived for forty-one years. (But she still thinks of Stockbridge, Massachusetts, as "home.") This is her tenth work of nonfiction.

Wendy's bachelor's degrees are in geology and natural science/technical communications from Virginia Tech and the University of Cincinnati, respectively. She has a master's degree in English and a graduate certificate in professional writing from UC. Wendy taught business, scientific and technical writing at the University of Cincinnati, and cultural diversity at Miami University. For many years, she tutored high schoolers in preparing for the ACT and SAT at a Huntington Learning Center. She is the mother of three sons, wife to Steve and grandmother to two adorable granddaughters.